D1565626

The Impeachment of Governor Sulzer

THE
IMPEACHMENT
OF
GOVERNOR
SULZER

A Story of American Politics

MATTHEW L. LIFFLANDER

excelsior editions
State University of New York Press
Albany, New York

Published by State University of New York Press, Albany

Excelsior Editions is an imprint of State University of New York Press

For information, contact State University of New York Press, Albany, NY
www.sunypress.edu

Production by Kelli Williams-LeRoux
Marketing by Fran Keneston

Library of Congress Cataloging-in-Publication Data

Lifflander, Matthew L.
 The impeachment of Governor Sulzer : a story of American
politics / Matthew L. Lifflander.
     p. cm.
 Includes bibliographical references and index.
 ISBN 978-1-4384-4337-9 (hardcover : alk. paper) 1. Sulzer,
William, 1863–1941—Impeachment. 2. Impeachments—New York
(State) I. Title.
 JK3459.Z5L54 2012
 974.7'041—dc23

                              2011037745

10 9 8 7 6 5 4 3 2 1

Politics is the most hazardous of all professions. There is not another in which a man can hope to do so much good to his fellow creatures. Neither is there any in which by a mere loss of nerve he may do so much widespread harm. Nor is there another in which he may so easily lose his own soul. Nor is there another in which a strict and positive veracity is so difficult. But danger is the inseparable companion of honor. With all the temptations and degradations that beset it, politics is still the noblest career any man can choose.

—Andrew Oliver (1706–1774); Member of
Massachusetts Provincial Council (1746–1765);
Secretary of the Province of Massachusetts
(1756–1771); Lieutenant Governor (1771–1772)

This book is dedicated to Helen Guelpa, in appreciation of my very good luck in having her as my assistant, secretary, office manager, confidant, researcher, editor, and wise advisor for more than three decades.

Contents

Illustrations

Prologue

Meeting Governor Sulzer

The doors to the elevator on the second floor of the State Capitol clanged open and crashed shut—loudly. They were heavy wrought-iron folding gates and the noise was especially jarring when it clashed with the quiet of the huge vacant corridor late at night. Bill Desmond, the elevator operator, enjoyed the commotion caused by his arrival or departure.

Desmond was Albany Irish through and through. Retired from some other job, he came to the capitol to be a guard and sometime elevator man because that is where his county leader, Dan O'Connell, sent him. Actually it was not Dan himself, but one of his lieutenants charged with taking care of the employment needs of loyal Democrats. Dan was the last of the big bosses. He had no need to see anybody personally in twenty-five years of controlling the Albany County Democratic machine. In exchange for loyalty and votes, Dan could get almost anybody a job in state government. Now that the Democrats were back in power again after twelve years of Republican Governor Tom Dewey it was even easier. "Uncle" Dan, as he was affectionately called, wasn't interested in the top commissioners' jobs or their deputies, assistants, counsels, among others. He wasn't interested in policy-making. It was the hundreds of maintenance men, drivers, elevator operators, building guards, clerks, assistants, and secretaries whose fate Dan controlled. Each one was a vote and the bigger their families were, the more likely they were to get a job. Dan always delivered a 90-percent majority in Albany County for any Democrat he supported and every governor knew it.

xiii

Bill Desmond's bright blue eyes had an impish touch of the devil shining through, and he spoke with a wonderful Albany Irish brogue, more Albany than Irish. His pink skin and bright white hair peeked out from the dull gray visor cap with the state seal that he wore on top of the dull gray cord uniform with silver buttons over a gray shirt with a black tie worn by the capitol guards. Not a very spit-and-polish group, but Desmond had charm, loved to be talking all of the time, and was the nearest thing to a tour guide that the Capitol had to offer in 1957. The tour guide aspect was a dimension of the job that Bill Desmond had added for himself, and most of us on the governor's staff appreciated his facility whenever we entertained a guest or constituent who was visiting Albany.

At least Bill had studied the small brochure distributed by the Department of Commerce describing the fascinating history of the ancient Capitol building. He was good enough as a natural storyteller that he could always add a few extra pointers of his own to enhance his beloved task of showing folks around the Capitol, which is how I first encountered William Sulzer.

It was just after 11 p.m. when I heard the crash of the elevator doors and knew that Bill had come for me as promised. It was a quiet evening in the Capitol building in late August 1957. The legislature had gone home before the end of April, as was the custom in those days. I was the last one at work on the second floor and had asked Bill to conduct a series of private tours of the Capitol for me when I came back to work after supper. I had deliberately left the front door of the governor's counsel's suite open so I would be sure to hear Bill.

"Are you ready," he said, greeting me from the elevator door in the great hall that ran along the entire south side of the Capitol's second floor. It was known as the Hall of Governors because it was lined with elegant portraits of most of the former governors hung next to the entrances of the executive offices, including the governor's counsel, the secretary to the governor and the governor himself, the large ceremonial office in the corner called the Red Room where governors over the years held public hearings and large meetings. The hall itself was floored in Spanish tile, walled in mahogany panels half way up the wainscoting over which the portraits were hung.

"Tonight we do the legislative chambers," Bill said, smiling as we went up to the third floor where he parked the elevator.

After leading me through the gorgeous red leather paneled senate chamber, and the opulent assembly chamber decorated in various marbles, we came to the room known as the assembly parlor paneled in oak and carpeted in light green with dull draperies. It was an especially beautiful chamber off the lobby to the actual legislative chambers, used for ceremonial events and group meetings or public hearings. This room was distinct in that the top third of its two-story-high walls were lined with oil paintings of most of the former Speakers of the assembly. The portraits were hung in guilt frames of nearly identical size, a neat and tight row along all four walls. Looking around, it was rather obvious that each of these men had been very important in his day. Nearly all of them looked formidable and the height at which the pictures hung made them look even more so. The Speaker is always the second most powerful man in state government and the more effective ones were sometimes even more powerful than the governor himself. Bill pointed out some who had become well known in New York history because they had eventually risen to become U.S. senators or governors themselves.

One portrait stood out. Obviously one of the older portraits, it showed a man who really looked very different from the others.

William Sulzer's deep-set eyes were piercing, staring down at me on the floor below, a forelock of his hair falling over his brow. High cheekbones gave his face a skeleton-like quality. The man was so obviously different from the others who had all assumed customary poses not looking directly at the portrait artist. Sulzer was staring directly at me if not glaring. Actually it would have been easy to convince yourself that he was somewhat crazed. I asked Bill Desmond if he knew who that one was. "Oh yes—that's Sulzer—he was trouble that one was. As a very young man he was Speaker in 1893 and years later he actually became governor—but he was impeached. That's why you don't see his picture on the second floor."

Bill had just told me all he knew about Sulzer. This became obvious when I asked him why Sulzer was impeached; "Don't know," he said, "but he was no good." Taking a last glance at his picture before we moved on, Bill said, "He was a crazy man."

That is how I discovered William Sulzer, and learned that New York had once impeached a governor, something that very few people are aware of.

When I got to my office in the Executive Chamber the next day, I was able to confirm from the *Red Book* on my desk, an almanac of state government information that, indeed, William Sulzer was the Speaker of the assembly at its 116th Session in 1893, that he had been elected the thirty-ninth governor of New York in November 1912 on the same day that Woodrow Wilson was elected president, and that he served from January 1 to October 17, 1913, when he was removed from office.

Because of a consuming interest in New York politics and the fact that I had just begun my career working in the office of counsel to the governor in the administration of Governor Averell Harriman, I was very interested in the qualities and characteristics of the various men who held the position of governor of New York. To me, Averell Harriman was a living legend who was following a number of giants who preceded him, names like Grover Cleveland, Theodore Roosevelt, Charles Evans Hughes, Al Smith, Franklin Roosevelt, to name a few. My interest in the history of New York's governors was shared by most of the people I worked with in Albany during those two years. Some of the clerical and support staff in the Executive Chamber had been there for many years and were quick to tell wonderful tales of their personal remembrances of Governor Franklin Roosevelt and Governor Al Smith and Governor Thomas E. Dewey, but when I asked, none of them were able to shed any light on Sulzer.

My own curiosity about the long-forgotten Sulzer story was sparked by the realization that, as a member of the governor's staff at the end of the 1950s, I was witness to the passing of an American institution, the political machine. Governor Sulzer's story, in retrospect, was the beginning of the end. His impeachment, what led to it, how it could happen at all, and, perhaps most importantly, what happened afterward, makes a fascinating tale of political intrigue and evolving public policy— involving many well-known men who were the star players on the political stage a century ago when Tammany Hall, New York's Democratic machine, was near the pinnacle of its power.

This story is an obituary to machine politics. Tammany no longer exists. It died after a long illness, and Averell Harriman was its last gubernatorial candidate. So that makes me an eye witness to its passing. Through firsthand experience, I saw Tammany Hall on its deathbed. I had the opportunity to participate actively and observe New York politics over a relatively short period of time when the party machine was in the process of being replaced by the television tube, leading to political candidates who could succeed without the machine if they raised enough money for themselves. Understanding the power of an effective political machine, the significance of the printed press, and the influence of business interests a hundred years ago is essential to understanding how each of these influences have transmuted to their present form, how they all come together in new and different ways to accomplish their objectives in the twenty-first century when the power of television's spotlight and, more recently, the efficacy of the Internet, has replaced both the need for party organization and the newspaper's capacity for intensive coverage. The most recent campaign finance regulation that emanated at the beginning of the twentieth century has been circumvented by bundles of "soft money," which is actually mimicking the "honest graft" of a century ago. The supreme court's recent decision to allow unrestricted independent corporate participation in political campaigns has undone years of restrictions and exacerbated our problems.

My up-close perspective began a half century ago as a very young lawyer working for a great governor in the same Executive Chamber and walking the same halls that served as the stage for most of this story about Governor Sulzer and the influences he dealt with.

I met Judge Daniel Gutman, who was counsel to Governor Harriman in 1956, when I was beginning my senior year in law school at Cornell. At the suggestion of one of my professors, we invited him to address the law students about the intricacies of state legislation. As the law school's official greeter, I was his host for the weekend. He was comfortable with my political credentials as I was also the president of the Cornell Young Democrats and obviously interested in politics and enthusiastic about having a Democrat as governor after twelve years of Tom Dewey, an excellent Republican governor who had the nerve to challenge presidents Roosevelt and Truman. When Judge Gutman asked me to come to Albany to serve on his small legal staff after graduation, he asked only one question about my qualifications: "How many hours of sleep do you need?" "Four or five is normal with me," I answered. "You will do fine," he said. Little did I know that I was dealing with the first workaholic I had ever met, and his major concern was to be sure I had the energy to keep up with the pace he set. For nearly half the year we worked from 9:30 a.m. until two or three in the morning, usually seven days a week. During the other half of the year, the "off-season," it would be only a six-day-a-week job and we could usually leave the office by 9 p.m.; except during the two summer months when we might get an occasional weekend off and left at 7 p.m.

The long hours were intense, but the work was so interesting and exciting by virtue of our significant responsibilities that the hours were never a problem, except for frequently feeling that there were not enough of them.

In my next meeting with Judge Gutman, just a couple of months before the job started, I learned that he had picked me to be the first lawyer on his staff who had not been sent to him by a political leader. He was trying, beginning with me, to assemble a staff that was selected on merit and professionalism, rather than political sponsorship exemplified by the blessing of a Democratic Party county leader.

While I did not really feel that I had a "leader," the way my New York City colleagues did, I was a Democratic committeeman in Westchester County since reaching voting age. I obtained a favorable recommendation from Bill Luddy who was Westchester's Democratic Party chairman. Because Democrats were then a vastly outnumbered minority party in Westchester who rarely elected anybody to any office, Luddy had never been important enough to the state party organization to justify placing one of his people on the governor's personal staff, which consisted of less than twenty people. My appointment actually gave Luddy a contact he would not otherwise have had, so he was happy to give me his endorsement.

Some of the other people on the governor's staff were also there without a leader's endorsement, because the governor had come to know them during his 1954 gubernatorial campaign. Among them was an especially impressive young man, a few years older than me, who usually dressed in very English- looking suits, spoke differently from most New Yorkers, and acted somewhat more worldly even though he constantly reminded us that he came from "Hells' Kitchen." His name was Pat Moynihan. He was the only member of the staff who was as tall as the governor. He was an assistant secretary to the governor and I was an assistant counsel.

From one of my colleagues on the counsel's staff I learned about leaders. It seemed that he had one whose name was "Milt." Senator Enzo Gaspari came from Bronx County and his county leader was Charles Buckley, the unchallenged Boss of Bronx County, and a major force in the Democratic Party because the Bronx always delivered big

Democratic majorities. Senator Gaspari, a former state assemblyman and state senator from the Pelham Parkway area of the Bronx, was a genuinely nice guy and good friend. He had a warm and friendly style, which went well with his portly figure. The "Senator," as he was always called, was about forty-five years old, round-faced, and bespectacled, with a thinning batch of curly black hair that never seemed to need combing. Enzo said of his job as assistant counsel to the governor, "they sent me here." The Bronx organization had secured the position for him after he lost his senate seat in a primary election.

Whenever Enzo and I went out to dinner together, which was often as we were two of the only bachelors in the office, Enzo always had to be back to the office by 7:30 to make a phone call. For many weeks I had no idea who he had to call and he was somewhat secretive about it. He would close the door to his office, which was adjacent to mine, load his ever-present pipe, take off his thick eyeglasses, wipe his brow, clear a yellow legal pad to take notes on and, with pen in hand, dial the number himself rather than ask the efficient Executive Chamber operator to place the call. Because Enzo was inclined to raise his voice when talking long distance, I could sometimes hear parts of his side of the conversation, although much of it was muffled, as the old mahogany doors in the Executive Chamber were very thick. The part I could always distinguish was "Milt, it's Enzo," "Yes, Milt," "Milt," "Yes Milt," "Yeah, Milt I got it," Okay Milt," etc., etc. The call would usually take about a half hour until Enzo emerged, looking flushed and relieved at the same time, sometimes grinning like a Cheshire cat and sometimes looking downtrodden as though he had been chastised, and not his usually effervescent self.

Eventually, Enzo admitted to me that "Milt" was his leader, the district leader for the Democratic organization in Pelham Parkway where Enzo came from. Every night Milt could rely on getting the call from his man in Albany and every night Enzo got his marching orders for the next day. The favors he was to seek or follow up on for Milt and the constituents Milt served. A special initial license plate for someone's car, an autographed photo of the governor, information about the status of a bill in the legislature that Milt was interested in, a call to some departmental official, a copy of the official state *Red Book*, a gubernatorial proclamation honoring some group or individual in Milt's district, a "pen certificate" neatly framed and testifying that the governor had used the old steel-point pen in the frame to sign a certain bill, an introduction for a constituent, or a message that Milt wanted Enzo to deliver to some state agency.

During my time in the counsel's office, I saw that the governor relied on Dan Gutman for his best advice on legislation, law enforcement matters, executive clemency, judicial appointments, extraditions, and all other legal issues. Gutman was highly respected by most of the governor's staff and by his colleagues throughout government for his good judgment and integrity, attributes that were recognized by most of the people he had encountered throughout his long and successful career as a prosecutor, legislator, and judge, before resigning from the bench to join the governor's staff at age fifty-five. For the most part, the professional politicians from Brooklyn or Manhattan in the Harriman administration or populating the legislature tended to despise Judge Gutman because he was hostile to political favor-seekers and he would not take the time to do even the most innocuous political favor, like making introductions, securing tickets to important events, or making calls to the Motor Vehicle Department to get a special license plate. In those days—unlike today—you had to know somebody to get your initials on your license plate. Governor Dewey had given out all of the two-letter plates to his Republican supporters, so, after eliminating dirty words in forty-three languages, Harriman's administration created the first three-letter plates—a bonanza for the Democratic county chairmen whose approval was usually required to get one, unless you happened to know someone on the governor's staff or the Motor Vehicle Commissioner.

When I asked Judge Gutman one quiet evening, "Why do those Brooklyn organization men hate you so?" he told me what he understood to be the real reason. "When I was a municipal court judge in Brooklyn, the district leaders would frequently send messages to me on the bench during a trial or as one was about to begin. It was a plain slip of paper with the name of the case they were interested in and it would say—for example 'Smith v. Jones,' with Smith's name underlined. I was supposed to take that as a request from this influential leader to make sure Smith won the case. While some other judges were helpful to them, I always tore up the slip and gave it back to the messenger—and some of them thought that made me unreliable and a bad guy, and they have so labeled me. Believe me, Matt, I am proud that they despise me, and I feel the same way about them."

Through Judge Gutman, I quickly began to gain insight into the moments of power politics that I was exposed to. At age twenty-five, there was a lot to learn about it as well as the more significant need to see how state government dealt with the great policy issues of the day.

The end of my first professional job was determined by the voters of New York on the first Tuesday of November 1958, when the far more telegenic Nelson Rockefeller defeated Averell Harriman who appeared to be too "stiff" in his outreach to voters, despite the respect his record deserved. The people gave us just seven weeks' notice. The governor's term, and my job, would end at midnight on December 31st—New Year's Eve.

Outside of personal career concerns, the only remaining tension had been created by the dramatic and well-televised political divisions that began at the state Democratic Party in Buffalo. The debacle of the State Democratic Convention was televised (for the first time), and it became the governor's albatross. Carmine DeSapio, Harriman's secretary of state, the last personification of Tammany Hall as the chairman of the Democratic Party in New York County, national Democratic committeeman, and the most influential political leader in state party politics, had defied the governor by rejecting Thomas Murray, a former chairman of the U.S. Atomic Energy Commission, who was the governor's choice as a running mate for U.S. senator. DeSapio also refused to consider Harriman's second choice, former Air Force secretary Thomas Finletter.

By providing initial support to elect Robert Wagner, son of the former U.S. senator, as mayor of New York City in 1953, and then Harriman as governor in 1954, DeSapio had assumed a major leadership position in the city and state Democratic Party. He was the new "Chief" of the heirs to Tammany Hall. Despite having to wear dark glasses due to an eye condition, DeSapio cultivated a favorable public image by supporting excellent, well-qualified candidates of impeccable integrity. At the 1958 convention, DeSapio defied the governor and forced the nomination of the highly respected New York district attorney Frank Hogan as the party's candidate for United States senator over Harriman's objection,[1] because DeSapio was convinced that Hogan, as a successful longtime district attorney of Manhattan and an Irish Catholic, would be a better balance on the ticket and have the best chance to defeat the popular Republican U.S. senator Jacob Javits. The governor's public humiliation and the resultant split in the party between "regulars" and "reformers" was effectively exploited by the Rockefeller campaign's resurrecting the image of the old Tammany Tiger controlling the governor of New York, an argument that contributed significantly to Harriman's defeat, however far-fetched it was in reality. The exchange of blame and bad feelings over losing the election continued in Albany on a day-to-day basis during the remaining weeks as it was acted out between the governor's staff and a few people in the government who supported DeSapio.

Among the absurd effects of this rift were several occasions when we had to make calls on behalf of the governor to a DeSapio deputy in the Department of State on routine state business. Before Election Day our requests were always received with a "yes sir" and prompt action. Now they were being responded to with "I can't do that without clearing it with the Bishop," which is how the DeSapio faithful referred to their revered chief.

This was an early lesson for me that would reverberate many times forty years later as I did the research for this book.

After lunch during our last afternoon in office on New Year's Eve, I prepared the official documents to appoint Judge Gutman to fill a vacancy that was about to be created in the Court of General Sessions, the highest criminal court in New York City, a vacancy to be filled according to law by appointment of the governor.

This vacancy was created by the election of its incumbent to the state supreme court in the November election. Normally the judge would be expected to resign prior to New Year's Day when he would assume his new office, thus leaving a vacancy to be filled by the outgoing governor of his own party. It was politically unthinkable that a judge elected as a Democrat would hold over until New Year's Day to resign and leave the vacancy to be filled by the new Republican governor. But, the incumbent had been nominated to both his existing position and his new one by Manhattan's Tammany political machine, so his loyalty was to his leader, Carmine DeSapio and no one else.

Word was that DeSapio had the judge's resignation in hand and it remained to be seen if he would present it to Governor Harriman or Governor Rockefeller. DeSapio had his last opportunity to let Harriman know who was the Boss and to punish Dan Gutman for his four years of loyalty to Harriman, during which he regularly refused to take "contracts" for DeSapio.

By 6 p.m. the governor had not received the resignation nor heard from DeSapio. Our official work was done, and both Harriman and Gutman assumed that DeSapio was taunting them by holding the resignation until later in the evening. The appointment papers were already signed by Governor Harriman and ready for filing, something that could be done at any time before midnight. Hopefully, the Democratic national committeeman would not want a judicial appointment to fall into Republican hands.

In late afternoon, Dan's wife Roz had come to the office to pick him up, and they invited me to join them for a quiet New Year's Eve dinner at their home in nearby Loudonville, while waiting for word from DeSapio.

Governor Harriman was spending his last evening in the Executive Mansion before turning it over to Nelson and the first Mrs. Rockefeller, who would move in on New Year's Day. He called Judge Gutman before we sat down to dinner. Harriman told Dan to keep in touch and they exchanged calls every half hour or so. Their conversations were very brief: "Have you heard anything?" "No word yet." At first each of them was confident that DeSapio would eventually call one or the other of them, and we would be able to file the nominating certificate before midnight.

There was a strong tradition that counsels to the governor could count on being rewarded with a supreme court judgeship at the end of their term. Governor Thomas E. Dewey had taken such care of his former counsels. Prior to that Governor Herbert Lehman had done the same; so had Governor Franklin D. Roosevelt and Governor Al Smith. Because Judge Gutman had come off the bench to serve Harriman, everyone assumed he would always have the opportunity to go back after his service. It was hard to believe that DeSapio would be so vindictive as to prevent it, let alone allow the Republicans to get one more judge of any kind.

The call never came.

All I knew when I left Albany after the election of Nelson Rockefeller in 1958 was that we once had a governor who was impeached and removed after nine and a half months in office and that he had been the youngest man ever to be elected Speaker of the assembly. I didn't learn any more about Sulzer until three years later. In June of 1961, while I was browsing in an antique shop in upstate New York, I came upon a small book entitled *The Boss, or the Governor*, accompanied by a two-volume set of bound books looking like a lot of law books, entitled *The Record of the Impeachment Trial of William Sulzer.*

On the cover of the small dusty green book was a photograph of Sulzer, looking very much like the portrait I remembered seeing in the Assembly Chamber.

The book provided my first insight into an amazing chapter in the history of American politics. It was published in 1914 (the year after Sulzer's impeachment) and its publisher was "The Truth Publishing Company."

The subtitle of *The Boss, or the Governor* was *The Truth About the Greatest Political Conspiracy in the History of America,* and its author was Samuel Bell Thomas, a New York lawyer who had been a Sulzer confidant and enthusiastic supporter.

Just a few lines from the author's preface will explain why it grabbed my attention and created a fascination with the subject of extreme relevancy to American politics today: "The removal of Governor William Sulzer marked the zenith of the arrogance and the brutality of corrupt bossism in New York State. Up to this time political bosses had controlled party organizations; they had commanded legislatures and administrative officers of the state government; they had nominated, for a consideration, justices of the Supreme Court, but it remained for Charles F. Murphy, the reigning boss of his period, to impeach a governor because that governor refused to do the bidding of the boss."[2]

The first chapter of the book was an introduction by Chester A. Platt, Sulzer's secretary to the governor, who had gone back to his job as the editor of the *Batavia Times,* an upstate newspaper in 1914. Platt had been intimately involved in getting the Democratic Party nomination for Sulzer to run in 1912—the same year that Woodrow Wilson was elected president of the United States.

Platt's introduction to the Samuel Bell Thomas book provided a few more details to motivate my desire to get to the bottom of this story: "Corrupt political bossism had shown amazing power in many ways, in many states, but never in such a startling manner as in the removal from office of a duly elected governor of the greatest state in the Union."[3] According to Platt, whose objectivity had to be questioned as he was head of the governor's staff, Sulzer's accomplishments before and after his election were monumental.

This introduction to Governor Sulzer motivated me to get to know more about him. I dug in. The result of which is this book telling the story from the perspective of its relevance to our current political institutions. I set out to find the truth. It was certainly relevant to my own experience in the Executive Chamber. I hope you will find it an interesting, relevant, and colorful story.

William Sulzer, inaugurated governor, January 1, 1913.
The New York Red Book (Albany: J. B. Lyon Co., 1913).

1

Inauguration Day

NEW YEAR'S DAY in 1913 was Inauguration Day in Albany. For people who lived in the state capital or those from elsewhere across the state whose involvement with the government justified their presence, it was a particularly festive occasion they looked forward to every two years. A new governor would take the oath of office in the Assembly Chamber in the state Capitol at noon and he was already especially popular with many people.

Fifty year old Democrat William Sulzer, more affectionately referred to by some of his constituents as "Bill," "Old Bill," or "Plain Bill," had been elected by what he called the largest plurality in the state's history—over 200,000 more votes than his nearest opponent in a three-way race. He defeated Job E. Hedges, the Republican candidate, a prominent attorney, and Oscar S. Strauss, the candidate of Teddy Roosevelt's Progressive Party, who was a well-known Jewish philanthropist and former diplomat who had served in Roosevelt's presidential administration. Woodrow Wilson was elected president in the same election and had carried the state with 41 percent of the votes.[1]

Sulzer came to Albany with superb credentials, a great deal of popular support, and a reputation as one of his party's best orators. During eighteen years in Congress he had distinguished himself as a very active, persuasive, and knowledgeable chairman of the Foreign Affairs Committee. He had achieved national stature by supporting a lot of progressive legislation, and was already well known to the state's voters. He enjoyed national stature as a result of some of the causes he identified himself with in Congress. He was a friend and supporter of William Jennings Bryan, and twice during his years in Congress his name had been mentioned as a possible candidate for vice president. He had also served five terms in the state assembly. Nineteen years earlier, at age thirty after only three years in the legislature, he was elected Speaker, the youngest in the state's history. He had sought the Democratic Party's gubernatorial nomination on at least seven different occasions before achieving it in 1912.

Inauguration Day was his day and Sulzer made the most of it. Capitalizing on the populist politics that had just elected Woodrow Wilson president of the United States, the new governor had already signaled significant changes from his predecessor, who was also a Democrat. To exemplify the simplicity and openness of the kind of administration that he promised to give New York, Sulzer had announced that he was changing the name of the Executive Mansion to the "People's House," a place where everyone would be welcome. He went out of his way to assure the press of his accessibility to reporters, day or night. On Inauguration Day he appointed a new head of the state's National Guard, a position of far greater interest in those days than today. He also announced that he was replacing the three-man state highway commission with a single commissioner.

During the period of preparation, between Election Day and Inauguration Day, the governor-elect had announced that, to save money, he would do away with the pomp and circumstance, including the customary military parade that had always been part of the traditional inaugural ceremony. He also eliminated the twenty-one-gun salute of Civil War cannons customarily fired on the Capitol lawn at the moment of his taking the oath. Both of these announcements had made people take notice. Sophisticates considered it to be ostentatious simplicity.

The governor-elect's official day began at about 10 a.m. Although cold, it was a bright and clear winter morning in Albany. A large crowd of enthusiasts and well-wishers had gathered outside of the Executive Mansion on Eagle Street. The mansion, a singularly unimpressive three-story wooden residence with a circular driveway surrounded by an equally unimpressive wrought-iron fence, was located in a rather ordinary neighborhood seven long blocks from the Capitol building.

At 10:15 the waiting crowd stirred at the sight of a handful of the state's National Guard officers approaching the mansion, attired in brilliant dress blue uniforms with much gold braid in evidence. A general, a major, and some junior officers had walked over from the Capitol.

They were the governor-elect's handpicked military staff. By tradition, they would escort their new commander-in-chief to the Capitol.

As soon as the guardsmen entered the governor's home, a string of carriages appeared on Eagle Street. In the first, wearing an elegantly cut dark blue suit, white shirt with a gold collar pin, black frock coat, and silk top hat, was New York's very fashionable, but not very popular Governor John A. Dix who was about to end his first two-year term. As a result of a dismal record, the party found him not to be reelectable. Dix had been picked to head the Democratic ticket in 1910 when he was the chairman of the state Democratic Party. The upstate Democrats had assumed he would not succumb to the dictates of Tammany Hall, the powerful Democratic Party machine in New York City. Except for a handful of political leaders who had made personal alliances, the Democrats from outside of New York City generally despised Tammany and resisted its efforts to control the state party organization. Dix had let his upstate supporters down and became quite unpopular with significant portions of his own party when his relationship with New York City Democrats led to the appointment of various party hacks and corrupt incompetents. He had also been plagued by poor judgment on some significant issues. In his carriage, Governor Dix was accompanied by another general and a naval officer who wore the stripes of a lieutenant commander and the gold shoulder braid of an aide to someone very important. They were from the military staff of the outgoing governor. Other military men followed in subsequent carriages and their full dress uniforms alone guaranteed a glamorous air to a festive occasion.

The crowd watched as the governor's resplendent entourage entered the mansion where their hero was waiting. Within minutes the people were rewarded by the appearance of two men at the front door—the stylishly dressed Governor Dix accompanying a somewhat taller man in rather frumpy attire. Governor Dix led the lanky six-footer down the porch steps to an open carriage waiting in the mansion's driveway where an attendant held open the door. At that point the taller man turned his back on the carriage and started walking down the circular drive from the mansion to the street where the new governor's fans were amassed behind the iron gate. A man in the front of the crowd shouted: "Three cheers for Bill," and the audience roared its approval. There he was—smiling at them and dressed in the same somewhat rumpled gray suit he had worn frequently during the last

campaign—and in several others previously. Plain Bill was not stylish.
He wore a dark gray overcoat for protection against the brisk air of an
Albany winter. His familiar soft slouch hat, barely concealing slightly
graying sandy colored hair, was black, and a fat black cigar pointed
upward from the corner of his mouth.

Someone in the crowd yelled out: "No high hat for Sulzer—He is
just plain Bill," and his supporters shrieked "Hurrah" after "Hurrah."
Just plain Bill smiled at his friends. Then, his face puckered in apparent
meditation, he walked a little bit bent forward but with long strides and
hands clasped behind his back leading the strange procession up on
Eagle Street toward State Street and the imposing gray granite Capitol
building—a half mile away. Governor Dix, carrying more weight than
his successor, and a smaller frame, had difficulty keeping up. Some of
the guard officers were out of breath by the time they got to State
Street, but the governor's fans brought up the rear continuing their
happy shouts and cheers.

At the intersection of State and Eagle they encountered five hundred members of the German Democratic Club of New York, including
a traditional "oompah-pah" band, led by thirteen of their officers all
wearing silk top hats and pink sashes astride white horses, waiting to
salute their man.

To enter the Capitol from that point, most people would turn left
and walk a few hundred feet up State Street to the main ground floor
entrance on the south side of the big gray, ugly building. But Just Plain
Bill Sulzer chose the much more dramatic path through the jubilant
crowd of onlookers in Capitol Park at the bottom of the stairway over
the Capitol's eastern portico, walking up the seventy-seven steps that
led directly to the second floor at the top of the steps. Reporters noted
that Teddy Roosevelt had used that long staircase entrance when he was
governor twelve years earlier whenever anyone was looking.[2]

The extravagantly decorated assembly chamber was packed with
people, plants, palms, and flags set between its glorious marble
columns and rich mahogany podium. The assemblymen had been
joined by the state senators, the black robed judges of the court of
appeals, Mrs. Sulzer and other relatives, high-level National Guard officers in their formal uniforms, state officials, legislative staff members,
press, and those important citizens fortunate enough to wangle a coveted invitation. It was notable that the most powerful leaders of Tam-

many were not there. Twenty thousand invitations had been sent for a chamber that could hold 1,500, including those crowded into the visitors' galleries and elegant foyers and crammed into standing room along the walls of the chamber. The overflow even stood inside the grand fireplaces.

Outgoing Governor Dix graciously introduced his successor, pointing out that "in this chamber a generation ago you were a familiar and important figure. The intervening years have afforded you a splendid opportunity to understand the needs of the human race."

While Dix spoke, Sulzer sat in a big stuffed chair in the front row and studiously maintained the look of a man in deep thought. After the oath of office was administered at 12:10 p.m., the military band struck up the "Star-Spangled Banner" and Governor Sulzer ascended the podium to give his inaugural address, which would be one of the shortest on record. On this occasion, he was uncharacteristically humble. Addressing the assembled leaders of New York, the new governor presented a picture of self-restraint that was unfamiliar to those who had followed his career, in which had distinguished himself as a forceful and colorful orator, always full of bombast and self-confidence. Capturing a theme of his gubernatorial campaign when he had said repeatedly, wherever he went across the state, that he had no boss except his own conscience, and he intended to have none, Sulzer told his inaugural audience: "Grateful to the people who have honored me with their suffrages, I enter upon the performance of the duties of the office without a promise, except my pledge to all the people to serve them faithfully and honestly and to the best of my ability. I am free, without entanglements, and shall remain free. No influence controls me but the dictates of my conscience and my determination to do my duty, day in and day out, as I see the right, regardless of consequences. In the future, as in the past, I will walk the street called straight, and without fear and without favor, I shall execute the laws justly and impartially— with malice toward none." Sulzer's Lincolnesque phrases had long been part of his oratorical stock and trade. His piercing blue eyes flashed as he dedicated himself to the maintenance of representative and Democratic institutions, promised an economical and business-like administration and "progressive reforms along constructive and constitutional lines." He "resolved to shirk no responsibility; to work for the welfare of the people; to correct every existing abuse; to abolish useless offices and wherever possible consolidate bureaus and commissions to secure greater economy and more efficiency; to uproot official corruption and to raise higher the standard of official integrity; to simplify the methods of orderly administration."[3]

When he finished, the governor left the third-floor Assembly Chamber, quickly descended the ornate "million dollar" staircase to the second floor, swiftly leading his entourage through several long halls, back to the top of the Capitol steps where he was cheered again by the large crowd that was still assembled in Capitol Park. He repeated his entire inaugural address for them, posed for some photographs, and then went inside to the elegant deep red–carpeted and mahogany-walled Executive Chamber, as the governor's ceremonial office on the second floor is called. There he held a reception and greeted hundreds of well-wishers who came to shake his hand, wish him well, and offer their suggestions about running the government and jobs for their friends. Hundreds more came to the official reception that afternoon at the Executive Mansion where Governor and Mrs. Sulzer greeted friends and members of the public to whom a general invitation had been extended, along with legislators and state officials gathered to celebrate the achievement of his lifelong ambition.[4]

Later in the day, the newly elected legislature convened and reorganized by electing new leaders as both houses were overwhelmingly Democratic for the first time in years. Resolutions were promptly introduced by the new Democratic leadership to ratify constitutional amendments providing for the direct election of United States senators and for women's suffrage. As required by the state constitution, the new governor delivered his first State of the State message, outlining in print the beginnings of the gubernatorial program, but promising more later on.[5]

Governor Sulzer proposed very progressive legislation. He asked the legislature to approve the proposed amendment that would require the election of U.S. senators by a direct vote of the people. (United States senators were then selected in New York by the state legislature, as was the case in many other states.) His position was rooted in his faith in the people. Sulzer's message said, "the people can and ought to be trusted. They have demonstrated their ability for self-government." Sulzer also asked that the amendment to provide for women's suffrage be submitted to the state's voters for approval as soon as possible, "in accordance with the pledge made to the people in the recent campaign." Actually, Sulzer had been a genuine longtime leader of this cause, and somewhat of a hero to the suffragette movement in New York as far back as the time he served as a leader in the assembly and then Speaker nearly two decades before.

His message also called attention to the importance of his party's pledge to reform electoral laws by enacting a direct primary bill to provide for the direct nomination of candidates for public office through a primary election system. Direct primaries had been a major platform for Progressive politicians across the country, and many states had already adopted such laws.

He called for legislative enactment of an extension of the civil service merit system in place of political appointments to many state jobs and for a litany of social programs, including laws dealing with minimum wages, worker's compensation, safety in the workplace, and restrictions on child labor.

All of these issues were in keeping with the program of his party, which was now in firm control of both houses of the legislature. Alfred E. Smith, the newly elected Speaker, and Robert F. Wagner, the newly elected president pro tem and senate majority leader, seemed to be similarly committed, so on the first day of his administration the new governor had good reason to be optimistic about a Progressive program that would assure his place in the history of New York, and perhaps the nation.

2

A Rural Childhood

WILLIAM SULZER, the forty-first governor of the state of New York, was born in an old brick house on Liberty Street in Elizabeth, New Jersey during the Civil War—on March 18, 1863, to be precise. William was the second son in a family of seven children, five boys and two girls.

The governor-to-be's father, Thomas Sulzer, was a German immigrant who arrived in New York City in 1851, having escaped from a German prison. Thomas had been captured while he was a student at Heidelberg University where he had joined a patriotic army fighting to establish a constitutional government. It is known that Thomas had a brother who remained in Heidelberg because William said his father had once offered to send him to the Heidelberg uncle for his education. His mother, Lydia Sulzer, who the governor says "always had her way," would not hear of it. Lydia, née Jelleme, was an American of Scotch-Irish ancestry from Passaic, New Jersey who married Thomas in New York City before the family moved to Elizabeth.

According to some of the very brief biographical sketches of William Sulzer that were circulated when he began running for public office, his parents wanted him to become a Presbyterian minister, but nothing in the extensive autobiographical descriptions of his childhood that the governor left behind would bear out that statement. Actually, Sulzer told a couple of stories of disappointment with organized religion that would certainly indicate that neither he nor his parents planned such a career for him.

Until now little had been revealed about Sulzer's childhood in New Jersey. Sometime in the 1930s, Sulzer began work on a rather pompous manuscript for an autobiography, which was never completed.[1] While it provides extensive detail about his recollections of his childhood and the years before he went into public life, most of the information has never before been publicly revealed. Interestingly, for someone from a large family, he rarely mentioned any of his siblings in the autobiographical notes, although some of the significant correspondence he left behind indicates that he maintained a warm family relationship with two of his brothers and at least one sister.

Sulzer's eloquent account of his childhood begins with a description of himself when he was about six years old: "my health was delicate, and I did not go to school. However, my mother, and my aunt who lived with us at that time, taught me a little, and often read to me, especially from the Bible. I was what unthinking people called in those days an odd boy. As a matter of fact, no one seemed to understand me."

Sulzer says that about that time the family moved from Liberty Street to a house in a better area of Elizabeth called "Quality Hill," which was being developed "for rich men from New York." His father was then a successful civil engineer who was doing construction contracting for the developer of Quality Hill, employing large numbers of people building sewers, streets, and houses, and building some houses for himself.

In December 1869, his parents sent him to a public school on Morrill Street in Elizabeth where he developed a reputation as "the game cock of the school," because he was constantly fighting with other boys. For such conduct he was whipped by the school principal and sent home so often with instructions not to come back that he eventually refused to go back. His father then sent young William to a German school where the headmaster soon told Thomas that he would not have his son in the school because he was always fighting with other boys there as well.

Soon after dropping out of school at such a young age, William went to work driving a mule team for his father at 75 cents a day, hauling materials for Thomas's extensive construction business. He liked working with the mules and horses, and the men who worked in the stable taught him a great deal about animals, beginning a lifetime interest in animal care that eventually manifested itself in a bequest to the Society for the Prevention of Cruelty to Animals in his last will and testament.

Young Will's parents had their own pew at the First Presbyterian Church in Elizabeth, where their second son was baptized and regularly attended Sunday services during his childhood. After services he attended the Sunday School. The young boy was favorably impressed by the minister, a Dr. Kempshall, who he would recall fondly as "a fighting clergyman and an intense Democrat. Besides, he was an eloquent preacher, and said what he means and meant what he said. I liked him for his fighting spirit, and his friendly manner to boys."

Sulzer described a contest that the minister ran to determine which boy under ten years old could most perfectly recite the Westminster catechism from memory. The prize was a neatly bound and duly inscribed copy of the New Testament. His mother encouraged him to go after the prize. He worked hard each day, with her help, to commit the catechism to memory. Sulzer won over nine other contestants and it was considered a great honor. On reflection toward the end of his career, he said, "I believe my mother thought more of me winning this prize than anything else I ever did in my life while she lived. Often when I became prominent in public life friends called on her and said she must be proud of the honors achieved by her son. Then she would take from her table the New Testament and say: 'The greatest honor my son ever received is this book.'"

When William was ten years old, the family suffered a dramatic financial tragedy. The total economic collapse of Mr. Dimoch, the developer of Quality Hill, at the beginning of the Panic of 1873 cost Thomas Sulzer several hundred thousand dollars according to the governor's recollection, and the family lost nearly everything it had except for a farm at Wheatsheaf, New Jersey, the deed to which his father had put in Lydia Sulzer's name. The Panic of 1873 caused five thousand businesses to fail that year and precipitated a five-year depression. Thirty-seven banks and brokerage houses closed the first day and two days later on September 20 the New York Stock Exchange closed for an unprecedented ten days. Railroads shut down and the future of thousands of merchants and farmers were adversely affected. It was the greatest economic catastrophe of the nineteenth century.

The Sulzers moved to Wheatsheaf. Wheatsheaf took its name from a public house that stood on the highway between Elizabeth and Rahway, New Jersey, during the eighteenth century. The Sulzers took special pride in the place because it was adjacent to a farm that had been owned by Abraham Clark, one of the signers of the Declaration of

Independence. From friends and neighbors they learned to farm and survive. Although they were now poor for the first time, their hard work made a new life possible.

On the farm, young Will began what might best be described today as a Tom Sawyer/Huckleberry Finn existence. He spent his time working the farm for his father, while eagerly absorbing everything he possibly could about plants and animals. His questions and curiosity knew no bounds and usually endeared him to adults he encountered. At Wheatsheaf the ten-year-old was sent to a one-room log cabin school attended by the children of the local farmers, nine boys and six girls to be precise. He describes the school as equipped with a blackboard, a desk for the teacher, and a pot-belly, word-burning stove surrounded by benches for the boys on one side and the girls on the other. The farmers afforded their children's teacher by having him live one month at a time with each farm family.

After the first year at the one-room schoolhouse, Will was sent to a modern school in Roselle Park where he behaved himself properly and was well motivated by a good teacher.

He adapted very well to farm life. In his spare time the boy learned to hunt and fish. He collected stones, learned about geology, and began a profound interest in minerals that would last an entire lifetime, culminating with his ownership of real mines in Alaska. Many years later, Sulzer reflected that "one of my greatest regrets in life is that I chose the law instead of natural history as my profession. I know if I had chosen natural history as my life work, I would have been happier, more erudite, and more useful to my fellow man."

As an amateur geologist all his life, the study of rocks was most appealing to Sulzer. Drawing on that experience, he would say "the rocks never lie," and he considered geology to be "the truthful record of the history of our planet."

On the farm, young Sulzer learned to grow things, to milk cows and distribute their products, to play musical instruments, to sing, and to participate in amateur dramatics, in which he really took great pride and played at very seriously. As he looked back on those wonderful and wholesome childhood years during an era that can no longer be reproduced, Sulzer recollected in great detail many of the people he met and the specifics of what he had learned from each of them. It is significant to note that even at such a tender age, Sulzer began to appreciate how each encounter with an adult was an opportunity to learn. Later as

Advertisement of the circus that young Sulzer joined in 1875,
The Great Forepaugh. Courtesy of the Library of Congress,
LC-USZ62-24112

a young professional, he would actively seek encounters with prominent men because he realized how much he might gain from their
experience.

By the time Sulzer was thirteen years old he became infected with
wanderlust generated by reading stories in the *Youth's Companion* about
adventures in far-flung places. In 1876 America held many fascinations
for a thirteen-year-old with curiosity and a spirit of adventure. The
nation was preoccupied with Indian affairs and the cavalry was fighting
Indian tribes in various Western Territories. Americans were considering how to develop the Great Plains and the Southwest. In Philadelphia
in May of 1876, President Ulysses S. Grant opened the Centennial
Exposition, the focus of which was a thirteen-acre exhibit of American
inventions. Ten million people attended the six-month-long exhibition.

In the later part of May 1876, when merely thirteen years old,
Sulzer announced to his mother that he was going away, but that he

intended to return. While Lydia certainly endeavored to dissuade him, she was unable to do more than provide some seed money as her rather iron-willed son was destined to hit the road. He traveled to various New Jersey cities, working from time to time to earn bed and board, first to New Brunswick, then Trenton, the Delaware River, and on to Philadelphia,[2] where he actually joined Forepaugh's Circus at $3 per week to help with feeding and watering the elephants. The circus traveled through northern Pennsylvania and the Southern Tier of New York, ending its summer tour in Jamestown in the far western corner of New York State, where young Will decided he had enough of circus life and headed for New York City on the Erie Railroad.

When he got to New York City, Sulzer set out to fulfill another boyhood ambition—to go to sea. He toured the South Street docks, which were then a mass of masts of the great sailing ships of the day that were anchored there between voyages bringing merchandise from all over the world to New York. South Street was redolent with the odor of spices, pitch, tar, fresh lumber, fruits, and sawdust. Sailors from all over the world filled the neighborhood. The prows of the oceangoing vessels sometimes stretched clear across the street, almost poking their noses into the office windows in the four-story buildings that lined the street. It was 1877 and the boy was going on fourteen. Although he was big and strong for his age, his attempts to get a job as a sailor on one of the ships were rebuffed because of his age. He was not considered old enough to become a sailor and was unable to find any ship's master who needed a cabin boy.

In New York City he rode the horse-drawn stages that went from the Wall Street ferry and the Fulton Street ferry up Broadway, then a dirt road only partially paved with cobblestones, to Twenty-Third Street, which was then a fine residential neighborhood with vine-covered houses and shade trees. In those days there were no tall buildings in the city, but the boy was in awe of New York, calling it "the greatest city I had ever seen. Everything in it, and about it, appealed to me and was educational." He frequented Trinity Church and would sometimes sit on the base of its iron fence looking across Broadway and down Wall Street, watching the people there.

One morning, while sitting in front of the church, he was discovered by a neighbor from New Jersey. This gentleman, Edgar Quackenbush, was his former Sunday School teacher who had heard from Sulzer's anguished parents about his running away from home. Mr.

Quackenbush was an executive at Daniel T. Hoag and Company at 92 Wall Street, then the largest tea broker in the city. After their encounter, Quackenbush secured a job for young Sulzer as an office boy at $3 per week, and then persuaded him to go home to his parents and commute from there by train to his new job on Wall Street.

Sulzer's parents were extremely happy to have him at home again and delighted in hearing about his adventures. His father tried to dissuade him from going to Wall Street and offered him a job at $75 per month on the family farm. But Will was a very determined, self-confident, and ambitious young man with a plan, and he preferred to take the 7 a.m. train each morning to New York to seek his future at the company where he would learn the rudiments of the tea business. He not only served as an office boy, but taking every opportunity to see how business worked, he quickly learned to prepare samples of the product for tasting by customers and accompanied the executives on trips to dockside wholesalers where he could observe how the tea was purchased. After several months, ambition compelled him to answer an ad for a position at $5 per week from Clark and Balch who were in the tea, coffee, and liquor business. There the management was so impressed with Sulzer's energy and intelligence that after only a few months they taught him bookkeeping and raised his salary to $8 per week. By the time he was fifteen he was earning $15 per week, which he rightfully considered a very good salary and he actually began to save money. He opened a bank account at the Seaman's Savings Bank with a $100 deposit, which he revealed in the 1930s had never been withdrawn.

Sulzer came home to New Jersey each evening. Two or three nights a week he would hitch up a horse and wagon and go out to sell his firm's products to business people in the various villages in Union County to supplement his income with commissions. Sulzer said later, "I was a good salesman and soon built up a lucrative trade. I never sold anyone that did not pay, so the firm never made a bad debt through me. I was doing well, making money, working hard, making progress, and getting along far beyond my most sanguine expectations. However, there were going through my brain all the time two things, viz: First, my desire to be a seafaring man. Secondly, my desire to be a lawyer."

A young lawyer he had befriended in New Jersey was working at the firm of Johnson, Phelps and White at 62 Wall Street. The firm had a successful practice with major financial institutions and he talked with them about studying law as a student in their office. "As I had then determined to be a lawyer, I concluded to resign my lucrative position with Clark and Balch, where I was making in the neighborhood of $50 a week, salary and commissions, and go to work as a law student for $3 a week. I had saved enough money to pay my tuition, and take care of myself until I could be admitted to the bar."

Considering the fact that New York was still in the depths of a terrible economic depression, with vacant stores, and closed manufacturing facilities scarring every street, Sulzer was really doing exceptionally well for himself.

3

Studying Law

SULZER'S INITIAL INTEREST in the law was sparked by an experience during his boyhood on the farm.

When he was only eleven or twelve years old, Sulzer met William A. Mulford, justice of the peace of the town of Roselle, New Jersey, where the Wheatsheaf farm was located. Judge Mulford's office was adjacent to the general store and post office that the boy visited frequently while doing chores for the family farm. The judge, intrigued by the young man's curiosity, welcomed him to his office and took time to answer his questions. He encouraged his young admirer to attend trials that were held in his office, and Will did so frequently.

One of the young farmhand's chores was to drive the family cattle to pasture across the land of a neighbor, a man named Dennis Crane. The crossing privilege was actually paid for by Sulzer's father. Crane objected to allowing Sulzer's cattle to pause to graze during the short transverse, but Will always took the side of a hungry cow and ignored the admonition. That resulted in an enraged Crane actually thrashing the boy with a hickory stick on one occasion after his warning went unheeded. Will kept the beating to himself and vowed to get even. His opportunity came when Crane's favorite white calf strayed over to Sulzer's farm. According to Sulzer's account: "I put a rope around its neck and led it into our barn, where we had, at the time, a big pail of green paint. . . . I painted this white calf . . . and when I finished the job it was the best looking green calf ever seen. Then I turned it loose, and it went back to the Crane place."[1]

17

Mr. Crane was furious and easily concluded that Will Sulzer had done it—a conclusion that Sulzer admitted was "well warranted." Crane lodged a complaint against the boy with Sulzer's friend, Justice of the Peace William A. Mulford. Sulzer vividly recalls Judge Mulford's reaction: "Judge Mulford . . . called me in, and told me Dennis Crane had made a complaint against me of painting his white calf green." Then the judge told him: "I do not want you to tell me whether you did it or not, but I want you to be here at two o'clock next Wednesday afternoon, when I will try the case." Sulzer promised him he would and the judge said: "I like you as a boy, and I am going to tell you the law. No one can be convicted of doing something he should not have done, unless there is direct proof. If no one saw you paint the calf it can not be proven you did it, unless you admit it. Crane can say all he likes at the trial, but if you keep your mouth shut, and do not go on the stand, and Crane cannot swear that he saw you do it, under the law of New Jersey I will have to dismiss the case. Do not forget this." Sulzer thanked him, and told him he would not.

That afternoon Tom Sulzer took his errant son to Elizabeth to get him a lawyer, telling his son: "Perhaps you did wrong in painting that calf, but you certainly were justified." William J. Magie, who was then the most prominent lawyer in Union County, was a friend of Tom Sulzer. He laughed when he heard the story and agreed to send a young lawyer from his office named Frank Bergen. The courtroom was packed with spectators at the trial. It had become a *cause célèbre*. After Mr. Crane testified, Mr. Bergen cross-examined him and then moved to dismiss the case, which the judge did. Mr. Bergen got the $5 fee he asked for. The culprit was very impressed with the proceedings. Outside of the courtroom he thanked Bergen and told him that he hoped some day he would be a lawyer like him. Years later, Frank Bergen became a leader of the bar in New Jersey and frequently recalled the "green calf case" as his first case and his first fee.

As a beginning law clerk at Johnson, Phelps and White in 1879, young Sulzer did what hundreds of others entering the profession did in those days. The Wall Street law offices at that time were generally located in three-story buildings that had once been residential. Some of the buildings on Wall Street rose to five stories. The gas-lit Wall Street was then cobblestoned and its sidewalks were punctuated with circular steel covers for coal chutes leading to each building's basement. There were no elevators, no telephones, no stenographers, and no typewriters. Law clerks began at 8 a.m. sweeping floors, dusting the offices, carrying coal to make the hearth fires in preparation for the lawyers' arrival between nine and ten o'clock. In exchange for these chores, as well as making tea and tediously copying legal papers by hand, the clerks were given the opportunity to study law books. Because there were few restaurants conveniently available, the lawyers and staff generally lunched in the office and the clerk had the additional chore of cleaning up after lunch. A would-be lawyer had the option of relying on the firm for all of his legal training or combining practical experience with attendance at law school classes, which Sulzer opted for, having already saved enough money to pay for his tuition. So at two o'clock he would take the stage to Columbia Law School, which was then located "uptown" on Washington Square. There he would listen to law lectures for one or two hours and make copious notes.

Sulzer described the system that was then in place for training lawyers: "The rule of the Supreme Court, at that time, was that a student should spend four years in a law office; or three years in a law office and one year in a law school; or three years in a law school and one year in a law office; as a qualification, and then be examined by the judges. The examinations were held before the General Term of the Supreme Court. One day was devoted to writing answers to written questions. The next day was devoted to answering questions propounded by the Judges."At that time Sulzer was going on sixteen years of age. He decided that he would put in as much time as he could in a law office, while attending the law lectures at Columbia College. He wanted to learn as much as he could, and become as proficient as possible, so that he would have no trouble in passing his examinations when he became of age.

Admission to the bar, then, as now, required the student to be twenty-one years of age. To maximize the time available for preparation at age sixteen, Sulzer took up residence in New York City, renting a room in the home of a physician who regularly rented to Columbia Law School students.

After a year at the Jackson law firm, Sulzer switched his employment to the firm of Evarts, Choate, and Southmayd, which had a far more active trial practice and offered him the opportunity to get experience in the courtroom. Already instilled with an excellent work ethic cultivated on the farm, Sulzer's ambition began to reveal itself in the early years of his legal training.

The next year Sulzer—now nearly eighteen years old—improved his position again, moving to a better job as associate managing clerk at the law firm of Parrish and Pendleton at $8 a week, $5 more than he had earned at his first two firms. There he was introduced to a general law practice firm that had an extensive theatrical practice, as well as a real estate and banking business. The theater was a great interest of his, and as an especially outgoing and personable law student, Sulzer got the opportunity to meet actors and actresses and attend many plays. Half his time at the firm was spent attending court cases. He was allowed to argue motions and participate in other pretrial activities. His hard work and self-confidence impressed his colleagues and, after six months he was promoted to managing clerk at $10 a week. Late in life he would look back on the experience with regret because his extensive duties and learning experiences at the firm required him to give up attending Columbia and he never got his law degree.

At Parrish and Pendleton, Sulzer also got the opportunity to meet some of the most prominent lawyers in the city as the variety of his duties increased with his experience. He assisted counsel in some important trials and worked on the actual preparation of briefs and other legal pleadings and began doing meaningful legal research.

One cold rainy night in December, near the end of his first year at Parrish and Pendleton, Sulzer was sent to serve papers at the town-house of a prominent man who was a defendant in a lawsuit. The papers had to be served by midnight in order to meet a legal deadline. The man was not home when Sulzer arrived at 8 p.m., and because there were so few hours remaining before the deadline, Sulzer dutifully waited outside of the house in the rain until the man returned. By the time Sulzer got his man, it was 11 p.m. and Sulzer was soaked to the skin. As a result, he contracted lobar pneumonia according to the diagnosis of the family physician in New Jersey, where Sulzer had returned to the family farm for treatment and family succor. Large doses of quinine and mustard plasters were the prescribed treatment. He was bedridden for six weeks and, at the beginning of his illness his life had actually been endangered. Sulzer described the situation: "I rallied on account of my youth and previous good health. After the fever broke I was so weak I could not get out of bed for two weeks. I was fed gruels and milk punches according to the doctor's advice. . . . As I got better I would sit . . . on the porch in the sun . . . but I did not recover my strength. . . . I was so weak I could hardly walk. . . . I had lost considerable weight and was as thin as a rail. The doctor recommended that I go south to recuperate. I talked it over with my parents, and finally concluded to go by sea to Florida."

Sulzer went to New York and explained matters to his employers at Parrish and Pendleton. While they were sorry to lose him, they promised to keep his position open for him until he returned. Sulzer withdrew money from his savings account, gave up his room in New York, and gave away his books and most of his clothes.

He went along South Street where rows of docks were jammed with two- and three-masted schooners and huge accumulations of wooden barrels of cargo, representing commerce from all over the world and the entire eastern coast of the United States. He found a ship preparing to sail for Florida. Its destination was Jacksonville. Sulzer asked the captain if he would take him aboard. The captain told him he could not take passengers, but if Sulzer would sign the articles as a sailor he would take him along, provided he would pay $20 for the voyage and do such work aboard ship as the mate instructed. Sulzer agreed and went aboard the three-masted schooner that night.

Sulzer was about to begin his great adventure.

Ships docked along South Street. Collection of the
New-York Historical Society, South Street, ca. 1884,
negative 47596. Courtesy of the New-York Historical Society.

4

Sulzer's Great Adventure

EVERY MAN SHOULD HAVE at least one great adventure in his life. Some seek it and fail. Others never have the opportunity. Most never try and wind up as hum-drum people in hum-drum lives. Those who manage to find a great adventure are the fortunate few. Their experience enriches their lives and provides a perspective that affords many advantages.

Sulzer was more than halfway through his training for the bar when fate in the form of pneumonia provided justification for a diversion that he had frequently expressed great interest in—going to sea.

The young man's self-confidence was unusually well developed. Embarking on an ocean voyage for the first time would be an intimidating challenge to most people, but young Sulzer was genuinely fearless and saw it only as an opportunity for adventure and an advancement of his knowledge. Of all the autobiographical notes he left behind, none are quite as interesting or unique as the story of his ocean voyage to Florida and the West Indies during his eighteenth and nineteenth years. Sulzer's observations provide a great insight into his attitudes and character at the time, and a valuable perspective on the status of the development of the places he visited.

About the middle of March, 1881, tall, sandy-haired young Sulzer sailed south on the schooner *Wm. H. Thompson*, celebrating his eighteenth birthday at sea. According to Sulzer's own account, "we headed South with a fair wind and all sail set. The captain and mate called all hands aft, and divided the crew in the watches of the captain and the mate." Sulzer was put in the captain's watch, and was assigned a bunk in the cabin instead of the forecastle with the cook and the sailors; serving food to the captain and the mate, helping the cook, and keeping the cabin spic and span were among his initial duties. His dream of being a sailor was coming true and he soon forgot all about becoming a lawyer. He described the captain as a kindly man, and an experienced sailor. "When we had leisure he taught me . . . to tie and untie sailor's knots and splice ropes, to steer the ship by the compass, and keep the sails full. He also taught me how to take latitude and longitude."

While the captain took a liking to Sulzer, the mate's attitude was very different. Sulzer described him as surly, brutal, and dictatorial, and said that he did not treat the men with much consideration. Sulzer called him: "The most profane man I ever knew, but . . . a thorough sailor. No matter how hard the wind blew he would never take in sail. . . . This mate had a peculiar saying which I have never forgotten. Whenever the wind blew hard, and the ship would sing, he seemed to be in his glory. He would pace the quarter deck, swinging his arms, and say: 'While she creaks she holds.'"

When the ship was off the Hatteras shoals, it ran into an unusually severe southwest gale. Young Sulzer captured the experience: "It was all we could do to keep the ship's head before the gale, while great seas washed over her sides and stern, so that one had to be careful and dexterous not to be washed overboard. This storm lasted about two days, during which time we had made no headway, except to the North. Later on, when we got off the coast of South Carolina, we ran into another severe gale, which tested the ship to its capacity, and the good seamanship of the captain saved the craft from destruction. I was on deck most of my time, where I watched everything, and learned how a ship should be handled in a storm. I found out that any good ship can weather almost any storm, if the ship is properly handled and maneuvered. Seamanship is a trade that can only be learned by courage, and long experience. When good weather came the captain told me that we had weathered two of the worst gales he had ever known in all his experience on the Atlantic Ocean."

When the ship finally reached the St. John's River in Florida, a tug towed it to Jacksonville where it anchored in the middle of the river. A health officer came aboard to examine the crew. He told the captain that there was yellow fever in Jacksonville and no one aboard the ship would be permitted to land. After they had been quarantined for about a week, Sulzer persuaded one of the other sailors to row him to the opposite side of the river. He made his way over land to St. Augustine.

In St. Augustine Sulzer's health began to improve. His self-confidence at sea had grown to the point that he bought a schooner for himself and learned to sail it like a veteran yachtsman.

According to Sulzer's own account, "I heard many stories about places in Florida on the East Coast from St. Augustine to Key West. There were very few white people, at that time, in this section of Florida, but many Seminole Indians. The thought occurred to me that if I could get a supply of merchandise, and run my schooner south, I could trade with these people, and make some money, besides seeing and studying the country." He persuaded Mr. Sanchez, who had the largest general store in St. Augustine, to trust him with a cargo of supplies to take south on a trading expedition. "Night after night I sat with him in his store explaining and accentuating my plan and purpose. I promised that I would come back, and pay him not only the cost of the merchandise, but 10% of whatever profit I made. He told me that most of the white people in that section of Florida were bad men, and fugitives from justice, and that the Seminole Indians were worse. He said that they would not only steal the schooner and supplies, but would kill me in the bargain." Sulzer told him he was confident he could overcome all obstacles. He eventually convinced Mr. Sanchez to trust him and they selected appropriate goods useful for trading purposes as practically all business was barter and trade. The bill for these supplies amounted to $2,350.00. Sulzer recruited two Negro sailors to help him. They were born in the Bahamas, and had been sailors practically all their lives. In September 1881, they sailed out of the harbor of St. Augustine. According to Sulzer, "Many people came to see me off, and most of them said I would never come back."

Sulzer, who was now an experienced and fearless sailor, encountered a major storm on his first night out. It lasted for thirty hours, severely testing his seamanship, and his ship was damaged. Eventually he made it to Mosquito Lagoon, noting, "Mosquito Lagoon is an expansive body of water. The few people who lived on its shores were mostly Negroes and half-breeds. . . . It was the first place, under the American flag, where . . . oranges were grown. . . . From these orange trees came practically all the orange trees in Florida, and other places in the southern part of our Country."

Sulzer left the Mosquito Lagoon and had his ship hauled through a small canal to the head of Indian River. He sailed down the Indian River, stopping at various places for days and nights at a time where he could do business with the white people and a few of the Seminole Indians. He did a profitable trade, exchanging his merchandise for various kinds of skins, egret plumes, and alligator teeth, which were valuable for different purposes at that time. He found plenty of fine fish and the most delicious oysters in the Indian River, and his party could also enjoy meat by hunting deer in the scrub and woods along the river. From Indian River he went up the Banana River to Cape Canaveral, and traded with the people there, then through Jupiter Inlet to Lake Worth. As Sulzer told the story in his autobiographical manuscript:

Many Seminole Indians came there from the Everglades to trade with me. I had a line of goods they desired. Sanchez had seen to this. . . .

I liked Lake Worth very much. It is a beautiful place with an ideal climate—winter and summer. I stayed there as long as I could. Then I . . . sailed south for Miami. Only one white man lived there at the time. He came from Australia. He had a small trading place at the mouth of the Miami River, and did a lucrative business with the Seminole Indians. . . . Both of us did a good business with the Seminole Indians, who lived in the back country, near Lake Okeechobee, and made frequent trips down the Miami River to the trading place. I became well-acquainted with these Indians. I liked them, and soon picked up enough of their language to carry on a conversation. Some of them could speak a little English. . . . They invited me to visit their Chief Tustenugee, at their homes on Lake Okeechobee. . . . The trader from Australia urged me not to go. He said I would not come back; but I went because I had no fear of these Indians, and I wanted to see this part of southern Florida. . . .

At sunrise, one morning, the Indians and I started up the Miami River. There were six Indians and myself in the party, and we had four large canoes, one containing the best things I could pick out from my merchandise, which I intended to present to the Chief, and the most important people of the Tribe. Going upstream was hard work. . . . We were soon in the Everglades, the greatest of their kind on earth. It was a revelation to me. Great stretches of tall saw grass in the swamps, and narrow, devious water passages through them. Then we came to the great cypress forests, and I could see that some of the trees were very old. In the cypress forests were the rookeries of many birds, especially herons, white and blue, from which came the beautiful plumes. Also pelicans, hawks, ospreys, and eagles. Some of these rookeries were very extensive, and the noise the birds made could be heard for long distances. I had never seen anything like this before. These Everglades extended for miles and miles north, south, east, and west. . . . That afternoon we came in sight of the Seminole Villages. I followed the Indians to the largest Village, and caught a glimpse of the Lake. The Indians had very good houses. Around each of the houses I noticed beautiful flowers, and gardens, and patches of tillable land under cultivation. . . . In the doorways I saw the squaws, young and old, and to my amazement some Negroes—men and women. When I asked about these Negroes I was told they were slaves. I found out afterwards that the Seminoles had acquired these slaves before the War Between the States, and that they knew nothing about that war, or the emancipation of the slaves. I also found out that they treated these slaves just as well as themselves, and were kindly disposed to them, and did not work them very hard. My Indian friends conducted me to the large Council House, where I was courteously and hospitably received by Chief Tustenugee. He was a fine looking man, tall and straight as an arrow. His hair was quite gray, and I judged then that he was over sixty years of age. The Indians brought up my presents, and I displayed them to the Chief and his head men and women. They were pleased beyond expression at the display, because the things were just what they wanted. The Chief's son and heir, Jimmy Tustenugee, acted as the interpreter, as the Chief spoke no English. I told him that all he saw was my gift to him, and that he could have whatever he desired for himself and his family, and the balance he could distribute as he saw fit to his friends and relatives, especially the children. He was very much gratified, and made quite a time over me. . . . I could see that I was welcome, and that I need have no fear.

Before I left the chief held a council celebration, and initiated me in the tribe, and made me a blood brother of the Seminoles. I was given an Indian name—Halpatha—which translated, as I was informed, meant alligator. I remained with the Indians for nine days, during which time I did some fishing, and hunting with them, and played different games.

When I took my departure I received a splendid farewell. Everybody—men, women, and children—came to see me off, and bid me a farewell. . . . They loaded one canoe with presents for me, consisting of skins, plumes, alligator teeth, and all sorts of beautiful things made by the Indian men, and their squaws. Some of these presents were invaluable. When I disposed of a few of them I got high prices, and made in actual money more than fifty times the actual value of the gifts I had presented.

The Australian trader, at the mouth of the Miami River, was amazed when I returned. He told me that I was the first white man, so far as he knew, who had ever been to the Lake, or the Indian community; he was gratified that I had received such a welcome and reception; and had been made a blood brother of the Tribe. The next day I bid the trader, Jimmy Tustenugee, and the few Indians who brought me back, a long farewell. . . . I then sailed for the Bahama Islands, as I wanted to see them, and perhaps do some trading there.

The trip to the Bahamas did not take long. He visited several towns, met many people there, and sold a good part of his cargo for cash—English money. He liked the Bahamas, the people, the climate, and the scenery. After leaving the Bahamas, Sulzer sailed south to Key West: "I liked the town, and saw about everything there was in it. I made some friends and acquaintances, and soon disposed all my cargo, at very favorable prices. So I had considerable money, all of which I had made since I left St. Augustine. I deposited $5,000 in the bank, and took a cashier's check for $3,000, which I mailed to Mr. Sanchez, in St. Augustine, with a letter telling him about my trip and its success, and squaring my obligation to him for the cargo."

When Sulzer left Key West, he set out for the West Indies, and some of the ports along the Spanish Main, from Colon to Rio de

Janeiro, intending to stop at the principal ports and do some trading. By careful investigation he found out just about the best goods and merchandise to buy for this purpose, and loaded them aboard his schooner. He visited several ports in Cuba, Haiti, Santo Domingo, Puerto Rico, Jamaica, Columbia, Venezuela, the Windward Islands, and finally to Rio de Janeiro. He saw much of the West Indies, much of the northern part of South America, and incidentally picked up enough Spanish to carry on a brief conversation with the people he encountered: "When I reached Rio de Janeiro I was amazed at its beautiful harbor. . . . In all my travels since I have seen few places that impressed me so favorably as the great City of Rio de Janeiro. I spent about two weeks there, and enjoyed every day and night. So did my crew, one of whom had been there before—in a sailing vessel. I disposed of everything I had to sell, and bought quite a supply of things I believed I could dispose of to advantage in Key West."

Sulzer returned to Key West and sold everything he had through his trading, and also sold his schooner. He had accumulated more money than he ever expected to have in his lifetime. He took a steamer to Tampa, Florida and then another to Tallahassee where he spent a few days before returning to St. Augustine.

> The first person I visited was my good friend Sanchez. He was so glad to see me that he hugged me and kissed me. He said: "I knew you would come back." Then he took me to his home, and after a good dinner, he made me remain until long after midnight telling him all about my adventures. I told him how much I had made, and that he was entitled to his share of it, and that I would pay him that the next morning. However, he said he had received my check for $3,000; that this sum was in full settlement; and that it was more than he expected; and I could not make him take another dollar, although I tried my best to make him do so.

Sulzer really considered Mr. Sanchez to be an especially good man and appreciated the faith he had placed in him. Up to the time of Sanchez's death, Sulzer corresponded with him regularly. As Sulzer described the conclusion of his great adventure: "After bidding goodbye to all my friends in St. Augustine I went to Jacksonville, and then leisurely north, visiting many places in the south until I reached Washington. Then I went home. I had been gone about two years. It was a great experience. I had grown older. My health was recovered. I had learned much. I was a different man—a man of the times, and all the times to me were beautiful."

5

Building a Law Practice

After a warm homecoming with his family and several weeks regaling his friends and neighbors in New Jersey about the details of his great adventure at sea, Sulzer decided that the time had come to make a decision about his future. His father encouraged him to buy his own farm and run it, and he actually tried to buy one he liked but could not do so on satisfactory terms.

Sulzer made some visits to the ships massed on South Street in New York City where he was advised that he was still too young to take the examination for a master's certificate. The red tape and pending delays that would be involved in pursuing a serious career at sea so discouraged him that he chose to end his interest in the sea as a career.

He also visited his old employers at Parrish and Pendleton, who were genuinely delighted to see him back in the city and looking so well. He was a very handsome young man, obviously mature beyond his years and attractive to his peers and seniors alike. His former colleagues were intrigued by the stories Sulzer told of his experience at sea during his absence. They offered him his former position as managing clerk. Several other acquaintances in the legal profession also offered him jobs and encouraged him to pursue his legal studies and take the bar exam. All this encouragement from respected professionals persuaded Sulzer to finally commit himself to pursue the law as his career. Because he had saved enough money, he decided that he would not take another job as a law clerk, but would continue to attend trials and study law independently so that he could be prepared for the bar examination when he reached the age of twenty-one in 1884.

31

Sulzer as a young lawyer, from
The United States Red Book, 1896.

When the time came, Sulzer left the family farm and established a residence in New York City. He went before the New York supreme court with fifty other applicants, thirty-seven of whom passed the written exam given to them on the first day. Sulzer was one of nine whose papers were so good that the judges waived the oral exam scheduled for the next day and admitted him directly.

Even though he was offered employment opportunities at several excellent law firms, his inherent self-confidence, enhanced by his passing the bar so easily, convinced him to decide to open his own law office and "never work for anyone again except myself."

His first office was located at the corner of Centre and Chambers streets close to all the courthouses that were then located in City Hall Park. Sulzer set out to become acquainted with politicians and newspapermen who gathered regularly in the area, as well as the lawyers, judges, clerks, and court attendants.

In those days, there were no computers, typewriters, or copying machines. No stenographers or typists were available to help. Like other lawyers of the time, Sulzer hand-wrote and prepared all of his legal papers. He served them himself. When the time came, he was well prepared, had done the appropriate legal research, documented his case with briefs on the facts and the law, and was ready to try each case himself. His various clerkships and his initial law school experience had stood him well. The high quality of his preparation and presentation led to frequent success in the courtroom, which created the foundation of a good reputation as a lawyer and enhanced his self-confidence.

Sulzer was dedicated to building a clientele to support his practice. He was always careful to dress well and began to join organizations that would enable him to meet prospective clients. Already admitted to the

Masonic Lodge in New Jersey, he had his membership transferred to a lodge in Manhattan and began a serious lifelong pursuit of Masonry. Sulzer developed a flair for catching clients and he worked hard at it—purposely doing all that he could to meet people, especially business-men, who might help him develop a successful practice. A young lawyer who wanted to build a successful practice could learn a great deal from Sulzer's methods. Today they would call it a marketing plan—but for Sulzer it just came naturally. He studiously sought and took advice from older lawyers who encouraged him and some began to refer matters to him to handle in the courts. Whenever he had nothing else to do he would methodically visit with people he knew and urge them to let him handle any law business they had. This approach landed him the Mer-chant's National Bank as a client in his first year of practice. It seems that the official cashier of the bank, Mr. C. V. Baila, had a farm adjacent to that of Sulzer's father, and Mr. Baila knew him since his boyhood. Mr. Baila wanted to encourage the young lawyer, which he was best able to do by delivering some of the bank's more routine business. Having the bank as a client was a very prestigious credential for a lawyer in his first year of practice.

At the same time, he also pursued his interest in politics, attending political meetings and getting himself known to judges and politicians. As early as 1884, in his first year as a lawyer, he had made "back of the cart" speeches on behalf of Grover Cleveland's presidential campaign. In that campaign he organized the Young Men's Democratic Club in New York and became its first president. Years later this club became the National Democratic Club.[1]

Toward the end of his first year in practice, Sulzer moved to a $20-per-month small suite in an office building at 71 Broadway that con-tained several large law firms and various business concerns. A principle reason for moving was a desire to expose himself to more people who could help develop his law practice. He made it a point to meet most of the office building's occupants in the hallways and elevators. This was in keeping with his objective to secure businessmen as clients. By diligently following up on every contact he made, he became quite successful as an attractive and outgoing young man who would not hesitate to intro-duce himself to everyone he met in a business context.

On one memorable occasion, the aggressive but quite charming young lawyer encountered Jay Gould, the railroad tycoon, as he left 71 Broadway where he had an office on the floor below Sulzer's. Sulzer walked him back to his other office in the Western Union Building on Dey Street. Gould was friendly and asked young Sulzer about how his law practice was getting along. Before taking his leave, Mr. Gould asked him to call upon him at three o'clock the next afternoon.

When Sulzer arrived, Mr. Gould invited him into his large and ornately paneled office, taking a chair at the side of the railroad tycoon's desk. "Mr. Sulzer," Gould said, "do you know anything about railroad law, and the court's decisions affecting railroads?" Sulzer frankly admitted that he knew very little about the subject, but expressed his confidence that he was well trained to find out anything he needed to know. Impressed with the candor and self-confidence that Sulzer had expressed, Gould gave him a small assignment involving the analysis of the legality of a Missouri Pacific Railroad bond. Sulzer offered to research and brief the issues within ten days. Mr. Gould said, "Take your time, but do it thoroughly." Sulzer appreciated the value of having Jay Gould as a client, and devoted the entire next week to doing the necessary research and provided a careful brief of some twenty handwritten pages. When Sulzer presented his brief, it so impressed Gould that he sent him a $2,500 check in response to Sulzer's $250 bill, along with a great compliment about the job he did.

By the end of his second year as a lawyer, Sulzer was doing so well developing his own clientele and receiving referrals from lawyers who retained him to do their trial work that he was "making ten times more money than I spent," while constantly pursuing more relationships with businessmen, lawyers, and judges. He became counsel to a major silk importer and, by making the acquaintance of the president of the New York Pie Baking Company, "got all of its business."

As part of his business-oriented self-promotion, Sulzer took up residence at the International Hotel on Park Row where he once again made it his business to meet as many people as he could. To Sulzer, the International Hotel afforded another opportunity to expand his contacts. There, for example, he met Henry George, the great teacher of economics, and dined frequently at his table and discussed economic theory. Ambitious and energetic, young Sulzer was out almost every night, making a point of frequenting the large number of leading hotels and restaurants (which he called "resorts") where he could count on encountering the rich and famous of old New York. On the second floor of the Astor House at Vesey Street and Broadway was one of his favorite spots, called "Room No. 1," where editors, newspapermen, lawyers, judges, and well-known politicians would gather every afternoon at the famous Rotunda Restaurant. There he met more important men and deliberately cultivated their acquaintance, which he claimed was a great help to him later in his career. For example, he made the acquaintance of W. S. Porter, the writer who became known as "O. Henry," who introduced him to Joseph Pulitzer, the famous publisher, another one of his early acquaintances. Among the favorite hostelries in the immediate area, which attracted Sulzer for companionship, food, and drink, was the Cosmopolitan Hotel on the corner of Chambers and West Broadway, and the Stevens House where Sulzer claimed to have made the acquaintance of Robert Louis Stevenson when he visited New York.

Throughout the early years of building his law practice in downtown New York, Sulzer also pursued his genuine interest in the theater, cultivating a theatrical practice and attending shows at such places as the Bailey Theater, Harrigan and Harts, Tony Pastor's, the Union Square Theater, the Academy of Music, and Daly's Theater, among others. Some of the actors and actresses he met in these days became clients of his law practice. Some of the theatrical cases he tried, in those early days, attracted a great deal of valuable newspaper publicity. That helped him get talked about as a lawyer by fellow members of the bar and the public in general. He knew the value of being known and talked about, and the young lawyer made an effort to be out more or less every night going around here and there.

Sulzer would frequently take the brightly colored stage drawn by two horses up Broadway. He considered Broadway to be the center of significant social activity because so many important people of his day walked up Broadway to their homes. There were a number of famous places where people would stop to socialize, have a drink, or break bread. The first place above Chambers Street was Niblo's Garden, which also provided legitimate theater, then part of the Broadway Central Hotel. As one proceeded further north, he or she would encounter the St. Denis Hotel, the New York Hotel, Sinclair House, and then the famous Morton House at Broadway and Fourteenth Street at Union Square, just a block over from Delmonico's great restaurant then at Fourteenth Street and Fifth Avenue.

In addition to deliberately cultivating the friendship of prominent lawyers, judges, and politicians, during that period Sulzer frequented second-hand bookstores, began building his own library, and took a keen interest in literature. During his early years at the bar, he was impressed with the quality of New York's newspapers and what he considered to be the courage of conviction evidenced by many of the editors and critics of the day who molded public opinion. Whenever he could do so, he also sought the acquaintance of newspapermen, both reporters and editors, which he did both by frequenting their favorite bars and restaurants and writing letters to the editor.

After successfully trying a significant commercial case in 1887, his fourth year as a sole practitioner, Sulzer was induced to join a law firm offering him an attractive partnership. The firm became known as Henderson, Sulzer and Forster and occupied the entire first floor of a large old brownstone building at 24 Park Place. He became the firm's leading trial lawyer and again went out of his way to make new contacts with all of the other tenants of the building.

At this time in his life, Sulzer, who would eventually acquire a justified reputation as an excellent speaker, worked at perfecting his speech-making ability by studying English classics in order to improve his command of the language. As he described it, "In my speeches I made it a rule to use plain, simple, well-understood Saxon words, and endeavored to confine myself to one, or two, or three syllables. I used short sentences, and eschewed foreign words, and their derivatives. In this way I acquired a good vocabulary, and a multitude of simple words and short sentences that could be utilized at any time for their effect on my hearers, not only in the courtroom, but at other places where I attended meetings and made addresses."

He made it a rule to attend every meeting he could, and if the opportunity was offered, "to deliver an address more or less appropriate to the occasion." As a result, he made new acquaintances and became known as an eloquent speaker.

In 1888, in his fifth year of practicing law, Sulzer moved his residence uptown to the Morton House—well known as a center of activity for prominent politicians, and business and theater people. It had an excellent bar and restaurant, as well as banquet rooms. Sulzer admitted that his object in moving to the Morton House was to meet people who he could make friends with and increase his law practice. Sulzer was shameless in his pursuit of people who could be helpful to him—and as he once said: "I was always busy, and I always worked fast." In general his early pursuit of power was succeeding.

After a year with the firm of Henderson, Sulzer and Foster, a relationship that had been very satisfactory, Sulzer nevertheless told his partners that he wanted to withdraw to have more time to pursue other interests. They were unable to dissuade him and, after an amicable parting, he opened his own office again, this time taking three rooms at 24 Park Place, and the twenty-five-year-old hired two younger associates to assist him with his growing practice.

It was 1888 and among the interests Sulzer wanted more time for was the pursuit of politics, an interest since childhood. His appetite for politics had been developed during his youth in New Jersey, his experience as a speaker in the 1884 presidential campaign, and his attendance at whatever political meetings he could attend. Years after, Sulzer recalled:

> Wherever there was a meeting, of any consequence, I endeavored to be invited, and called on for a speech. Speech-making was my ambition. I was then a ready and a fluent speaker. I never spoke too long, but always to the point, and tried to say a few things that would stick like burrs in the brains of my hearers, so that they would never forget what I said. Besides, before I was admitted to the Bar, and afterwards up to this time, whenever I could attend a political meeting I did so, and delivered a speech more or less effectively. In this way I became acquainted with some of the leading politicians, and office-holders, of the city. I cultivated their acquaintance, and whenever I could be useful to them as a speaker I gladly volunteered.

Sulzer claimed that he had a genuine relationship with President Grover Cleveland who ran for reelection in 1888. As he describes it:

> I did all I could for him in 1884 and in 1888. I often saw him. We became great personal friends. I always liked him, and admired him, and supported him. . . . I called to see him twice, while he was in the White House in 1885 and 1887. I attended his inauguration in 1885. On one of these occasions he offered me a political appointment, but I declined it on the ground, as I explained, that my law business needed all my time, and would not permit me to accept a political office as I could not

do justice to its administration. Besides, I then told President Cleveland that I would never accept an appointive office; that if I had any ambition in politics it was to be elected by the people to the New York Legislature, so that I could make an intensive study of how the laws of my State were made, and that would help me in my legal career. Mr. Cleveland was very nice about it, and gave me good counsel. He said: "Mr. Sulzer, we need able lawyers like you, not only in the Legislatures of our States, as well as in the National Legislature, in Washington." He told me to take his advice and go to Albany when the opportunity presented itself, and after making a record in the State capitol to go to Congress and make a record there. He said the legislative branch of the Government was its greatest branch, and the people's branch, and the people should take more interest in the sort of men they sent to the Legislatures, and to the Congress of the United States.

During the 1888 presidential campaign, he attended the convention, which renominated Cleveland. Sulzer offered his services to the Democratic State Committee of New York, and the Democratic National Committee as a speaker on behalf of Cleveland's reelection campaign, and made a very good impression on those who heard him. After Cleveland lost, Sulzer was so disappointed that he could not get over it. On reflection years later, Sulzer opined that Cleveland did not receive the support he should have received from some disgruntled factions in his party. "I knew this, and I never forgot it."

6

Politics Rears Its Head

As the son of Thomas Sulzer, young William's interest in politics came very naturally. Thomas, who the governor-to-be described as a "liberal and intense Democrat,"[1] had participated in the presidential campaigns of 1868, 1872, and 1876, when the family lived in New Jersey. In those days, long before the impact of television or even radio, a much greater percentage of the citizenry involved themselves in election campaigns than is the case today, and many people took active parts in political campaigns. As an observer of his father's activity and sharing his father's interests, Bill saw and overheard a lot of talk about the intricacies of politics, and he shared his father's enthusiasms and his deep disappointments. Sulzer always remembered that his father took him to campaign rallies and exposed him to speeches of Horace Greeley, Samuel J. Tilden, and others.

The year 1876 was a tumultuous one in America. Post–Civil War Reconstruction was coming to an end in the South. General George Armstrong Custer, a national hero, and six hundred members of the U.S. Cavalry were slain by Chief Crazy Horse's Sioux at the Battle of the Little Bighorn on June 25. The presidential election was an unusual and exciting one, which pitched New York governor Samuel Tilden, the Democrat, against Ohio governor Rutherford B. Hayes, the Republican. Tilden won the popular vote by a substantial margin, but fell one vote short of winning the electoral majority. However, the votes in four states were challenged on the basis of allegations of fraud and intimidation of voters. The viciousness of the allegations nearly brought the

39

country to the brink of another civil war, and the election was eventually decided by the House on a narrow party vote. Hayes was declared the winner as a result of a swap of votes with to Southern interests who were promised that the last federal troops policing the South would be withdrawn.

The entire Sulzer family in New Jersey were ardent Democrats. In July 1880, young Sulzer, then seventeen years old, wrote a long, eleven-page letter addressed to his Aunt Leticia, his grandparents, and cousins describing the details of a vacation he took by himself earlier that summer aboard the handsome Hudson River steamer *Mary Powell*, a two-stack side-wheeler that was then the fastest boat on the river and was known as the "Queen of the Hudson." The boat went from New York City, north through the Tappan Zee, visiting the villages of the lower Hudson Valley and on to West Point where Sulzer and the other tourists saw the campus on the high ground along the Hudson, and watched the cadets on parade. Before coming home, Sulzer spent a few days at Coney Island, which, although the amusement parks had not yet been built, was then a major attraction for the city's masses seeking a variety of recreation. Coney Island offered sideshows, gambling of all kinds, the delights of clam chowder at five cents and fabulous food at the better hotels lining the boardwalks, clam digging, a huge bathing beach with an evening fireworks show, and music provided by some of the great bands of the day. Apologizing for not having written sooner, and begging his aunt's forgiveness for not coming to visit her in Passaic, Sulzer said that if she did not accept his letter in exchange for the visit she expected, he would "take the scolding like a Jersey Democrat," indicating the teenager's involvement in politics.

After describing the sights encountered on his trip in great detail, and extending his mother's greetings and invitations to the Passaic relatives, Sulzer concludes his letter with his first recorded political observation, obviously referring to the 1880 presidential campaign. "The Democratic platform is rotten. Independence now, independence forever. We do not want to pay $200,000,000 Southern war debt. Dixie! A cold day for Hancock & English!" (Winfield S. Hancock of Pennsylvania and William H. English were the Democratic candidates for president and vice president who were defeated by James Garfield and Chester A. Arthur.)

With so much interest in politics in his formative years, it comes as no surprise that, upon becoming a lawyer and acquiring the skills of oratory, the young attorney should gravitate toward political activities and eventually public office.

Sulzer developed a reputation as an excellent speaker, beginning with his service to the Democratic Party as a "cart tail" orator on behalf of Grover Cleveland's presidential campaign; first in 1884 and again in 1888. His speeches, beautifully delivered from the back of a horse-drawn cart, which provided the speaker's platform as well as the transportation, eventually attracted the attention of a number of prominent political leaders, including John Reilly, then the Tammany leader of the old 14th assembly district in Manhattan's Lower East Side. Reilly, one of the politicians Sulzer befriended at Morton House, treated Sulzer as a protégé and a resource, and he sent him stump speaking on behalf of other Democratic candidates. Sulzer warmed to his political tasks and soon became known as "Reilly's boy spellbinder." The young lawyer's reputation as an orator was growing. Sulzer fully appreciated the fact that was as true then as now—as he increased his circle of friends and acquaintants, he also enhanced his prospects of obtaining legal business, which was his primary goal. Sulzer, who had become an exceedingly ambitious young lawyer, had been changing his residential address with some frequency; he saw that by moving into Reilly's 14th district, he would be in a position to take greater advantage of Reilly's warmth and enthusiasm. The 14th ran from Eighth Street to Fourteenth Street on the Lower East Side of New York City. So, with Reilly's encouragement, Sulzer changed his residence again. In September 1889, he moved from Morton House, taking two sunny rooms on the second floor of a large brownstone on Twelfth Street near Second Avenue. The house was owned by a German family who warmly welcomed Thomas Sulzer's son as a member of their own family.

Sulzer's affinity for John Reilly was enhanced by the fact that Reilly and his brother, Bernard, were strong supporters of his hero, Grover Cleveland. Bernard, the older brother, had already served as sheriff of New York County, and he was also a friend and political aide to Governor Samuel Tilden, who ran unsuccessfully for president in 1876. As sheriff, an unsalaried but much sought after political position in which the incumbent earned fees for his services, Bernard had secured his financial future with the help of the Tammany Democrats.

The Reillys promised Sulzer that they would help advance his career if he moved into their 14th district. They explained to him that he would have a political future in the 14th and could expect a judgeship whenever he desired to go on the bench. In those days, the district was still predominantly Irish-German and Sulzer's ethnic background made him very attractive to the constituency. European Jews and others were moving in as new tenement buildings were constructed. As important members of the Tammany organization, the Reilly brothers were in a position to back up such promises. John Reilly had the new resident of his district elected as a member of the Tammany Hall General Committee for the 14th district, which was a politically prestigious post for such a young man. It's not clear if Sulzer knew that he was taking on obligations when he accepted the enthusiastic support of John Reilly—who was a significant Tammany power. When a district leader wielded his constituency behind a candidate, that candidate was expected to be loyal to the organization. What such loyalty entailed would depend upon the public office that the candidate held and the extent of the particular leader's involvement with people who might need the help of the elected official.

New York was an especially exciting city in 1889. President Benjamin Harrison came to the city in April to join in the three days of festivities celebrating the centennial of the United States. Fifty thousand New Yorkers marched in the grand parade.

New York's Lower East Side had become the Mecca for the great wave of European immigrants who began to arrive in the beginning of the previous decade. By the time Sulzer sought his first elective office, the area had become the most densely populated place in the times, crowded with the new immigrants then arriving from Southern and Eastern Europe. Because the tenements were so crowded, city life easily spilled into the streets, which became a vast open-air bazaar, swarming with peddlers of every kind, hawking their wares in a great cacophony. Nearly 25,000 pushcarts lined the Lower East Side streets, selling everything from clothes to food.

During the summer of 1889, Sulzer was invited to the outings, excursions, clambakes, and chowder parties that were regular events sponsored by political leaders in the various assembly districts. These were occasions for great fun for the constituents and opportunities to meet the people who were prominent in politics, and those who supported them at all levels of the community. Five-dollar tickets were given away to constituents and the events were financed by selling tickets to saloonkeepers, storekeepers, prostitutes, gamblers, and business people who might need political help from time to time.

These summertime affairs were traditionally held in popular picnic groves in northern Manhattan, the Bronx, and Westchester to which the faithful would usually be transported by the hundreds and sometimes thousands in large excursion steamboats.

A typical summer outing organized by a successful assembly district leader started at 9 a.m. and involved several steamboats, staffed with musicians. On board, the leader provided candy and quarts of ice cream, as well as sandwiches, chicken, pies, soft drinks, and nursing bottles of milk for the babies when women and children were included. The steamboats were loaded with roulette wheels, faro and poker tables, dice and other portable gambling devices, which appeared just as soon as the hawsers were loosed from the piers. Some staterooms were set aside for the distinguished guests with names like "Big Tim" Sullivan, "Silver Dollar" Smith, and some with titles like "alderman," "sheriff," "senator," and "commissioner," who were given playing cards and served champagne at special receptions. A bar was always open where whiskey and beer were served to those who were gambling or just enjoying the fresh air.

There was a large, happy, and already grateful group debarking at the park at the end of the excursion, where the beer would flow and grills would be set up around the portable dance floor, surrounded by long rows of picnic tables. While the gambling continued during the afternoon, every sort of outdoor game was available to the merrymakers—and there were plenty of contests of skill and athletic prowess. Some men played baseball and some rushed to the water for swimming. Men splashed each other with seawater and roared raucously. Amateur prizefights were set up for the entertainment of the crowds. Teams of nine fat men played baseball against teams of nine lean men; bachelors were pitted against married men. Offish laughter was generated by footraces between the fat men. Con men were also a constant presence, demonstrating their ability with a shell game or loaded dice at the risk of getting caught and suffering a punch in the nose. Fireworks were usually set off on the way home.

When the revelers got back to the city in the evening, the party would usually end with a torchlight procession through the assembly district where the sponsoring Tammany association would have its headquarters. The people would be handed souvenir buttons with ribbons attached commemorating the occasion, amid more fireworks and exhortations of glory to the local political boss and the grandeur of

Tammany Hall, as well as suggestions as to who deserved their next vote. By the time the exhausted people of all ages returned to their homes, the occasion was memorable and nobody would forget their sponsors when they asked for their vote on Election Day.

A barbecue given by a well-known Tammany leader named William S. Devery, who was also the police commissioner,[2] on an empty lot in his district just before the September primary was eloquently described in *Tammany Hall*.[3]

> Shortly before the primary election in September Devery gave a barbecue on an empty lot in his district. It was said that twenty thousand glasses of beer were given away that hot summery day on the dusty lot. Men scrambled over each other to reach the refreshments. The beer was brought up in kegs, and the drivers of the brewery wagons wore red-white-and blue rosettes, and the wagons were draped with Devery banners. Each keg was marked "Special Devery Brew." Fifteen bartenders served the large crowd, and butchers cut bullocks to make sandwiches. Devery had ordered that no beer should be given to children, but a *Sun* reporter saw small bodies crawling between the legs of the men in order to get where the beer was distributed. The police were forced to drive back with pieces of rubber hose some of the pushing crowd.

In those days, and for years to come, the assembly district leader was a very pivotal figure in the body politic. The secret of success of the Tammany Hall organization, like its counterparts in many of the great cities across America at that time, was the fact that the organization was led by men who were working at the business of politics every day of the year.

Supported by a group of hard-working, handpicked precinct "captains," the district leader was known to everyone in the district and it was his business to know everyone who lived there and to understand their personal problems. As most successful leaders perceived their role, it was their duty to get jobs for the people in their neighborhood, to pay their rent when they were unable to do so, to get them out of trouble when they got arrested, and to keep them amused with outings in the summer and dinner dances in the winter.

The famous Chronicler of Tammany, George Washington Plunkitt, a state senator and district leader, once described the typical day's work of a Tammany district leader. Starting with an interruption to his sleep at 2 a.m., the leader is called on to bail out a saloonkeeper who was arrested for violating some liquor law. He is back in bed at 3 a.m., but at 6 a.m. he is awakened again to attend a fire where he meets several of his election district captains and helps find hotel rooms, clothes. and food for victims. Fires were considered to be great vote-getters. During the day, the leader helped six constituents with problems in police court, securing the discharge of four after a few words with the judge, and paying the fine for two others. He then went to another court and paid the rent for a poor family about to be evicted. Back at his district office, he met with four men looking for help in getting or keeping jobs with the city or a utility company, all of whom he was able to help.

In the late morning he attended funerals at different churches and synagogues, and then had several meetings with his election district captains on campaign matters. In the afternoon he attended wakes, weddings, and bar mitzvahs, and in the evening he made shivah calls.

In the evening he attended a Jewish wedding reception and went to a Catholic church fair after holding a meeting with a dozen pushcart peddlers who needed his help with policemen who were harassing them.

All that was expected for these various services was that the constituent would support the Tammany candidate on Election Day, which, as Plunkitt said with colorful clarity, they usually did because most of them did not care who they voted for anyway.[4]

In the fall of 1889, the Reilly brothers encouraged Sulzer to run for the state assembly. The Tammany faction of the party was then in the minority in the 14th district and the Reillys told him that, although he might not win, running for public office would bring him some prominence and would certainly help his law business. So, Sulzer, not really expecting to win, decided to give it a try and took the nomination on the regular Democratic ticket, the local branch of the Tammany organization.

Early in October of 1889, a few Democrats under Reillys' auspices assembled at the corner of Second Avenue and Fourteenth Street and, with very little enthusiasm, nominated Sulzer. The regular Democratic candidate was pitted against a Republican candidate who also had the support of those Democrats called the County Democracy, a rival to Tammany, who formed a Fusion ticket that was the favorite in the race.

Sulzer approached the opportunity to get elected with every bit of his energy and ingenuity. He made a good platform issue for himself with speeches against the Broadway railway franchise being granted in perpetuity to a private corporation; the issue of public versus private ownership of city franchises was a hot one, and Tammany usually found itself on the other side—supporting their friends in businesses that supported their candidates. The Democratic organization in the district was not strong enough to be very helpful in a situation in which they did not consider their prospects to be good enough to be assured of success. Sulzer was not to be discouraged and he decided to go door-to-door and meet as many people as he could, relying on the force of his personality and the self-confidence of a young man who had generally succeeded in whatever he undertook up until then.

His family in New Jersey was very supportive and they were delighted to see his picture in the hometown newspaper. His sister, Lillie, wrote to him a few days after the nomination to express their prayers for his success and conveying his mother's concern about his being out at night and overdoing it physically. She obviously had not heard about his experience in the neighborhood in his district that was known as "Mackerelville," two blocks on Thirteenth Street between First Avenue and Avenue B. It was named for its many fish businesses and fish peddlers. These particular blocks consisted of small brick houses on both sides of the street, with a saloon on the ground floor of almost all the houses, with people living above. Until 1880 it had been almost exclusively populated by poor Irish immigrants, but new tenements were being built there and were attracting European Jews to the neighborhood. Criminologists of the day described it as one of the most wicked places on earth, with more burglaries, robberies, and criminals than any other place in America.

Disregarding advice, Sulzer decided to go there on the third night of his campaign in order to find out if it was as bad as it was reported to be.

Sulzer entered the first saloon he encountered on the north side of Thirteenth Street just east of Third Avenue. He intended to introduce himself to all the bartenders on the block, convinced that they might become valuable allies in his quest for votes. Continuing his practice of always being well dressed, Sulzer wore his customary high silk hat and cutaway coat; the room was empty except for the bartender. Sulzer laid a dollar bill on the bar and asked for a drink. He announced that he was a candidate for the assembly and if the bartender had any friends in the back room, he would like to buy them all a drink and shake their hands.

The bartender looked at the young lawyer, said nothing, and whisked the bill into the cash drawer. Then he gave a low whistle. Suddenly, Sulzer was surrounded by a dozen tough guys who without a word began to pummel and kick him, and throw him through the batwing doors of the saloon into the middle of the street. When he picked up his bloody and bruised body, he saw that his coat and trousers were torn and his hat was gone. After that experience, Sulzer wore old clothes and an old felt hat whenever he campaigned for political office.

As soon as he recovered from the beating after two days' rest, he went door-to-door and visited every store he could reach in the district without going near Mackerelville again. He attended every meeting that took place in the district to introduce himself and make a speech whenever he was given the opportunity. He called on newspaper editors, including Joseph Pulitzer, editor of the *New York Times*, and earned the support of that influential paper.

He took advice from his old friend, former president Grover Cleveland, who had moved to New York City after he was defeated for reelection in 1888. Cleveland introduced him to the editor of *New Yorker Staats-Zeitung*, the leading German newspaper in the city. That paper was influential in the district and helped him though its columns. Germans were at the time the largest block of immigrants in the city and in his Lower East Side district, although some had already started to migrate uptown to what is now Yorkville.

Sulzer's personal campaign was unique to that district and to the surprise of supporters and adversaries alike, Sulzer won the election by an eight hundred–vote majority.

He was the only Democrat on the ticket to carry the district and political leaders outside of the 14th took notice of what he had accomplished. Soon he began to receive speaking invitations from political and civic organizations around the city. Sulzer's political star was rising.

7

A Connected Assemblyman

Although his unexpected victory on Election Day made him an immediate minor celebrity among Democrats and journalists, Sulzer concentrated on the clients of his thriving law practice from Election Day until year-end. On the first of the new year he would have to start attending sessions of the legislature in Albany for a couple of days each week until the legislature adjourned in early spring.

In the middle of December 1889 the assemblyman-elect was summoned to Tammany Hall by Richard Croker, who by that time had been the leader of the New York City Democrats for three and a half years.

The new Tammany Hall building on Fourteenth Street was erected in 1867. As he entered Tammany's headquarters, Sulzer looked up at the elegant façade adorned by a white marble statute of the Delaware Indian chief Tamanend, from whom the Tammany name is derived. (Tamanend was a great Delaware warrior famous for his sagacity and love of liberty. Before the American Revolution, he ruled over thirteen tribes of the Lenni-Lenape [Delaware] Confederacy in the area that became New York, New Jersey, Delaware, and Pennsylvania. Tamanend was an exemplary leader.)

America's oldest political organization, the Tammany Society was incorporated in New York in 1805, although branches already existed in most of the original thirteen colonies. Long before the term "networking" became popular, the Tammany Society was primarily a social association that existed to enhance the financial interests of its members. Its Civil War regiment, the 42nd New York Volunteers, organized in 1861, was among the earliest to go to war on behalf of the Union.

These New Yorkers bore the brunt of Pickett's Charge at Gettysburg and the monument to Tammany's soldiers can be viewed there to this day. Over the years before the Civil War, the organization broadened its base to service new immigrants, and it developed into a political powerhouse.

Richard Croker's predecessor, "Honest John" Kelly, managed Tammany and much of city government from 1872 until his death in June of 1886. Kelly inherited the organization from the infamous Henry Marcy Tweed, "Boss Tweed," the Tammany leader who died in the city jail in 1878 after being convicted in 1871 and sentenced to twelve years for leading what was known as the "Tweed Ring," a group of Tammany politicians who literally stole over $50 million of city funds and very nearly bankrupted the city. Out of the ashes of this mother of municipal scandals rose Honest John Kelly, who succeeded in putting a clean new face on the discredited old machine. He did it by attracting some people of excellent reputation to join him in revitalizing the tarnished Tammany organization and set out, with considerable success, to bury the Tweed Ring stigma. Under Kelly's vision, Tammany became synonymous with an effective Democratic Party machine for electing public officials. Kelly perfected Tammany into the model of an efficient political organization, determining nominations, controlling city government, and rewarding the faithful district leaders, captains, and other workers with city jobs and contracts. It was Kelly who first created the concept of requiring the party's candidates for public office to contribute campaign funds to the organization in order to secure a nomination and leaving it to the organization to decide which of its slate of candidates it really needed to spend money on. The amount of the tariff varied with the significance of the office they sought. Personal campaign finance efforts were not permitted. Once elected, officeholders, including judges, were required to contribute a percentage of their salaries to the party organization, a practice that lasted in some places for nearly a century and in a few instances is still going on in one form or another. Kelly's people understood the importance of organizational loyalty and cooperation. It is far more efficient to have the party decide where to spend its money because it can ignore those candidates who are sure winners while marshalling its resources for those whose elections are closer contests, even though they may not be as attractive as fundraisers. This same concept is employed today by United States Senate and Congressional Campaign Committees, as well as the state legislative campaign committees. It allows the leadership of the House to use its incumbency and its collective ability to attract the money to allocate to marginal districts in the hope of electing additional loyal members and enhancing party control of the particular house.

Honest John Kelly kept his administration of Tammany Hall free of scandal. Although Kelly accumulated a personal fortune of half a million dollars during his years as a leader, his personal integrity was never questioned.

As Kelly's longtime protégé, Richard Croker almost automatically took his place as Grand Sachem, the official title of the leader of the Tammany Society and chief of Tammany Hall, which was effectively the Democratic Party organization in New York County. Croker ascended to the Tammany throne almost by default because, at the time of Kelly's rather sudden death in 1886, Croker was his right-hand man, conveying the boss's orders to the Executive Committee during Kelly's final illness. Because of his obviously close relationship with Kelly, the sachems assumed that Croker was Kelly's heir-apparent, and he was readily accepted by the Executive Committee. Croker secured his support among the other district leaders by wisely assuring those who supported him that they would share in whatever patronage he acquired. Tammany grew and prospered under Croker's strong leadership and he presided as undisputed chief for nearly two decades, growing very rich in the process, while always allowing his loyal district leaders to enjoy a prosperous share of the opportunities.[1]

Croker had just begun to accumulate his enormous power as chief of Tammany Hall when he sent for the young man who had surprised everyone by getting elected as a Tammany Democrat from the 14th district. Until then, Sulzer had no contact with Croker, although he assumed Croker's blessing when he was nominated to run for the assembly by his district leader, John Reilly. The politicians thought Sulzer would only be a sacrificial lamb in a district where Tammany was outnumbered by a coalition of Republicans and anti-Tammany Democrats. But, Sulzer won the seat without the organization's active participation by virtue of his own dogged determination, eloquence, and hard work. In doing so, he had vanquished Tammany's enemies. Sulzer owed nothing to Croker.

Before going upstairs to Mr. Croker's office, Sulzer looked into the main hall, which featured a nearly life-size portrait of Richard Croker over the huge fireplace adorned with three-foot-high brass andirons and a tiger skin rug. The tiger's massive head looked up from the floor and his wide and open mouth faced the door to greet visitors. On the great mantle there was Tammany's symbol, a large bronze tiger, about three feet long and a foot high, standing at the base of the Croker portrait. On each side of the fireplace were four large leather easy chairs. Two matching leather couches at an angle to the fireplace wall on each side of the room completed the clubby furnishings.

Sulzer was ushered into the chieftain's mahogany-paneled office. Wearing his customary dark, pinstriped vested suit with a white wing-collared shirt and white pocket handkerchief, forty-six-year-old Croker, despite his relatively short, stocky stature and relatively large head, managed to be a commanding presence, exuding authority. Known to be a man of few words, he spoke directly and openly. He was always focused and persuasive. The chief rose from behind the large rolltop desk of dark mahogany to greet the clean-shaven and elegantly dressed young man who towered over him. Sulzer was well over six feet tall. Croker's full beard was a neatly trimmed mixture of gray and dark brown. His gray eyes were kindly and sympathetic, and contrasted dramatically with the deep-set piercing blue eyes of his youthful visitor, who was strikingly handsome but still somewhat baby-faced. Sulzer's neatly combed sandy hair, contrasting with his dark blue suit, made him appear more elegant. He exuded the self-confidence of a young man who had been very well accepted by the people of his own community, spoke eloquently, and won his first election when the experts did not think he would. While in awe of Croker's position as Tammany's leader, Sulzer was not intimidated in his presence. To Sulzer, Croker was another important person on whom he must make a good impression.

Croker motioned Sulzer to sit down in one of the dozen identical ornate oak armchairs that lined the wall of the large room dominated by a huge chandelier and several heavy oil paintings, a room which was better designed for large group meetings than it was for intimate interviews. As he seated himself in the similar oak chair that matched the mahogany desk, the city's most powerful politician took the measure of this potential new star on the Democratic firmament. Croker was friendly and began the conversation by graciously congratulating Sulzer on the unexpected success of his first election campaign. Then, with no further preamble, Croker said: "Mr. Sulzer, you enjoyed the nomination of the Tammany organization, and you made the most of it. We are very delighted. Now I need to know if we can count on you to stand by the

Assemblyman Richard Croker, from Alfred Henry Lewis, *Richard Croker* (New York: Life Publishing Co., 1901).

organization." Sulzer, who would later claim that he didn't fully grasp the significance of Croker's question, responded grandiloquently: "I am a Democrat through and through, and I will always stand by the Democratic Party when I believe it is right and I hope it will always be right."

Sulzer appreciated Croker's cordial and friendly attitude and he was very pleased at his reception. Before Sulzer took his leave, Croker, apparently satisfied with Sulzer's response, told him, "You can always call on me whenever I can be helpful. Call me here or at the city Chamberlain's office. I will be available to you."

The city chamberlain handled deposits of public money, maintained the city's financial records, and made quarterly financial reports on the condition of city finances. In addition to his considerable salary, the chamberlain also legally received commissions on the bank accounts he supervised and enjoyed a splendid opportunity to be wined, dined, and rewarded by the banks that competed to hold city funds.

Sulzer was confident that he had made a powerful friend. It is unlikely that he really appreciated just how powerful Croker was. Although only twenty-six years old, Sulzer had already proven himself to be a capable person by so quickly learning enough to become a rather successful lawyer in the big city at a relatively young age, and cunning enough to appreciate the importance of cultivating influential people in order to build his law practice. He was not yet so sophisticated as to understand the totality of the city chamberlain's place in the New York power structure. Some of Croker's power was already apparent, generating frequent criticism from political adversaries, the responsible press, and the several groups of formidable municipal reformers. It was the very same power appreciated by the district leaders who comprised the Tammany Executive Committee from which the power was derived, and by the voters who gave their constant support. It would take the revelations of years of journalistic inquiry and public investigations for only a portion of the extent of Croker's influence to become known. To those who participated in Tammany's operations, or those who benefited from them, Croker was already an impervious hero, an outstanding political operator and wise leader of men who won elections for people who appreciated the help they got and loyally shared some of the benefits he disbursed among his many supporters who did not begrudge him his share.

The story of Croker's rise to the stewardship of Tammany Hall and all that went with it is a fascinating one that exemplifies the assimilation and success of immigrants to America at the turn of the century, and especially so of the Irish who dominated Democratic politics.

Richard Croker was only three years old when he was brought from Ireland's County Cork by his father, a veterinary in the old country who eventually practiced in America as a blacksmith with a horse-drawn street railway company. With only a few years of primary school education behind him, young Richard acquired a reputation as a tough guy in the Lower East Side neighborhood. He was a successful amateur boxer and rose to leadership of the then-infamous "Fourth Avenue Tunnel Gang," one of the many gangs populating that part of the city who made themselves available for nefarious chores, including support of political candidates. America was already engaged in the third year of the Civil War when Croker entered politics at age twenty by working for Tammany Hall on Election Day in 1864, leading a gang of "repeaters"—men who would roam from one polling place to another casting votes wherever they went, but Abraham Lincoln was reelected to his second term as president. By 1865, Croker's enthusiasm for the Democratic Party was so great that he voted seventeen times for one Democratic candidate, according to an admission he proudly made to an investigating committee of the legislature some years afterward. He was elected to the city's Board of Aldermen in 1868 and again in 1869. His political efforts were rewarded by the machine with one city job after another, becoming city coroner in 1873 due to Honest John Kelly's patronage, a position that allowed him to collect $15,000 a year in fees.

No story of Croker's rise in Democratic Party politics can omit the fact that during his days as city coroner, Croker got involved in a fist-fight arising from an exchange of heated words with a political adversary. During the fight, some shots were fired and a bystander was killed. Croker and eyewitnesses claimed he never had a gun, but Croker was identified to the police as the shooter by the dying gasps of the victim. He was arrested and tried before a jury, which was unable to agree on a verdict after seventeen hours of deliberations. Croker was released and never retried and his image was helped not hurt. Subsequently, based on the trial testimony, it became the accepted view that Croker had not fired the shot, which was actually fired by one of his close friends whom Croker would never finger.[2]

The highlight of 1886 in New York City was the dedication of the Statue of Liberty on Bedloe's Island in New York Harbor. Thousands of New Yorkers turned out on a rainy afternoon in October to witness President Grover Cleveland unveil the famous gift from France. People lined the storefronts of lower Manhattan, ships of all kinds circled the site, cannons were fired, and steam whistles blew. It was a glorious day for New York. For years to come, boatloads of new immigrants would thrill to the sight that symbolized liberty as they arrived in America, and many of them would replenish the base of the Tammany organization that would be sure to welcome their support. This was the climate in New York City when Croker ascended to the throne of the chief of Tammany Hall in 1886.

Croker's first major decision as the new leader was to enhance the image of Tammany and of himself as a wise leader by electing his first candidate for mayor, Abraham S. Hewitt. Croker led Tammany into a coalition of other political forces to elect Hewitt, a man with an excellent established reputation. Hewitt had served five terms in Congress and was once chairman of the National Democratic Committee. The mayoral campaign was a dramatic three-way race in which Hewitt, with Tammany's help, defeated economic reformer Henry George and Republican Theodore Roosevelt, who had already distinguished himself as a state assemblyman. Observers of the election said that rarely had so much fraud been employed on behalf of a candidate as those perpetrated on Hewitt's behalf.

After his election, the new mayor was somewhat standoffish toward Tammany and was certainly not tractable enough when it came to fulfilling Tammany's desire to control most public positions. Dedicating himself to demonstrating his independence of character was a prime objective for Hewitt, and he concentrated on ending corruption and improving municipal services, especially in the area of developing the rapid transit system and helping the poor. Mayor Hewitt also managed to offend some important constituencies—especially the Irish—when he stubbornly rejected the custom of flying a green flag over City Hall or the honor of reviewing their St. Patrick's Day Parade, which was already a New York City tradition. The mayor's troubles were compounded by the great blizzard that struck the city in March of 1888, dropping twenty-two inches of snow over three days, leaving hundreds of New Yorkers marooned overnight in their cold offices. Some had to pay bystanders to be rescued from the halted cable cars or elevated trains.

Even though President Cleveland lost his bid for reelection, Croker had restored Tammany as a power in National Democratic politics by supporting Cleveland at the National Democratic Convention in 1888.

In 1888 the next time around, Croker dumped Hewitt and elected his old friend, Hugh Grant, the first reliable Tammany man to be elected mayor since the days of the Tweed Ring. Grant was a wealthy son of a prominent Irish-American family. He had been elected sheriff of New York County in 1885, and he enjoyed a deserved reputation for personal integrity. Grant's election gave Tammany and Croker complete control over city patronage jobs, and city contracts, and assured Croker that he would become a rich man in a very short time. Croker operated from the office of city chamberlain a $25,000 a year mayoral appointment and from the chieftain's office at Tammany Hall.

As city chamberlain under Mayor Grant and leader of Tammany Hall, Croker was in a very influential position on the day in 1889 when he met Sulzer. He was riding high. The city of New York was expanding northward rapidly. The competition for city favors in the area of transportation alone was tremendous. Four lines of elevated railways ran from the tip of Manhattan to Harlem and were already overcrowded. Entrepreneurs with powerful connections were competing for franchises to run electric cable cars and horse cars over the crowded city streets. Croker could pass out many construction contracts and have lots of jobs to award his faithful. As always he maintained the loyalty of his district leaders by having them share in the patronage and giving them a piece of the action.[3]

The range of financial opportunities was enormous, most of it what the colorful George Washington Plunkitt called "honest graft."

Because he spoke out without shame and in colorful language, George Washington Plunkitt became one of the most well-known examples of a Tammany Hall boss in his heyday, which ran from 1868 to 1904. During most of his career he was a state senator and a district leader. At one time Plunkitt served simultaneously as magistrate, alderman, county supervisor, and state senator. His "office" was the bootblack stand at the New York County Courthouse, from which he earned his special reputation by speaking frankly and publicly about how he and Tammany worked. Many of his public statements were gathered in a particularly colorful book published in 1905 by a newspaper reporter named William J. Riordan. The most everlasting chapter in *Plunkitt of Tammany Hall* quoted Plunkitt on "Honest Graft and Dishonest Graft."

Everybody is talkin' these days about Tammany men growin' rich on graft, but nobody thinks of drawin' the distinction between honest graft and dishonest graft. There's all the difference in the Times between the two. Yes, many of our men have grown rich in politics. I have myself. I've made a big fortune out of the game, and I'm gettin' richer every day, but I've not gone in for dishonest graft—blackmailin' gamblers, saloon-keepers, disorderly people, etc.—and neither has any of the men who have made big fortunes in politics.

There's an honest graft, and I'm an example of how it works. I might sum up the whole thing by sayin': "I seen my opportunities and I took 'em."

Just let me explain by examples. My party's in power in the city, and it's goin' to undertake a lot of public improvements. Well, I'm tipped off, say, that they're going to lay out a new park at a certain place.

I see my opportunity and I take it. I go to that place and I buy up all the land I can in the neighborhood. Then the board of this or that makes its plan public, and there is a rush to get my land, which nobody cared particular for before.

Ain't it perfectly honest to charge a good price and make a profit on my investment and foresight? Of course, it is. Well, that's honest graft.

After going on to give several specific examples of how honest graft was earned by those who knew where bridges would be built or park land acquired, and so on, Plunkitt said:

I've told you how I got rich by honest graft. Now, let me tell you that most politicians who are accused of robbin' the city get rich the same way.

They didn't steal a dollar from the city treasury. They just seen their opportunities and took them. That is why, when a reform administration comes in and spends a half million dollars in tryin' to find the public robberies they talked about in the campaign, they don't find them.

As a matter of policy, if nothing else, why should the Tammany leaders go into such dirty business, when there is so much honest graft lying around when they are in power? Did you ever consider that?

Now, in conclusion, I want to say that I don't own a dishonest dollar. If my worst enemy was given the job of writin' my epitaph when I'm gone, he couldn't do more than write:

"George W. Plunkitt. He Seen His Opportunities, and He Took 'Em."[4]

While bribery and skimming public funds were even then prohibited by law, Plunkitt's formula for honest graft was not then illegal, any more than the ability to influence legislation or government action that is purchased through the influence of "soft money" from undisclosed contributors is in America at the turn of the current century.

Croker went on to become the most powerful leader that New York politics had ever known until that time, controlling the Democratic Party and most of its officeholders in all of New York City, including most of its state legislators when he needed them. When he first got involved in Tammany politics Richard Croker was a poor man. When he retired in 1901, he was a multimillionaire. During his last years as the chief of Tammany Hall, Croker attempted to run the organization during long absences abroad by sending international cables to convey his decisions to his Executive Committee in New York—a practice which eventually lost him their support. Resentment about his absences was exacerbated by his marriage at age sixty-five to a widowed teenage American Indian princess who his colleagues referred to as "Pocahontas," to whom Croker left most of his $5 million estate when he died at age seventy-nine in 1922. She was only twenty-nine.

By designating successful candidates for mayor, Croker was rewarded with well-paying city jobs. More importantly for his pocketbook, he was rewarded with a lot of good investment opportunities and perhaps even cash. A few of the facts about Croker's business dealings were revealed during various investigations that took place during his reign and afterward. Rarely did these revelations surprise the public, and even more rarely did they affect the ability of Tammany to turn out the vote. After all, these revelations of Croker's business were no different than the "honest graft" described by Plunkitt and usually accepted by sophisticated people in those days as nothing illegal, however inappropriate. As a matter of fact, many of the city's business leaders participated heavily and profited from Tammany's practices and enjoyed opportunities that were not there for them whenever a municipal reformer got into public office.

Croker's New York was about to enter the gay nineties, a colorful period made familiar in film and literature for its culture of pleasure, gaiety, fun, and bawdiness. The nightlife of the city flourished. Its restaurants, theaters, entertainment, and dance halls became its hallmark. In 1895 there would be 135 dance halls in New York City, mostly in Manhattan. Ragtime music was capturing people's hearts, and dance bands were taking their place on the New York City scene. Dancing schools were teaching social graces to the daughters of the wealthiest families as people believed that proper dancing techniques and etiquette would help to refine society. Other elements of society were attracted by taxi dance halls, where men could meet women for 5¢ a dance. Splendid carriages carried elegant men and beautiful women to the city's nightlife. But, it was also a time when gambling and prostitution would be raised to a more socially acceptable level by virtue of widespread police corruption that not only condoned it, but participated in it, and some of the Tammany district leaders held the franchise for these illicit activities.

While Croker himself was never accused of participation in the take from the gambling dens, bordellos, or police corruption, this business was specifically franchised to other district leaders who supported Croker. Among them was the most powerful of the district leaders—"Big Tim" Sullivan, a state senator, a member of Tammany's Executive Committee, who, along with several other Sullivans dominated the Bowery. Sullivan also supervised government relations for the entrepreneurs who ran much of the gambling that thrived in the mid-Manhattan area known as the Tenderloin, where bordellos and gambling rooms were operating openly under the watchful eye of friendly police officers whose protection was dependent on favors from Tammany leaders. Sullivan had been a state senator for many years. His name survives today as the author of New York's Sullivan Law, which effectively prohibited concealed weapons without a permit from the police department. Sullivan's people were not above carrying guns—he just did not want his adversaries to be able to carry them to facilitate holdups of his bordello operators, so he got his law enacted. Sullivan's colleague Bill Devery, who would eventually become a district leader himself, was chief of police in 1898. He earned his fortune by controlling the police who allowed prostitution to prosper because their proprietors paid their protection money to the police who shared with the district leaders who designated police captains and inspectors who bought their rank from the Tammany leaders who controlled the police. At the time, police captains in Manhattan were reported to have paid $30,000 for their positions, which paid only $15,000 per year.

It is important to understand what kind of a man Richard Croker was because it helps us to appreciate what Sulzer and all the others who encountered him were able to see and relate to one way or another.

Croker surely knew what was going on. Yet, through his own sophisticated business dealings he nurtured the climate in which such basic corruption could survive.

Yet, in 1890, when he gave up the job as chamberlain and no longer had any visible means of support (the position of Tammany chief paid no salary), Croker was able to move from a simple home in the then-middle-class uptown community of Harlem to a large and pretentious house on East Seventy-Fourth Street, just off Fifth Avenue. At that time the neighborhood was one of New York's finest, inhabited by some of the most successful business leaders in the city, who were building large limestone mansions. At the same time, he began to invest serious amounts of money in thoroughbred racehorses in upstate New York and in Tennessee, and started emulating the lifestyle of the very rich. Eventually, Croker would own estates in Florida, England, and Ireland. He would frequently travel among his American estates by rail in a private car. During his term as Tammany's chief, Croker had become a partner in a real estate firm that made some of its profits selling city lands under the control of superior court judges who chose the referees who organized the sales. When asked about this business under oath at an 1899 state legislative hearing of the Mazet Committee, which was investigating the connection between political appointments and lucrative fees, Croker's candid testimony was most revealing. The committee counsel, Frank Moss, put it to Croker:

Q. So we have it then that you, participating in the selection of judges before elections, participate in the emolument that arises down at the end of their proceeding, namely, judicial sales?
A. Yes, sir.
Q. Then, you are working for your own pocket, are you not?
A. All the time—the same as you.[5]

There were many lucrative ventures in which knowledgeable politicians enjoyed the opportunity to make ground-floor investments in the stock of street railway corporations whose franchises were awarded by the city or the elevated railways franchised by the State Public Service Commission. Croker admitted to having participated in some of them, but always refused to be specific. During this same investigation, he told Frank Moss: "I have got nothing to hide at all, and if anyone tells me of a nice stock to buy, and I can make a little turn on it, I am going to do so, and I have done so. . . . But any questions you ask me about my personal business, I decline to answer."[6]

It has been reported that Croker received extraordinary amounts of stock free of charge during his tenure as leader of Tammany Hall. Some of those who made these valuable gifts to Croker were the owners of construction companies who had obtained huge contracts from the development of various aspects of the expanding city roads, buildings, schools, and so forth. Croker owned one building on Park Row, which housed city offices at above-market rents. He had stock in the Roebling Company, which built the Brooklyn Bridge in 1893. When Croker's son Frank, at age twenty-one, became a stockholder and corporate secretary of Roebling, the company was able to sell its fireproofing systems to city public school building projects. Other published stories about Croker's influence that were never proven and were denied by Croker involved cash payments for certain key votes of the city Board of Aldermen. Croker would only admit that he was an expert practitioner of "honest graft" as espoused by Plunkitt, but he was also a superb political leader and organizer who understood how to win elections and who relied on his own strength and leadership skills in doing so, and nobody was ever able to make a charge of illegality that would stick.[7]

Lincoln Steffens was one of the most accomplished newspapermen of the day. He was deeply involved in revealing the worst aspects of municipal corruption, and became the most highly respected of the "muckrakers" who revealed the worst elements of the structure and system that ran New York and other major American cities. Steffens's autobiography is a classic that needs to be read by any student of politics. His perspective of Croker is very revealing. Steffens described his firsthand interview of Richard Croker.

> "Now, then," he said that day as we crossed Union Square, "what do you want to ask me?"
>
> "Well, about this boss-ship," I began. "Why must there be a boss, when we've got a mayor and—a council and . . ."
>
> "That's why," he broke in, "it's because there's a mayor and a council and judges and—a hundred other men to deal with. A government is nothing but a business, and you can't do busi-

ness with a lot of officials, who check and cross one another and who come and go, there this year, out the next. A business man wants to do business with one man, and one who is always there to remember and carry out the—business."

"Business? Business?" I repeated. "I thought government was all politics."

He smiled, turning to look into my face.

"Ever heard that business is business?" he teased. "Well, so is politics business, and reporting— journalism, doctoring— all professions, arts, sports—everything is business."

"But business hasn't any bosses," I said.

He stopped, serious, and as I stopped with him to face him, he protested.

"Now, now, you ain't talking for publication either, and you tell me you have been a Wall Street reporter. If that is true, then you know as well as I do that Wall Street has its bosses just like Tammany and just like the Republican machine."

My blundering answer was the confession, first, that I did know that, and second, that I did not know it till that very day. Recounting to him the thoughts I had had on my way uptown about the parallel of dummy directors and dummy police commissioners, and banker bosses and political bosses, I felt ashamed of the fact that I had not seen those things while I was in Wall Street. My humiliation was wasted. Perhaps my chatter was naïve. Anyway it seemed to please Mr. Croker. He put his arm through mine, saying, "I guess you are on the square all right."

The change of subject embarrassed me; so I blurted out another question.

"But they don't have graft in business. They don't take bribes from saloons, and they don't take away the earnings of the women of the street. How can you stand for that in politics?"

We were walking again, slowly up Broadway, and he strode along in silence for so long that I was about to repeat my question, when he answered.

"There is graft in Wall Street, of course. You don't mean what you say about that. You mean that there isn't any dirty graft, like the police graft, don't you?"

"Yes, that was what I meant."

"Police graft is dirty graft," he said as if to himself. "We have to stand for it. If we get big graft, and the cops and small fry politicians know it, we can't decently kick at their petty stuff. Can we now?" He was looking at me again as he added with sharp emphasis, "We can't be hypocrites, like the reformers who sometimes seem to me not to know that they live on graft."

Again he stopped, and again he wanted to be believed. "This I tell you, boy, and don't you ever forget it: I never have touched a cent of the dirty police graft myself."

I believed it; I never forgot it. It turned out to be true. Richard Croker never said anything to me that was not true unless it was a statement for publication, and then, if it was a lie, he had a way of letting you know it. He had morality. He was true to his professional ethics. And he said things that could be used against him; that day, for example.

"But you do make money out of politics," I said as we paused to part at Madison Square.

"Like a business man in business," he answered, hard as nails, "I work for my own pocket all the time."

He faced me down with it, waiting to hear what I would answer, and when I did not answer, when he saw that I was thinking in a whirl, he turned warm and sweet again, held out his soft, small, white hand, and bade me good-by.

"Come and see me again," he invited, holding my hand. "Mornings are best, after breakfast, at the Club, but come whenever you like, and if I have time we'll talk it all over."[8]

Croker truly believed that it was his responsibility as a leader to make himself available to all those who considered themselves to be his constituents and to meet everyone with respect unless and until they showed that they didn't deserve it.

"Yes," said Croker, on a day when his habit of open-door to all had undergone a comment; "Yes, I see everybody. And particularly I haven't the heart to turn these poor people away. They squander my time, and often I can do them no good. But they don't know these things; and their small affairs are of as much interest to them as the business of any money monarch is to him. Were I driven to name what I regard as most to my credit, it would be that, during the sixteen years I've been at the head of Tammany Hall, every man, rich or poor, small or great, who wanted to see me, did see me, and was listened to. And when I could I helped him. I wouldn't want a better epitaph."[9]

One of the qualities that made Croker such an effective leader was his willingness to deal honestly in his relations with other people. Croker was quoted as saying: "The first element of leadership is honesty—perfect honesty. The honest man will prevail. Because other men can trust him. A rascal can trust an honest man; and a rascal can't trust a rascal. You might take one hundred men, ten of them honest and ninety of them false, and put them away on an island. Come back in two months, and, for the reasons I've given you, you'll find the ten honest men dominating the rest."[10]

He believed and understood the power of organization as applied to politics especially: "Every successful enterprise must have organization and a head. Everything which succeeds must and does have organization; without it all things fall to pieces. Be it a store or an army, or a church, or a party in politics, it must have organization and a head. If I'm a "boss"; and a president is the big 'boss' of all."[11]

The fact was that during the 1880s and 1890s, all of New York City's vast transportation system was privately owned. The older systems were elevated railways and horse car lines, strewn willy-nilly across and up and down various Manhattan streets. More recently, street surface systems that were powered by electricity in the form of overhead lines, or batteries, steam engines, compressed air, or cable power were being introduced. In the 1880s, cable lines were the favorite. The Broadway cable line stretched all the way from the Battery to Fifty-Ninth Street.

The newly enlarged city was a dynamic place. In March of 1900, it embarked on construction of the underground subway to enhance the surface cars and elevated trains, which were relied on until then. With the advent of a subway looming in the near future, Croker and his Tammany cronies became deeply involved with the wealthy owners of various transportation companies in the competitive battle between those who advocated a municipal subway against the private interests, frequently allied with Croker, who worked to expand the surface and elevated railway systems that already existed as more desirable because they would offer more immediate relief to New York City's commercial and residential development needs.

In 1898, New York City was expanded to include Brooklyn, Queens, and Staten Island with Manhattan and the Bronx into Greater New York, a city of three million people. Robert Van Wyck, the first mayor of the enlarged city, was the third mayor selected with Boss Croker's support. Tammany district leaders in the Van Wyck administration included a police commissioner, two former police commissioners, the commissioner of corrections, commissioner of docks, the parks commissioner, the bridge commissioner, the commissioner of water supply, borough president of the Bronx, several state senators, city councilmen, and Croker's old job, the city chamberlain, a list that in itself evidences the reach of Tammany Hall's ability to influence contracts and favors.

The story of the Ice Trust illustrates just how brazen the Tammany leadership could be during Croker's time as leader of Tammany Hall.

On April 4, 1900, the *New York Times* carried a front-page item, which astonished even those who were accustomed to the evil machinations of Tammany Hall. The price of a block of ice, an essential item in city life in those days before refrigeration, was about to double from thirty to sixty cents, according to an announcement by the American Ice Company, a recently formed company that enjoyed a monopoly by owning most of the ice plants in the city and with the support of the three Tammany dock commissioners, controlling access to the city piers where ice was unloaded.

American Ice, popularly known in the yellow press as the Ice Trust, had achieved its monopoly with the help of high-ranking members of Tammany Hall who controlled the city government. In fact, the *Times* revealed that certain Tammany men were part owners of the ice company, and stood to reap huge profits from the increased revenue.

Without electric refrigeration, each apartment, hospital, and every restaurant relied on ice to preserve food and other perishables, including milk and certain medicine. While the well-to-do could absorb the increase, the extra thirty cents could mean the difference in subsisting or going hungry to the poor who lived in squalid tenements on the Lower East Side and regularly supported Tammany.

The *Times* revealed that through preferential treatment the ice company had become a monopoly by awarding large portions of the company's stock to important Tammany Hall officials, including Croker and his handpicked mayor, Robert Van Wyck. The mayor and his brother had reportedly received a half million dollars worth of the Ice Trust stock without laying out a penny. Other shareholders revealed by the newspaper and never denied were each of the three dock commissioners, members of Croker's family, and Hugh McLaughlin, who was the Democratic leader of Brooklyn.

The *Times* initiated a lawsuit in which the mayor was forced to testify and admit his ownership of the company's stock. The testimony ruined his career and the Ice Trust was forced to rescind the price increase and give up its monopoly. While Croker and his dock commissioner who had provided the monopoly with exclusive access to city docks were damaged by the revelation, Croker survived the embarrassment, just as he had survived other embarrassments.[12]

Among the dock commissioners at that time was Charles F. Murphy, a significant Lower East Side district leader who would eventually succeed Croker in 1902.

It is not clear whether Sulzer understood how significant his good standing with Croker would be when he first met him before embarking on his legislative career, but it would soon become very apparent when he took his seat in Albany and a relationship grew between Sulzer and Croker.

Assemblyspeaker Sulzer, *The New York Red Book*, 1893.

8

Assemblyman Rising

The newly elected state legislature convened on January 1, 1890 with Republicans in the majority in both houses. David B. Hill, a Democrat, was then governor. Sulzer paid him a courtesy call and was invited to call again whenever he needed advice. When Grover Cleveland, a former reform mayor of Buffalo, resigned as governor of New York upon his election as president in 1884, Hill, who was the lieutenant governor, succeeded him. Hill, who subsequently won election to two three-year terms as governor in 1885 and 1888, dominated the state Democrats. In March of 1891, Hill was elected by the legislature as U.S. senator from New York, but he did not begin his service in the senate until the end of his gubernatorial term in December of 1891—a unique situation.

It is interesting to note here for reasons that will become more apparent as this chronicle unfolds that Sulzer says in his autobiographical notes that the only committee assignment he received in his freshman year in Albany was to the Committee on Public Institutions, which was known to be a committee that never met. However, according to the official records in the *New York State Assembly Journal*, 1890, volume I, page 52, he was placed on the very important Committee on General Laws, which, according to at least one historian, was an unusual honor for a new member and came about as a result of the influence of Tammany Hall.

Sulzer was an unusually dutiful legislator, attending every session, studying each bill that was introduced, and making it his business to meet and befriend as many of the other members of both houses as he could, including the Republicans.

Being an assemblyman was much more of a part-time job in those days than it is today. Sessions usually lasted only two or three months and frequently adjourned after two or three days each week, leaving time for Sulzer and most of the others to pursue their law practices or other business interests. Sulzer was genuinely surprised to learn that there was a great deal of corruption. While many members were honest and pursued their work with sincerity and integrity, others were there to cash in. Lobbyists for industry would pay to assure enactment or defeat of bills their clients were concerned about. The practice of introducing what were called "strike bills" or "ripper bills" against particular business interests was rampant and the introducer knew he would be rewarded for killing his own bill, which was his prerogative as the bill's sponsor by making a motion to strike the bill from a committee calendar.

As a freshman, Sulzer had little influence, but he was sufficiently clever and ambitious to ingratiate himself with more senior members by supporting their legislation.

Late in his first session, Sulzer introduced a resolution calling for an investigation by his dormant Committee on Public Institutions of the facilities where the insane and feeble-minded were confined. Until that time the state left that function entirely to county government for those who could not afford private institutions. The county hospitals were infamous for abuses, inhumane treatment, and corruption, and Sulzer saw the situation as a disgrace. Sulzer succeeded in getting the committee to meet and report favorably on his resolution. When the resolution came before the house, Sulzer made his maiden speech and was so effective and impassioned that his resolution passed the House over the objections of the Republican speaker and other assembly leaders.

His eloquent speech brought him attention from the Albany reporters and earned him considerable publicity for the first time as a legislator, including a story in the influential *New York Herald*, written by its legislative correspondent, Thomas G. Alvord, who was much respected as a knowledgeable old hand in Albany. His father had been Speaker of the assembly in 1879.

According to Sulzer's own account:

> In writing his story for the *New York Herald*, Mr. Alvord called me: "Henry Clay, the Mill Boy of Mackerelville," because of some resemblance to the favorite son of Kentucky. The *Herald* played it up and, much to my discomfiture, the name stuck. I always disliked being called "Henry Clay," whether I looked like him or not, because I never was in sympathy with most of the Whig politics of Henry Clay of Kentucky. But the name stuck,

and I could not get rid of it. Other newspapers followed it up, and the more I tried to shake it off, the worse it became. Many people believed my name was not William but Henry Clay Sulzer, and I received many letters so addressed. I used to beg people not to call me "Henry Clay."[1]

Shortly thereafter the legislature adjourned and Sulzer, then not quite twenty-seven years old and despondent over his experience in Albany, determined he would not seek reelection. He looked forward to returning to his thriving law practice. Before leaving town, he called again on Governor Hill who was the party's real leader.

The governor and I talked for more than two hours. He was rather sympathetic with my viewpoint, but he urged me to be a candidate again. He told me he, and the Democratic leaders of the State, were determined to make every effort they could to defeat the Republicans in the coming election, and secure a Democratic majority in the Legislature. He urged me to come back, and said if the Assembly were Democratic, and he believed it would be, that I would be most useful to the Democratic party, and the people of the State, on account of my ability and experience. In his talk with me he said something I have never forgotten: "You know, Sulzer, there are two kinds of men; honest men and dishonest men. They are in every walk of life, including the Legislature. In a general way politics is more or less corrupt; but we cannot change human nature. In a Democratic form of government the best we can hope for is that the honest people will far exceed in numbers those who are dishonest. As Governor I must get along the best I can with all sorts and conditions of human beings, but in so far as I can I separate the sheep from the goats, and always stand by men of honesty, ability, and character."

Eventually Sulzer was persuaded to run again and the coalition of Republicans and insurgent Democrats that opposed him two years previously were unable to agree on a candidate to run against him. In November of 1890, he won his district by a large majority and the Democrats won control of the assembly.

After his election, Sulzer again turned his attention to his law practice and, again, took a partner, a new lawyer named Thomas W. Smith who was the son of a very successful real estate operator in his assembly district who promised a lot of business to the new firm of Sulzer and Smith. The firm was successful and young Smith proved honest and helpful. The relationship lasted several years until Smith went off to Europe, married a young lady in London, and decided to stay there.

Sulzer's interest in taking a partner was influenced by the fact that during his first year in Albany, important clients were already beginning to miss his personal attention and expressed complaints about the way matters were handled by his associates.

Sulzer was becoming an influential member of the majority. With active support of Tammany Hall that continued throughout his service in the legislature, he was able to create an impressive record of successfully enacting major legislation and he played a significant role in defeating the passage of many bad bills. With Governor Hill's help with the new Speaker, Sulzer got his legislation enacted to provide for state care of the insane and New York became the first state to create a modern system of state mental hospitals. The concept was to be emulated across the nation.

As a member of the legislative majority, Sulzer now found his work in Albany personally fulfilling and, although returning to his very successful law practice at the end of the session, he had no doubts about running again. In November of 1891, he was reelected by an even larger majority, and returned to the 1892 session as a leading Democrat who was considered by some to be a potential candidate for Speaker because Blue Eyed Billy Sheehan had been elected lieutenant governor on the ticket of Roswell P. Flower, whose nomination for governor had been seconded by Sulzer at the State Democratic Convention.

At the inauguration of Governor Flower, Senator Hill, who was still the most influential leader of the party, asked Sulzer to withdraw his own candidacy for Speaker in favor of Dr. Robert P. Bosch who was the assemblyman from Chemung County—where Hill came from. In deference to Hill, the twenty-nine-year-old Sulzer agreed to support Bosch and was rewarded with the chairmanship of the assembly's powerful Judiciary Committee.

As chairman of Judiciary, Sulzer became the de facto majority leader and he was able to enact a great deal of important progressive social legislation. Many of the bills he introduced were assigned to him by the Democratic Party machine. Among the laws he was responsible for was the law for the creation of a women's reformatory, the law providing for free lectures for working men and women in New York City, the law abolishing sweatshops, the law abolishing imprisonment for debt, the law to limit the hours of labor, the law to open the Metropolitan Museum of Art to the people on Sunday, the law providing for the prevailing rate of wages, the law abolishing corporal punishment in the penal institutions of the state, the law requiring weekly payment of wages, the law establishing an epileptic colony, the law establishing the Bronx and Van Cortlandt parks, the law establishing the Aquarium in New York City, the law establishing the Public Library in New York City, a law to codify the statutes of New York, a ballot reform law, the law to enlarge and strengthen the Civil Service, and the law for the celebration, in New York City, of the four hundredth anniversary of the discovery of America. He was a strong advocate of women's suffrage. He worked closely with Susan B. Anthony of Rochester, New York, who headed the national movement, and his enthusiasm for their cause made him one of the darlings of the suffragettes.

By this time, Sulzer was achieving meaningful recognition in state politics and was a delegate to the National Democratic Convention in 1892 that would renominate Grover Cleveland as president of the United States. Although Senator Hill challenged him for the nomination, Sulzer's loyalty to President Cleveland was long-standing and caused him to break with Hill, who enjoyed the support of Tammany and all seventy-two New York delegates except for Sulzer and his close friend, Patrick Keenan, the other delegate from Sulzer's congressional district.

Prior to the vote, the Hill forces had circulated a letter to all of the national delegates, claiming that Cleveland could not carry New York, then the most populous state in the nation. Sulzer and Keenan were the only ones to refuse to sign it, much to the chagrin of Tammany boss Richard Croker who had facilitated their designation as delegates.

After Cleveland won the nomination, Sulzer was one of his very few friends in the New York democracy, although Croker's party machine and Governor Hill did eventually work for Cleveland's election. Cleveland carried New York and won the presidency for the second time.

Sulzer's defection was forgiven. Whether this was due to his insignificance or to his popularity in his own district is unclear, but 1892 continued to be a year of political advancement for the twenty-nine-year-old assemblyman from the Lower East Side and Tammany continued to be supportive.

The celebration of America's four hundredth anniversary was coming up, and Chicago had been selected over New York as the site for what became known as the Colombian Exposition in 1893. When New York failed to get the designation for the national exposition, Assemblyman Sulzer's bill (enacted with the help of Tammany) to have an official celebration in New York City to commemorate this event was important to the business and political leadership of the city. Because Sulzer had been sponsor of the bill, New York City mayor Hugh Grant, Croker's protégé, designated the assemblyman to organize the celebration, an honor that gave Sulzer tremendous exposure among the city's business interests and the press. The New York event, lasting an entire week, included a huge military parade, an international flotilla of warships, and a variety of public festivities culminating in a great banquet.

Sulzer was reelected to his fourth one-year term in the assembly in 1892 by an even larger majority than previously. It was a Democratic year, Cleveland was elected president, and the Democrats again won control of the legislature.

Sulzer claimed that he secured his ambition to become Speaker by traveling around the state after Election Day to meet with some of the upstate Democratic leaders and assembly colleagues who were favorable to him. He also got important support from Governor Flower and Edward Murphy, the State Democratic Party chairman, although Senator Hill preferred to see an upstater get the post. Many years later Sulzer said that Croker had another candidate, but if that was so, Croker certainly did not exercise his capacity to veto Sulzer's candidacy. The fact is that the major Democratic leaders assembled in Albany the day before the legislature convened and allocated the leadership positions among their supporters on a territorial basis, and made no pretense about it. This meeting resulted in an assembly caucus of record-making brevity when the elected members met and designated the Speaker, the clerk, the sergeant-at-arms, and three others. According to the January 3, 1893 *New York Times* account: "Each of the five Barons in the party received his share of the patronage. New York was given the Speakership, in the person of William Sulzer of New York." However, commenting on the editorial page of the same day's issue, the *Times* editorial said of Sulzer's election as Speaker: "This shows the absolute control of the machine in the organization of the Assembly, though in Wm. Sulzer, it has chosen a candidate not likely to excite opposition. He is fairly well qualified and rather popular, but he will be obedient to his masters."

When the assembly convened in January of 1893, his Democratic colleagues unanimously elected Sulzer Speaker. Three months short of his thirty-first birthday, Sulzer was the youngest man in the history of the state to be elected Speaker, a record that stands to this day.

In New York State, the Speaker and his counterpart in the state senate, the president pro tem, are the two most powerful officials in government except for the governor. Each has the capacity to rule his house with near total discipline because they control committee assignments, legislative staff, the legislative budget, and they can usually decide which bills pass and which do not. Any governor who wants to enact his state budget and his programs must deal with the leadership that controls the majority vote in each house. It is a very rare occasion when a bill can be enacted that is opposed by the legislative leadership.

When Sulzer was elected Speaker, some elements of the press reported that he had shown a disposition to serve the party machine and appeared to be a ready tool of Boss Croker. Whenever Sulzer would describe his role years after he left the legislature, the influence of the party machine would never be mentioned, but there can be no doubt that both his election as Speaker and his very real and extremely impressive record of legislative accomplishment could not have been achieved without the active support of the Tammany organization in New York City, which in 1893 meant the support of Tammany's chief— Richard Croker. Any doubts about Richard Croker's influence that would be created in the years ahead by Sulzer and his most loyal supporters is dispelled by a handwritten letter found among Sulzer's papers in the archives of Cornell University during my research for this book. Written on Tammany Hall letterhead, it is interesting because it is great evidence of the political reality of the times, a reality that would last in various forms of intensity for many more years.

Tammany Hall,
New York, February 29th 1892
Hon Wm. Sulzer

My dear Sir:
A Resolution has passed the Senate to sell the Salt lands at Syracuse, and is now in the Assembly Judiciary Committee. I think it is for the interest of the Democratic Party that the same be smothered, and I trust you will use your influence to accomplish same.

There will be two or three local bills for Syracuse introduced in a few days, which if passed will give our friends

control of the Public Works, Police and Excise Boards therein, and I believe them to be for the best interest of the Democratic Party also, and therefore respectfully request that you give them your support, and also get the support of our friends in the Legislature to pass the same.
With best wishes.

I am Sincerely Yours,
Richard Croker

As Speaker, Sulzer reduced the usual number of Republican members on the various assembly committees and put most committees under control of members who were loyal to Tammany Hall or its allies from the Kings County Democrats who controlled the party in the then-independent city of Brooklyn (which was incorporated into the city of New York five years later). According to the most objective newspaper accounts of the day, Sulzer let the political bosses make up the committee structure.[2]

In describing the opening day of the legislature on January 3, 1893, the *New York Times* reported on some of the initial activity in the state senate. In case anyone doubted the blunt honesty of New York County's infamous state senator George Washington Plunkitt, they ought to read that account of Senator Plunkitt's introduction of two bills to mark the beginning of his last year in the senate. Plunkitt's proposed legislation was characterized by the *Times* as "two bills which ought to yield handsome revenue, should they become laws." One of the bills proposed to establish a park in a location where the senator already had the contract to fill in a large tract of the land where the park was to be established. The other bill proposed to improve the grade of three Manhattan streets for which it was already known that the senator was slated to get the contract for the work the bill required to be done when it became law.

Another example of Croker's involvement in legislation during Sulzer's term as Speaker became public early in the session. The *New York Times* reported that the Speaker was working with the governor on a ballot reform proposal that was presented as a reform measure. Speaker Sulzer told the press that the amendments, which were going to be added to the law, "are according to the suggestions and ideas of Mr. Richard Croker."[3]

At the time there were a large number of daily newspapers in New York City and across the state, and the papers were not reluctant to slant their news stories to reflect their strong editorial positions, especially positions for or against the political machines that dominated the municipalities in which they were published. It is, therefore, not unusual to find contradictory press accounts of some events that reflect the editorial bias of the newspaper that is doing the publishing.

By some accounts, Sulzer's term as Speaker produced the lowest tax rate and the most economical budget in forty-seven years, and the cleanest and the shortest session of the legislature in fifty-one years.[4] There is no denying that his legislative record was unusually impressive and important.

Others described his term as Speaker in far more negative terms. To some, it was a disaster. The legislature of that year is reported to have been most scandalously partisan and its effect was to end the Democratic Party's rule in Albany until 1910. According to the *New York Evening Post*, "the session of 1893 was remarkable for the number of pet measures that were rushed through, for incompetent committee, for 'snap' hearings, for strangled measures, for the surreptitious, tricky, jamming of 'ripper bills' with graft as the goal, and with Speaker Sulzer frankly, naively, and unquestioningly obeying every nod and beck of the Croker-Sheehan-Murphy triumvirate. . . . The legislature represented a small group of political bosses, and it served the machine they constructed."[5]

The *New York World*, with somewhat more forbearance, remarked: "On the whole its record is not essentially better or worse than that of its predecessors for some years past. It was machine-ridden. . . . The legislature has done the will of the bosses with a shameful but by no means unprecedented servility."[6] The *New York Tribune* acknowledged that "all legislation came from Tammany Hall and was dictated by that great statesman, Richard Croker."[7] This frank acknowledgment is particularly revealing in view of Sulzer's latter-day contention that his public career had been wholly free from Tammany influence and that he had won his way solely by serving his constituents.

The fact remains that Sulzer was extremely popular, not only among the voters of his assembly district, but among a lot of the influential Democrats and newspaper editors across the state. He was reelected to the assembly in 1893 and served an uneventful term as minority leader in 1894.

Congressman Sulzer, *The New York Red Book*, 1894.

9

The Congressional Years

The year 1894 was a very bad year for Democrats. A year before, a national economic depression had begun with the stock market crash that became known as the Panic of 1893. It would last four years. A Democrat, Grover Cleveland, was the president of the United States. His administration was racked by problems in the economy, highlighted by falling gold reserves and a lot of industrial strikes, the most infamous of which was the Pullman strike in Chicago in July 1894. Federal troops sent by President Cleveland to maintain order were eventually withdrawn after their presence provoked serious mob action and extensive destruction including millions of dollars of damage from fires. William Jennings Bryan, a Democratic congressman from Nebraska, began his rise to national prominence in June of 1894 proposing, with great eloquence, to free silver to alleviate the gold shortage that was threatening the economy. In New York, the Republican controlled state senate had created the Lexow Committee to investigate and publicize the scandalous relationship between Tammany Hall, the business community, and the police department.[1] The damaging revelations made for months of headlines. In September, twelve thousand tailors went on strike in New York City to protest sweatshops, the latest symbol of social injustice. It was no surprise when Republicans prevailed on Election Day.

Levi P. Morton, the Republican candidate for governor of New York, ended twelve years of Democrats living in the governor's mansion by defeating David B. Hill, the former governor who had promoted himself to the U.S. Senate. Sulzer had actually turned down an offer from Senator Hill to join his ticket as the party's candidate for attorney general.

He knew that it was not going to be a good year for Democrats as the people had turned against President Cleveland's administration. Sulzer figured out that he would have a better chance to survive a bad year for his party if he ran locally. He became a candidate for the U.S. House of Representatives from the 10th congressional district on the East Side of Manhattan, which included Sulzer's 14th assembly district and so many other areas that were predominantly Republican that it was generally considered to be a safe Republican seat. Sulzer's self-confidence and ambition drove him to the challenge. He had already won each of his five assembly district races by an increasing majority and he had developed a genuinely energetic personal following. Fully aware that the Democratic Party was in deep despair, he decided to run a very personal campaign against Ferdinand Eidman, a popular Republican who shared Sulzer's German-American background. Eidman was also a proven vote-getter who had been elected city coroner when all of the other citywide elections had gone Democratic. Eidman's support came from not only Republicans, but from the remnants of the anti-Tammany "County Democracy" group as well. Sulzer believed that the odds against him were 5 to 1 and even his best friends were betting against him.

Many years later, Sulzer reminisced about his first congressional campaign: "I made a house to house canvas. I worked in the District among the people from sunrise to midnight." He knew he could rely on most of the regular Democrats, but needed to meet his opponents' people. "This I did quietly and unobtrusively by personal visits and conversations with the people. I saw every man, and woman, I could. It was a personal canvas. I organized every block. Every night I addressed several meetings." Meetings were held in halls, and outdoors. He spoke from the tail-end of vehicles, and on all kinds of hastily erected temporary platforms. Some of the newspaper reporters wrote that he was the most eloquent "cart-tail orator" in the country.

When the votes were counted on election night, November 6, 1894, Sulzer won. The Democratic state ticket lost his district by more than twenty thousand votes. Sulzer carried it by an eight hundred–vote majority. This is how campaigns were conducted before television, radio, and computerized mailing lists made them so much more impersonal. It was a personal triumph. Sulzer went on to describe the situation he encountered:

The election, of 1894, was an uprising of the people against the Cleveland administration. The Republicans gained 120 seats in the House of Representatives. . . . There were only five Democrats elected to the House, in the United States, north of Mason and Dixon's line [two others were from New York City]. It was one of the greatest defeats the Democratic Party ever sustained. . . . I was showered with congratulations on my victory. When they analyzed the vote they knew it was a personal triumph— not a political victory. Of course, I was gratified that I had won, and that my boyhood ambition to be a Member of congress had come true.

The 10th congressional district in the heart of Manhattan's East Side was extremely cosmopolitan and reflective of the rapidly changing urban scene in New York. In the beginning of Sulzer's congressional service the district was largely composed of Irish and German immigrants. Over the years of continuing population shifts, it became predominantly Jewish. Sulzer earned the confidence of his constituents through constant attention to their needs. The pride they took in his representation made him enormously popular and he was consistently one of the most successful vote-getters in the state, repeatedly running ahead of his party's ticket. Sulzer's political success in his own district was truly impressive. In his second race for Congress in 1896, Sulzer increased his plurality to 1,400 votes, while Bryan lost the presidential contest in the district to McKinley by over 17,000. Four years later with the Tammany organization's active support (which was missing in 1896), Bryan lost the district to McKinley again, but by only 11,000 votes, while Sulzer was elected by over 5,000. Sulzer continued to do better each year regardless of how well the Democratic ticket did for governor or for president. By 1906, Sulzer carried his district by over 11,000 votes, receiving 75 percent of the vote.

Sulzer's depiction of the meaning of his election to Congress in 1894 was indicative of the man. He was full of himself and justifiably enamored of his ability to win elections, especially when the odds were against him. At a time when great oratory was especially meaningful, he believed in his enormous oratorical skills and he exuded self-confidence. Empowered by his victory from the time he was first elected to Congress, Sulzer's ambition for higher office became rapidly apparent. He worked hard to demonstrate his effectiveness in a great variety of important issues that interested him and vigorously pursued every opportunity he could create to build political relationships and broaden the base for support of his ambition. His single-minded pursuit of political advancement paid off as people far beyond his own constituency took him seriously as a public speaker, a leader, and an effective legislator. There is no doubt that he built an impressive record during his years in Congress. Sulzer's ample accomplishments embraced a wide range of important areas, both foreign and domestic, and the record reveals that he had a meaningful impact on legislation and government action.

When Sulzer first arrived in Washington to take up his duties as a member of the House of Representatives, he renewed acquaintances with Judge David B. Culbertson who was then a very senior member from Texas. Sulzer had met Culbertson some years before when he was involved in a real estate case in Texas on behalf of one of his New York City clients. Sulzer and two of his freshmen colleagues, Oscar W. Underwood of Alabama and Joseph Bailey of Texas, were invited to dinner at Judge Culbertson's apartment at the old Metropolitan Hotel near the Capitol. After a pleasant dinner, the judge offered the three freshmen some sage advice. "If you want to amount to anything in Congress," he said, "you have to study, work hard, and give your entire time to your duties." The older man advised them to "take up some subject, and become better posted on it than any other man in Congress, so that whenever the subject comes up, you could discuss it more intelligently and more exhaustively than anyone else."

After the judge approved of Bailey's desire to become an expert on the Constitution, Underwood was advised to make himself expert on tariff and taxes. (Bailey soon became a U.S. senator. In 1910 Underwood became chairman of the House Ways and Means Committee and a candidate for the 1912 presidential nomination.) Culbertson steered Sulzer to foreign affairs, a subject which was already of great interest of the New Yorker who pursued that advice. Sulzer credits this meeting as eventually leading to his chairmanship of the Foreign Affairs Committee when the Democrats took control of Congress in 1910 and Champ Clark became the Speaker.

Sulzer maintained his active law practice in New York City throughout his service in the assembly and in Congress. It is obvious from the correspondence in his files that he was able to maintain some lucrative matters to handle when he did not have to be in Albany or Washington, although some clients objected to being handled by colleagues and wanted Sulzer's personal attention. During his first term in Congress, Sulzer's younger brother Ray managed his office and juggled his appointments.

Sulzer became an influential congressman within his party when the Republicans controlled the House and within Congress itself when the Democrats were in the majority.

On the domestic side, he introduced legislation in 1904 to create a U.S. Department of Labor, a bill that was eventually enacted into law and signed by President Taft in 1913 as one of the president's last official acts. Then-governor Sulzer was invited to attend the signing ceremony. At the beginning of his career in Washington, Sulzer had also introduced the legislation that created the U.S. Department of Commerce.

He introduced bills to reorganize the U.S. Merchant Marine through favorable tariffs at a time when America was losing out to foreign shipping. He brought attention to forgotten colored soldiers. He wrote the statute that created an excellent copyright law and another that created the U.S. Patent Court of Appeals. In 1904 he introduced legislation that eventually led to amending the Constitution to bring about the direct election of U.S. senators. Ironically, as it would later turn out, he also sponsored federal legislation to publicize political campaign contributions.

He sponsored statehood for Alaska. Alaska was a major interest in Sulzer's life and he visited there several times. He was well-known among Alaskans as "Sour Dough Bill." He invested in mines and his brother Charles became Alaska's nonelected territorial delegate to Congress. Sulzer Mountain still exists in Alaska outside of a town called Sulzer.

During his years in Congress, Sulzer introduced legislation to create a graduated income tax, to create a Bureau of Corporations to enforce antitrust laws, to increase the salaries of letter carriers, and to provide pensions for the widows and orphans of Civil War veterans of the Union Army.

Sulzer's bill to create a parcel post service in the U.S. Post Office became law in his last year in Congress, and one of the first parcels was delivered to him at the Executive Mansion in Albany during his first week as governor. A picture of Mrs. Sulzer receiving the package made the *New York Times*.

Despite the fact that the Democratic Party was in the minority in the House of Representatives for the first sixteen years that Sulzer served, he was, nevertheless, considered to be a respectable force to be reckoned with. This was due in part to his acknowledged eloquence, his most impressive record as a vote-getter who consistently survived Republican landslides, and his commitment to the causes he espoused or the issues that interested him. He proudly positioned himself as a champion of the underdogs, although his critics considered it posturing or even demagoguery.

Sulzer's significance is evidenced in *Men and Issues of 1900*, edited by James P. Boyd. Articles were published by seventeen senators and eight members of the House, with Sulzer among them, along with ten articles by top government officials, including the president and the leading members of his cabinet, former presidents, and presidential candidates. Sulzer's erudite article was entitled "Trusts Must Go," in which he revealed his own philosophy when he laid out in a lawyer-like fashion the argument against extending the authority of national banks and the menace of the trusts. He said, "today about 200 trusts control, wholly, or in large part, every conceivable product and industry of the country. These gigantic combinations constitute, in my judgment, the greatest menace at the present time to our Democratic institutions." Sulzer went on to say, "out of a total population of 70,000,000 less than 40,000 persons in the United States own more than one-half of the entire aggregate wealth of the land." Further, he notes, "the centralization of wealth in the hands of a few by the robbery of the many during the past quarter of a century has been simply enormous, and the facts and figures are appalling. Three-quarters of the entire wealth of our land appears to be concentrated in the hands of a small minority of the people, and the number of persons constituting that minority grows smaller every year." This case is not unfamiliar to all those who listen to congressional debate today.

Congressman Sulzer never hesitated to use his influence vigorously on behalf of any cause that interested him which he deemed to be worthy, and his causes were many and his interests varied. He said he had a boyhood fascination with American Indians. Throughout his life, Sulzer considered the American Indians to be "a brave people who were treated unjustly by our government." His teenage trip to Florida by sea had exposed him to the Seminole Indians. Sulzer was very proud of his initiation into their tribe that made him a blood brother. He took pride in the fact that during his service in the state assembly he also became a blood brother of the Six Iroquois Nations. In 1885 he made a trip to southern Arizona where he says that he met Geronimo, the infamous Indian chieftain, who impressed young Sulzer with his "intelligence, bravery, honesty, ability and sincerity." In the material that Sulzer developed in the 1930s for his unpublished autobiography, he tells the following story:

> In 1885 I was in Southern Arizona, and in Sonoma, Mexico. At that time Geronimo and some of the Chiricahua Apaches were on the warpath, as it was then expressed, and doing some damage in Arizona. It was at this time that I first met Geronimo and a few of his warriors. He told me about his grievances, and boiled down, they amounted to about this. When the United States gave the Apaches a Reservation, in Arizona, they were satisfied and went there. However, the Indian Agent there, at the time, had very little vision and lacked good judgment. He refused to permit Geronimo to go on the Reservation because he had three wives. The Indian Agent said he could only take one wife with him. Geronimo refused to abandon his wives.
>
> Shortly afterwards he collected a few Apaches, and began to make trouble, which lasted for nearly fifteen years. When he and his braves finally surrendered to General Nelson A. Miles, in command of the Department of Arizona, it was on the express understanding that they should be permitted, without molestation, to return to the Reservation with their wives, horses, cows, and personal property, and that none of them should be punished. They were never subdued or captured. They surrendered on the agreement, or treaty, as above stated, which treaty was violated by the U.S. Government. Geronimo was sent as a prisoner to Fort San Marco, St. Augustine, Florida. This was contrary to my sense of justice.
>
> When I went to congress I took up the case of Geronimo's imprisonment with the President, and the secretary of war. I also went to St. Augustine and had a conference with Geronimo. I promised him that I would do all in my power to have him released and allowed to return to the Apache Reservation. To this end I used all my influence with the officials in Washington, and finally got a compromise from the War Department, at

the instigation of the president, that Geronimo be released from the San Marco Prison, and sent to Fort Sill Indian Territory, now Oklahoma. I visited him at Fort Sill on two occasions. He longed to return to Arizona, but he died there where he was virtually a prisoner.

The last time I saw Geronimo he gave me a silver ring which he said had been given him by his third wife when they were married. He put the ring on my finger and told me to wear it in remembrance of him. I promised, and have kept that promise. It is the only ring I wear.

His service in Congress was conspicuous for his championship of people's rights. In several eloquent speeches he pleaded the cause of the Cuban insurgents before the House. He introduced the first resolutions sympathizing with the Cubans, the first granting them belligerent rights, the first favoring their independence, and the first declaring war against Spain. He also championed the rights of the Boers in South Africa by introducing a number of resolutions of sympathy for their cause and eloquently denouncing the conduct of the war by the British.[2]

By 1910 as chairman of the Committee on Foreign Affairs, the congressman from the 10th New York District had accumulated sixteen years of seniority and a voice that was listened to in foreign affairs of the nation. Among his most serious accomplishments in this area, Sulzer took pride in the fact that in 1910, when President Taft massed twenty thousand American soldiers on the Mexican border and threatened to invade to protect the interests of American businessmen who were concerned about a potential change in power, the new committee chairman steadfastly rejected the possibility of congressional approval of such an invasion. He stood up to a personal appeal from the White House and tremendous pressure from the business community. Sulzer took his stand in favor of nonintervention and the meaning of that principle throughout Latin America. He argued successfully that America's word was more sacred than its dollars; we had a treaty to live up to, and President Taft had given nonintervention assurances to other Latin American countries.

Another triumph for Congressman Sulzer was achieved when he succeeded in enacting a congressional resolution persuading the United States government to abrogate its diplomatic treaty with Russia because the Russians were refusing to admit Jewish-Americans as visitors. At the time, the czarist government was discriminating against former Russian-Jewish citizens who had immigrated to the United States and became U.S. citizens, many of whom were desirous of returning for a visit. Sulzer organized a huge public hearing in Washington that was attended by nearly every identifiable major Jewish leader. That hearing certainly cemented Sulzer's popularity with New York's Jewish voters who played a major role in his own congressional district and in the Democratic Party in New York City. He succeeded in adopting a resolution by a vote of 300 to 1—calling on the State Department to abrogate the 1832 diplomatic treaty with Russia because they were violating basic rules of diplomacy by discriminating against American citizens due to their religion. The State Department acted and the Russians changed their practice. This resolution would eventually have a profound impact on Sulzer's election as governor.

In 1895, Joseph Pulitzer, publisher of the *New York World*, increased its circulation by publicizing a cartoon that featured a slum child wearing clothes that were tinted yellow by a brand new color printing process. Pulitzer's archrival and competitor, William Randolph Hearst, lured the *Times'* cartoonist (Richard Felton Outcault) to come over to Hearst's *New York Journal*. Not to be outdone, Pulitzer replaced the cartoonist with George Luks, who would go on to be renowned as one of America's most important artists. The two papers also competed for news, the more sensational the better, and both papers became famous for their "yellow journalism," which came to mean opinionated, nonobjective, emotional, and sensational reporting intended to increase circulation.

The rivalry of those two papers, and others of the same type, led to development of a big story about things that were alleged to be going on in Cuba. Throughout 1896 the stories of atrocities by the Spanish against the Cubans began to develop sympathy for the oppressed Cuban people, some of whom were talking revolution. While President Cleveland, at first, and then President McKinley, resisted the newspaper pressure for intervention, Sulzer and others in Congress were initiating their resolutions of support for Cuban rebels. Eventually McKinley ordered a battleship, the USS *Maine*, to Cuba to protect American citizens and property there.

On February 15, 1898, the *Maine* exploded while anchored in Havana Harbor. Two hundred and sixty-six of the ship's 354 officers and men were killed; because almost all of its officers were ashore attending balls, dinners, and bullfights, most were enlisted men. The cause of the unfortunate explosion has never been clearly determined, a fact that did not dissuade the yellow journalists who were hell bent on creating a war. In April of 1898 Congress authorized an invasion of Cuba and recognized Cuban independence. Spain declared war on the United States.

An American fleet under Admiral George Dewey defeated the Spanish fleet in the Philippines on May 1st and U.S. troops invaded the Spanish-held Philippines. Subsequently, U.S. troops invaded Cuba in June, leading to a decisive victory by Colonel Theodore Roosevelt's Rough Riders at San Juan Hill in July ending the war by the end of that month. Cuba was freed and the United States acquired Puerto Rico, the Philippines, Guam, and Wake Island.

After the war was over, Sulzer sponsored legislation to "Remember the *Maine.*" His bill was enacted, resulting in raising the battleship from the waters of Havana Harbor in 1912. The examination of the hulk did not reveal the cause of the explosion and the ship was towed into the Caribbean and re-interned.

After introducing a resolution in Congress to express support for the oppressed Cuban revolutionaries, Sulzer wrote to Frank Black, governor of New York, on April 9, 1898:

> In the event of war with Spain, which now seems inevitable, I desire, through you, to place my services at the disposal of the State to serve my country in any capacity I can in defense of the national honor, for the glory of the flag, and for Cuban independence.
>
> You and I served together in Congress, and you know how intensely I feel regarding the Cuban question.
>
> When hostilities begin, if you will give me authority, I can organize very quickly a good volunteer regiment in the city of New York, and appeal to you for leave to go to the front.

Having Colonel Roosevelt organize the Rough Riders was enough for Governor Black because he ignored Sulzer's request. Sulzer persisted. On May 20 Sulzer wrote again telling Governor Black that he had succeeded in raising a regiment in New York City, claiming it consisted of good men, ready for service in Cuba, Puerto Rico, or elsewhere, and that Sulzer should be named as colonel.

While Sulzer was seeking a commission appropriate for a member of the House Committee on Military and Naval Affairs, his younger brother, Ray Sulzer, who had been managing the congressman's New York City law office, enlisted in the army.

Ray's letter of appreciation to his brother from Fort Hancock, New Jersey, dated June 28, 1898, is poignant:

My dear Will:

Yours just received. I am very glad to hear that you succeeded in getting my appointment confirmed by the Senate. I shall never forget your kindness in obtaining my appointment and I know you had to work hard to get it.

I shall anxiously await my official notification, and presume I will receive my commission and assignment when I report to the Adjunct General.

I received a letter from Charley yesterday in which he told me of your visit at Elizabeth and how pleased Mother and all were over my appointment as Captain.

I have been highly congratulated by all the officers here who saw my appointment in the newspaper and army and navy journal.

I hope I will be notified so I can get away from here soon as possible and when on my way to Washington can stop off at home for a short time.

As ever.

Your affectionate Brother,

Ray

Ray was killed in action in the Philippines.

Sulzer's oratorical skills were such that he was always in demand as one of the greatest speakers in the Democratic Party. His appearance was sought in political campaigns across the country and he took great pleasure in accommodating many party organizations and Democratic candidates, thereby ingratiating himself and building support for his own ambitions. As Sulzer was fond of saying, he was available "for every cause that lacked assistance, and against every wrong that needs assistance." He also made himself available on the lecture circuit to supplement his income, a practice that exists today and has helped make ends meet for New York governor George Pataki and his predecessor Mario Cuomo. Like these two recent governors of New York, professional lecture bureaus organized Sulzer's lectures.

Sulzer was well known in Congress for his bursts of eloquence. By 1902 Sulzer's congressional colleagues nicknamed him "Seltzer" because of his effervescence and tendency to pop up at unexpected times. From the book of *Congressional Anecdotes*:

THE COMPANY HE KEEPS

New York's William Sulzer ('Old Bill') dressed as much as he could like Henry Clay, strode into the House through the door beside the Speaker's desk as though he were a famous actor appearing on the stage, and, if the galleries were crowded, always found some way, no matter how contrived, to get into the debate going on in the House. One day, when the House was discussing a bill to appropriate $5000 to erect a monument to Baron Steuben, Prussian officer who had drilled George Washington's troops during the American Revolution, Sulzer got the floor and proposed an amendment substituting Washington's name for Steuben's. Someone quickly made a point of order against the amendment on the ground that it was not germane, and Speaker Cannon sustained it. "Mr. Speaker," roared Sulzer dramatically, "am I to understand that George Washington is out of order in this House?" Visibly irritated, Cannon brought his gavel down heavily and cried: "He certainly is when he is in the company he is keeping today."[3]

Despite his achievements in Congress, there were always some detractors in the press, if not in his constituency, and some of their negative attitudes persisted despite or because of his consistent success as a candidate for Congress, the constant acclaim he achieved for his speeches for the Democratic Party outside of his own district, the fact that his name was mentioned as a potential running mate with William Jennings Bryan in 1896 and 1900, that he was even considered by a few of his colleagues to be a potential candidate for president in 1912. Besides, since 1896 there was a constantly growing group of upstate New Yorkers who considered him to be a good candidate for governor.

His friends considered him to be a spellbinding orator, but his critics accused him of demagoguery. Their problems were enhanced by the fact that Sulzer took himself and his work very seriously and there is little evidence on record of a sense of humor or any humility. Part of the ridicule he got from certain newspaper reporters emanated from the Henry Clay resemblance, and part came from his eloquent and dynamic speaking style, which seemed to flow forth in private conversation as well as public.[4]

Friedman concluded that "his brass-band methods and Fourth-of-July oratory stamped him as a demagogue. He was adept in all the devices of popularity and was endowed with all the bombastic qualities of the typical spellbinder. Even in an interview with newspapermen he would orate."[5]

In his 1922 autobiography, *All in a Lifetime*, Henry Morganthau said that Sulzer studiously set out to enhance his Clay image by growing a long forelock and training it to fall over his forehead in the Clay manner. However, when Morganthau described Sulzer's appearance in his office in 1912 to solicit a campaign contribution, he said, "Sulzer was evidently seeking a theatrical effect—made up to portray the part of 'a statesman of the people.' His coat was of one pattern, and his vest of another. His baggy trousers were of a third. The gray sombrero which he always affected was rather dingy; his linen just a trifle soiled. Familiar as I was with Sulzer's political poses, through our acquaintance, I mentally noted the skill of the morning's costume in dressing the part of 'a friend of the people.'"[6]

Friedman said, "Sulzer's eloquence bubbled forth at the slightest pressure." Speaking on his bill calling on the government to keep the Statue of Liberty in New York Harbor lit every night in the year, Sulzer indignantly asked,

[W]hy it is that after all this time this light must go out? Is liberty dead? I hope not. I am a friend of liberty here and everywhere. As a citizen of this Republic, I take a just pride in the grandeur of Liberty Enlightening the World and for all it typifies here and symbolizes to people in other lands. I would not darken its effulgent light, but I would make it burn brighter and brighter as the years come and go. It stands at the gates of America, a magnificent altar to man's faith in liberty, whose

WILLIAM SULZER and H. M. GOLDFOGLE, members of Congress from New York, are close friends. When Congressman Sulzer bursts forth in eloquence on the floor ex-Judge Goldfogle is usually an appreciative listener. Mr. Sulzer fondly imagines that Henry Clay looked like William Sulzer. Some of his friends have sought to console him by assuring him that he would eventually grow out of it.

From Thomas Fleming, *Around the Capital with Uncle Hank* (New York: Nutshell Publishing Co., 1902).

light should penetrate the darkness of tyranny throughout the times and guide men from oppression to our hospitable shores of freedom.[7]

Sulzer always called himself "a man of the people." When asked to define the term, he said, "A man of the people is one who loves his fellow man, and who is in sympathy with his hopes, his aims, his aspirations. He is the man who gets up in the morning and works hard all day and feels that he has earned his day's wages if he has done one man a good turn."[8]

"When it comes to preserving our liberties," said a Washington correspondent in a post-impeachment story in *Current Leader*,

William is a whole canning factory. He can scent an outrage on those liberties all the way from the Capitol to the White House, or vice versa, as the case may be. . . . It makes no difference what the outrage on our liberties may be. The whole boundless universe is Bill's. He lets go at the Czar and at King Leopold with equal vigor and with equal output. He is a little brother to the oppressed of all the times. "Our" to him means all nations, all creeds, all colors and all conditions. He is for the universal conglomeration of man.[9]

Another newspaperman wrote similarly:

From the tall, thin, pyrotechnical figure of the impassioned congressman a dithyramb was always to be expected when any issue that arose could be construed as an assault upon popular liberty. Freedom shrieked in that spare, restless figure with the keen blue eyes, the Napoleonic lock with a charter to rove at large over his forehead, the singular likeness to Henry Clay when the Great Pacificator was young. He was accused of bombast, and certain it was that the moment he scented an invasion of the people's privilege in any quarter, he launched into an amazing oration. Oratory is the breath of his nostrils. The pose is the man. He confutes objections with what has been compared to an avalanche of speech. His opponent releases a verbal deluge upon himself. . . . He gyrates and brandishes and fulminates when roused to action.[10]

[T]he inimitable Mr. Dooley had a great admiration for his old friend Bill and was moved to praise for "a man who has to blow his nose ivry time he thinks iv th' troubles iv ithers." Said Mr. Dooley with his matchless wit: "It's always been a great relief to me whin bowed down undher th' yoke iv oppressyon to know that ol' Bill was weepin' or runnin' f'r office or makin' some other sacrifice f'r me. He has always been a frind iv th' people. He has lavished his sobs on thim an' has ast nawthin' in return but their votes. While he was in Washing'ton no poor man ivir called on Bill an' came away empty handed. He always clutched in his emacyated fin a bag ov sunflower seeds an' a copy iv Bill's last appeal f'r humanity.[11]

A severe critic was Norman Hapgood, who wrote in a *Harper's Weekly*: "He never stood up for his opinion against his immediate advantage. He never relied upon reason, but placed his trust in pose and rhetoric. He had no element of superiority, and yet the people trusted him. He posed and screamed, and the people took him at his word... Sulzer has never done an unpopular thing that I know of. He never had any morality except to seek cheap success at any cost."[12]

There were harsh criticisms from journalists, most of which came after his congressional service and not during it, and much of that came after or during the impeachment process. The very language of the critics themselves is almost as bombastic as that of Sulzer, of whom they are so critical.

What is really so much more significant is that these harsh words did not seem to have any impact on the nature of Sulzer's relationship to the voters who consistently expressed themselves in his support. By winning an election every two years, by ever increasing majorities, and building his own impressive political organization in his district, Sulzer assured himself of re-nomination and election without having to rely on the Tammany organization, even though he continued to maintain generally good relations with the Tammany leadership who sought the congressman's helpfulness with their needs in Washington.

During the early years of his term in Congress, Sulzer maintained an active correspondence and a relationship with Richard Croker. Croker retained the leadership of Tammany Hall until 1902 when Charles Murphy succeeded him after the very brief term of his handpicked successor, businessman Lewis Nixon, who resigned because Croker had continued to try and run things for him by cable from his home in England.

The governor's correspondence file during his first term in Congress revealed an 1895 letter from Croker who was vacationing in Florida, thanking Sulzer for his help on a particular "real estate exchange bill" in the House and asking him to contact three other specific friends for their help in defeating the bill in the Senate. In the following year, Sulzer organized five other Tammany friends to contribute $50 each to pay a well-known portrait painter, C. B. Tempelsman, to do a crayon portrait of Mr. Croker.

In national politics he was sent as a delegate from his New York congressional district to the Democratic National Conventions of 1896, 1900, 1904, 1908, and 1912; and was one of the active supporters of W. J. Bryan in each of his presidential campaigns.

There can be no doubt that Sulzer was always accepted as a "player" on the national scene when he was in Congress and a significant participant in Democratic politics nationwide as an influential New York congressman. While he was sometimes considered by fellow congressman and candidates from outside of New York as a link to New York's powerful Tammany organization, he was also known for his independence from Tammany and his willingness to make his own decisions apart from Tammany.

During his eighteen years in Congress, Sulzer sought his party's gubernatorial nomination every two years. While this effort did not succeed until 1912, his early and constant forays to upstate New York allowed him to build a following around the state that eventually helped him secure his goal. On September 9, 1896, Walter Scotto, a friend of Sulzer's from Buffalo, sent him an eleven-page handwritten report of his efforts to line up convention support in Syracuse and Rochester among active Democrats, newspaper editors, and political leaders.

Sulzer's personal files contain a handwritten letter from Richard Croker dated August 11, 1896 from the Moat House, the Tammany leader's home at Wantage in England, acknowledging a letter from Sulzer and telling Sulzer that he "would be pleased to help you for whatever your ambition might desire if I was on the ground to do so. I hope the party will not forget you, as you have been true in every respect so far as I know. I got a letter from [unreadable] in which he spoke of you for governor. It would please me very much to see you in that high office and I am sure you would do credit to the party."

There was one occasion due to congressional redistricting in 1902 when Tammany actually made an unsuccessful attempt to oppose his nomination, but, by that time, Sulzer's mentor John Reilly had died and Sulzer had taken control of the political apparatus in the district and his re-nomination was assured.

Sulzer became a player on the national political arena by befriending and supporting congressional colleagues, including William Jennings Bryan, who was the Democratic Party's unsuccessful presidential candidate in 1896 and again in 1900. Starting in July 1896, Sulzer participated in the creation of Bryan clubs around the state in defiance of the wishes of his friends at Tammany Hall. The relationships he built among Bryan supporters around the state and the nation added another dimension to Sulzer's personal following. Sulzer's importance in the Bryan camp was such that he was actually considered as a vice presidential nominee with Bryan. In 1900, campaign buttons depicting Sulzer and Bryan were distributed. While that became another unfulfilled ambition for Sulzer, the mere mention of the possibility enhanced the congressman's stature. Sulzer's unsuccessful 1896 campaign for the gubernatorial nomination was significantly enhanced by his own activities on behalf of Bryan's presidential campaign, especially his work in organizing the Bryan/Sewell clubs around the state that were independent of Tammany Hall. The first-term congressman was acknowledged by Bryan in his book about the 1896 campaign where Bryan said that Sulzer was a powerful influence in the campaign and one of the first New York Democrats to take up the fight for the endorsement of the platform.

In the fall of 1899, Sulzer made a bid for the post of minority leader of the House when it reorganized in 1900. Despite Sulzer's early efforts on behalf of Bryan's presidential candidacy—southern and western members were aligned against Sulzer because Tammany Hall had not been helpful enough to Bryan in 1896—Tammany's failure was held against Sulzer.

Understanding Sulzer's handicap, Richard Croker tried to be helpful and get beyond this problem of the past by writing to Sulzer:

> In the interest of our party, I sincerely hope you will succeed in your candidacy for the minority leadership of the next House of Representatives.

All our friends will stand by you loyally, in my judgment, concurred in by the leaders here, your selection will strengthen the party in the east, especially in the States of New York and New Jersey, and aid us to carry those states in the next presidential contest. This should be the wish and desire of every Democrat.

I want you to show this letter to our friends from the south and the west, and I appeal to them to help you because I know how important this matter is to the party at this critical time. You can say to them for me, that anything they do to help you, will further Democratic success in the great contest next year, and will not be forgotten whenever we can reciprocate.

The letter foresaw the fact that Croker and Tammany would make up for the mistakes in 1896 and reliably support Bryan in 1900, which they did. As the time for the Democratic Convention approached, Sulzer, as an intermediary between Bryan and Tammany, received a letter from Richard Croker who wrote from his home in Ireland.

I received your very kind letter and was pleased to hear from you. You can say to Col. Bryan I will leave nothing undone for him. I trust he will keep his health. I have written to John Carroll asking him to see to it that the delegates be instructed for Col. Bryan. I will be back in due time to take part in the national convention.

Sulzer passed the letter to Bryan who responded:

Your favor at hand. Am glad to learn of your correspondence with Mr. Croker. His interview in the Journal the other day was very strong and will go far toward unifying things there.

Am gratified to hear so good a report of the outlook.

Your attitude on the question of Vice President is the correct one. Some of the candidates will have instructions from their own states, but when the delegates meet in Kansas City they will be in a position to go over the whole ground and so to act as to promote the success of the party.

Bryan's letter reveals that Bryan was not going to assert himself on behalf of Sulzer's ambition for the vice presidential nomination, a possibility that Sulzer had already succeeded in getting some newspaper attention to. Sulzer, or somebody on his behalf, was also circulating Bryan/Sulzer campaign buttons.

Actually, Bryan had written to Sulzer about Sulzer's vice presidential candidacy on April 20, 1900, telling him that he has not participated in vice presidential talks, but he has heard Sulzer's name discussed. "I think it is all right for your name to be discussed. You take the right stand. You are ready to run if the delegates think you are the most available and ready to stand aside if someone else seems more available. That is patriotic." It is certainly not an encouraging letter. The publicity about a possible vice presidential candidacy enhanced Sulzer's stature at home as well as in Congress.

The convention gave the vice presidential nomination to Adlai E. Stevenson, governor of Illinois, and the party lost again to the McKinley-Roosevelt ticket. Theodore Roosevelt became president at age forty-two when McKinley died in September from injuries received at the hand of an assassin.

In August and September, Sulzer was deluged with speaking requests from other states asking him to make an appearance for the ticket. Because of the network of nationwide contacts he acquired as a congressman, and his eloquent oratory, which attracted campaign speaking opportunities on behalf of others, both in New York and outside, Sulzer became a popular and even a formidable ally to party organizations and candidates outside of New York City and an asset to colleagues he befriended.

Throughout the late winter, spring, and summer of 1900, Sulzer heard continually from people in New York and some upstate newspapermen editorially implored the Democrats to nominate him for governor.

Sulzer's campaign for upstate support was built on relationships he developed with Democrats outside of the city of New York and reinforced with an energetic schedule of public appearances in response to their invitations generated by his fame as an inspiring public speaker. Because he was operating without the benefit of modern media coverage, Sulzer's ability to make an indelible impression on those who wielded political power and on potential voters required him to get around the state on an active schedule of public appearances.

A Poughkeepsie, New York, newspaper account found in one of the scrapbooks that Sulzer had delivered to the New York Public Library in 1904 told a wonderful story of the congressman's Labor Day excursion to Dutchess County in September of 1901. The newspaper account of the day told so much about the happy nature of such an outing, the way in which such events were reported in simpler times, and the response to Sulzer himself. I am reproducing it here in part to convey all the colorful flavor of such an event in 1901:

> Sharply at 1:45 o'clock yesterday afternoon the members of the trade and labor council of Poughkeepsie and their invited guests formed a line on Cannon Street. First came the police and then Peabody's band. Following these came the different organizations. In one of the trucks of the teamsters union were a number of small boys with a banner on which was the inscription "We will be union men by and by." Each union carried a handsome banner with the name of the organization it represented upon it . . .
>
> The scene as the line passed down the streets was an inspiring one. Thousands of persons thronged the streets . . . the members of the different organizations bared their heads as they passed the carriages which contained the city officials who in turn bared their heads to the working men. . . . On Main Street every available spot was filled. Windows and balconies and door steps all were packed to the utmost capacity. Many had . . . understood that the speech by Congressman Sulzer on the labor question would take place in the afternoon, but . . . were much disappointed when arriving at the grounds they learned that the speech would not be until 7:30 o'clock in the evening. The procession filed into the grounds at about 2:45 o'clock and for the remainder of the afternoon, the people sat in shady nooks or walked about the grounds. There were many features which took up the afternoon. One was the greased pole on the top of which was a five dollar silver watch. The trials for the watch were mostly made by small boys. One would stand on another's shoulders and a third would get up on the pole by being pushed with a stick until the others could reach no further. Then he would slide down to the ground. Some would take handfuls of dirt, but to no avail. Dozens of boys would get almost to the top and then slip and slide to the ground. Finally about half past five o'clock a boy named Lizzy got to the top. But what was his consternation to find the watch

nailed. He was nothing daunted, however, and at last slid to the ground, watch in hand, the envy of all of his boyfriends. Then there was the tug of war between six members of the labor organization and six from Young America Hose Company. The contestants pulled and tugged and their friends became so excited that many would grab hold of the rope and start to help the losers when they would be stopped by the referee. The tug lasted three minutes and was finally won by Young America's team. The greatest attraction and one which interested more people than anything else, outside of the dancing, was the black woolly head of Ignacious Peas stuck through a hole in a large canvass and anyone was allowed three throws for five cents and every time you hit the coon you got a quarter. Ignacious got many a hard crack. One time he was out of business for a few minutes, but only for a few minutes, when he bobbed up serenely with the same old cry, "Hit the only Nigger on the grounds, if you can."

At four o'clock the orchestra began. This was the signal for dancing and many a lad and lass hurried to the dancing pavilion where they were soon whirling to the pleasant strains of the music. . . . those who wished to stay had only to sit down and eat their supper and thus save the time and trouble of going home. . . .

During the afternoon, Mayor Hull escorted Congressman Sulzer around the city in his carriage and to the fair where the congressman was shown the many productions of Dutchess County.

It was a happy afternoon, everyone being in the best of spirits and not the semblance of hot words between anyone. Everyone wore an air which seemed to say we've come for a good time and so let's have it, and have it they did.

Over a thousand people went to Darryl Park in the evening to hear Congressman William Sulzer speak. Mr. Sulzer went to the grounds accompanied by Mayor Hull. He was introduced by John Bailey and was received with excited cheering. He said in part:

"Before the Civil War people heard little about organizing labor. After the war when efforts were being made to organize monopoly labor organizations sprung up as labor's self defense." Applause. "Labor unions were at first decried as being inimitable to the country, but now there is not a monopoly or trust which dares to deny labor the right to organize. Labor has as much right to organize as others have. I believe with Lincoln when he said if you destroy all the capital in the country labor will recreate it, but if you destroy labor the land becomes a waste" Applause. "We are living in the greatest land in the times. A land where he who plods succeeds. There are hundreds of thousands of working men who belong to no organization, but if they were all united and stood united for a reform, that reform would be successful. If labor stood united without jealousies and wrongs, labor could demand from the federal government all the rights to which it was entitled. Without unity nothing can be accomplished. Many statutes on the books of New York have been put there by organized labor. This is true of sister states and even the federal government. But there is much yet to be done. You little comprehend how much you can accomplish if you unite and stand firm for some principle. If I had my way I would decrease the hours of a legal working day. I believe that by doing this just as much can be accomplished and just as much material can be turned out. I believe the day is not far distant when the length of a working day in the United States will be six hours. Knowledge is power. I would have the humblest working man as well posted on the question of political economy as any professor. I encourage you to give your spare time to the study of the public questions. You would soon be able to decide rightfully for yourselves." Applause. "I would have you give at least two hours out of the twenty-four in the study of economic questions. I encourage this because I want to see American working men the most intelligent working people in the *Times*. I want you to put away all of your differences as between federal and Knights of Labor and you will stand as firm as did our solemn army before Santiago. If you would only set your standard high, aim worthy and high and you will succeed. If you will say that you want to accomplish something pick out what you are going to do and then struggle some more and persist and you will succeed. Everything that was ever accomplished in the *Times* that amounted to anything was done by hard work. Fix your ideal high in this land of opportunity and freedom. This will dignify your labor and your character." Applause.

Mr. Sulzer closed with a quotation from Goldsmith's Deserted Village. He closed amid applause and cheers.

Sulzer's role in the 1912 Democratic convention in Baltimore evidenced the culmination of all these activities, and was, to some extent, illustrative to the future problems between Sulzer and Murphy. According to Sulzer, the inside story of the 1912 Democratic convention had never been told. As Sulzer recalled the incident during the 1930s, his role at the convention made history.

There were four candidates for the presidential nomination, Champ Clark of Missouri, Woodrow Wilson of New Jersey, Oscar Underwood of Alabama, and Judson Harmon of Ohio. Champ Clark, the Speaker of the House, was the leading candidate as the convention convened. He had more committed delegates than any other candidate. Sulzer, who had been a member of Congress for years with Champ Clark, was one of the prominent Clark advocates in the country. He believed that Clark wanted him on the ticket for vice president.

Sulzer was elected a delegate to the convention from his own congressional district ticket, despite the efforts of Charles Murphy of Tammany Hall. Murphy was for Harmon because the big business interests of the country wanted Harmon nominated. Murphy controlled the delegation and had the Unit Rule adopted against the protest of Sulzer, who knew Murphy was for Harmon. By virtue of this Unit Rule, when the State of New York was called in the convention, Boss Murphy rose and said, "New York casts 90 votes for Harmon."

Sulzer pointed out that if Clark wasn't nominated, Woodrow Wilson would get the nomination. Murphy was bitterly opposed to Wilson. After about a dozen ballots, Murphy saw that what Sulzer said was coming true and he switched the delegation from Harmon to Clark, to head off Wilson.

Sulzer presided as permanent chairman during most of the convention. As a member of the House of Representatives for many years, Sulzer knew the house rules, which governed the convention. He was considered to be an able presiding officer and an experienced parliamentarian. Besides, he had a voice which could be heard throughout the convention hall.

Charles F. Murphy at the 1912 Democratic Convention.
LC-DIG-hec-01256. Courtesy of the Library of Congress.

After many roll calls, William Jennings Bryan, the party's previous candidate and a delegate from Nebraska, wanted to change his vote. Sulzer, as the presiding officer, ruled appropriately that Mr. Bryan could not do this because, under the rules of the House of Representatives, no member can explain his vote on a roll call. Besides, the delegation from Nebraska had been instructed by the Democratic voters of Nebraska to cast their votes for Champ Clark for president on every ballot. Mr. Sulzer ruled that these instructions were binding on each delegate unless a majority of the delegation decided otherwise.

The convention was deadlocked. U.S. Senator William J. Stone of Missouri, who was a friend of Bryan, as well as of Champ Clark, asked unanimous consent of the convention that Mr. Bryan be heard. Sulzer put this motion before the convention and there was no objection. The rules of the House permit anything to be done by unanimous consent.

Bryan's speech changed enough votes on the succeeding ballots to defeat Champ Clark and eventually bring about the nomination of Woodrow Wilson. It changed the course of American history. Sulzer was convinced that if it hadn't been for Bryan changing his vote to Wilson when he did, Clark would have been nominated. Bryan brought about the nomination of Wilson. (Wilson knew this and rewarded Bryan by making him secretary of state.)

When the Clark leaders in the convention realized the importance of the Bryan switch, they knew that Clark could not be nominated and Wilson would get the nomination unless something heroic was done. They called a secret meeting.

Attending this meeting were Senator Stone of Missouri (the Clark leader), Senator John Bankhead of Alabama (the Underwood leader), Senator Smith of New Jersey, Tom Taggart of Indiana, Roger Sullivan of Illinois, Fred Lynch of Minnesota, and several others. These men not only controlled the delegates from their own states, but many other delegations. About two o'clock in the morning they roused Sulzer out of bed and had him come to the conference. They said to Sulzer: "We are satisfied Clark can't get the two-thirds majority. To stop Wilson's nomination, we must all agree on a new candidate. We believe you are the best man. All that is necessary for you to do is have the New York delegation vote for you. Can you get Murphy to do this?"

Sulzer told these Democratic leaders that Murphy had never liked him and that he felt confident that Murphy would not be for him. He told them that it would be a mistake for him to speak to Murphy. Sulzer suggested that it would be much better to have Roger Sullivan of Illinois, a friend of Murphy, talk the matter over with Murphy. This was agreed upon and Roger Sullivan saw Murphy at 7:30 that morning and tried to convince him that the only way to defeat Wilson was to throw every delegation they possibly could to Sulzer on the next ballot to stampede the convention.

Murphy listened to him, but finally said that, under no circumstances, would he go for Sulzer. Roger Sullivan then told Sulzer if he wanted to be president to see Murphy and make peace with him. Sulzer made the effort and saw Murphy about nine o'clock that morning. He talked with him briefly, explaining the situation in the convention that was about to open its proceedings for the day. He explained that it was a critical moment in the history of the Democratic Party. When Sulzer finished, Murphy said: "New York is not for you—and that's that."

When the convention assembled later that fateful morning, Senator Bankhead, Tom Taggart, Senator Stone, and others went to Murphy on the convention floor and appealed to him again for Sulzer. They said in so many words, "If you will vote the New York delegation for Sulzer on this ballot, we will do the same with our delegations and bring about his nomination, and he can be elected." Murphy told each of them: "I'm against Sulzer."

On the next roll call that day, the tide turned to Wilson. Then Senator Bankhead again went to Murphy and said, "It is Sulzer or Wilson." Murphy answered, "We don't want Sulzer." Then Bankhead said, "Very well, I shall now take the platform and throw the Underwood vote to Wilson." Murphy made no reply. Wilson was nominated.

Triangle Shirtwaist Fire, *New York World*,
March 25, 1911.

10

The Tragedy That Changed New York

William S. Shepard was a reporter for United Press who happened to be walking in New York City's Washington Square at 4:45 p.m. on Saturday, March 25, 1911, when he witnessed a tragedy in progress: the Triangle Shirtwaist Factory Fire. From a street corner telephone booth, Shepard called his office with details as he saw them. His vivid descriptions were flashed by telegraph to the agency's member newspapers around the nation:

> I was walking through Washington Square when a puff of smoke issuing from the factory building caught my eye. I reached the building before the alarm was turned in. . . . I learned a new sound—a more horrible sound than description can picture. It was the thud of a speeding, living body on a stone sidewalk.
>
> Thud—dead, thud—dead, thud—dead, thud—dead. Sixty-two thud—deads. . . . I call them that, because the sound and the thought of death came to me each time, at the same instant. There was plenty of chance to watch them as they came down. The height was eighty feet.
>
> The first ten thud-deads shocked me. I looked up—saw that there were scores of girls at the windows. The flames from the floor below were beating in their faces. . . .
>
> I looked up to the seventh floor. There was a living picture in each window—four screaming heads of girls waving their arms. . . .

We cried to them not to jump. We heard the siren of a fire engine in the distance. . . .

"Here they come," we yelled. "Don't jump; stay there."

One girl climbed onto the window sash. Those behind her tried to hold her back. Then she dropped into space. . . . Then came that first thud. I looked up, another girl was climbing onto the window sill; others were crowding behind her. She dropped. I watched her fall, and again the dreadful sound. Two windows away two girls were climbing onto the sill; they were fighting each other and crowding for air. Behind them I saw many screaming heads. They fell almost together, but I heard two distinct thuds. Then the flames burst out through the windows on the floor below them, and curled up into their faces.

The firemen began to raise a ladder. Others took out a life net and, while they were rushing to the sidewalk with it, two more girls shot down. The firemen held it under them; the bodies broke it. . . . Before they could move the net another girl's body flashed through it. The thuds were just as loud; it seemed, as if there had been no net there. It seemed to me that the thuds were so loud that they might have been heard all over the city. Thud—dead, thud dead—together they went into eternity. . . .

I heard screams around the corner and hurried there. . . . Up in the [ninth] floor girls were burning to death before our very eyes. They were jammed in the windows. No one was lucky enough to be able to jump, it seemed. But, one by one, the jams broke. Down came the bodies in a shower, burning, smoking— flaming bodies, with disheveled hair trailing upward. They had fought each other to die by jumping instead of by fire. . . .

On the sidewalk lay heaps of broken bodies. A policeman later went about with tags, which he fastened with wires to the wrists of the dead girls, numbering each with a lead pencil, and I saw him fasten tag no. 54 to the wrist of a girl who wore an engagement ring. A fireman who came downstairs from the building told me that there were at least fifty bodies in the big room on the seventh floor. Another fireman told me that more girls had jumped down an air shaft in the rear of the building. I went back there, into the narrow court, and saw a heap of dead girls.

The floods of water from the firemen's hose that ran into
the gutter were actually stained red with blood. I looked upon
the heap of dead bodies and I remembered these girls were the
shirtwaist makers. I remembered their great strike of last year
in which these same girls had demanded more sanitary conditions and more safety precautions in the shops. These dead
bodies were the answer.[1]

The Triangle Shirtwaist Company employed five hundred garment
workers on the eighth, ninth, and tenth floors of a "fireproof" building
on Washington Square's east side. Fifteen minutes before the workday
was scheduled to end at 5:00 p.m., someone had dropped a still burning cigarette into a pile of discarded fabric under the sewing machine
worktables on the eighth floor. The workshop floor consisted of three
narrow lines of tables for sewing machines, with fabric for the operators parked on the table between each machine, which was as close to
the next one as possible to allow the maximum number of machine
operators to squeeze in. Underneath the tables were piles of waste
materials from previous cuttings. Overhead in a rope line hung the finished goods. In just a few seconds, the entire crowded floor had
become an inferno, and the panicked employees began to rush for the
distant exit doors, some with their clothes and hair already on fire. But
the doors were locked—a common management practice designed to
keep the employees from sneaking unauthorized breaks and to prevent them from taking any extra needles, a length of thread, or finished merchandise. Quickly the fire spread upward. Most of those on
the tenth floor were able to escape to the roof. During the first ten
minutes some on the ninth got out by elevators before they stopped
running. A few women on the eighth floor pushed their way to a fire
escape, but less than twenty got out that way before the rusty fire
escape collapsed from the weight of the frightened young workers
plunging to their deaths. The eighth floor was already engulfed in
flames when the city's fire department arrived within ten minutes
bringing some thirty-five pieces of the most modern equipment, most
of it horse drawn. Their ladders could reach only to the sixth floor as
young women started to appear in the windows. Fire and police horses
balked at the scene because they were not used to the smell of blood
that was already running in the gutters from the broken bodies lying
on the sidewalk or on the street.

Burned bodies were found piled up before locked doors. By 5:30 the fire was all over.

A makeshift morgue was established on an East River pier and the bodies of those who jumped and the one hundred people found inside after the fire was subdued were laid out for the families to try and identify the 146 dead, a process that took three days.

The victims were mostly young women, ranging in age from fourteen to thirty-five; their average age was nineteen. Most were immigrants, mainly Jewish and Italian. They earned from $7 to $12 a week, depending on their productivity.

The outrage and emotion was such that 120,000 people joined the unions, social welfare organizations, immigrant societies, and church groups in the funeral procession, which marched past 400,000 silent onlookers.

The largest industrial tragedy in history left the city outraged and the public demanded that such an event must never happen again. New Yorkers were shocked, especially so when they learned that there were no sufficient laws governing the conditions in factories that made it possible for the scope of this disaster to happen again. The few laws that did exist were never enforced.

OUTRAGE, THEN ACTION

Out of the ashes of the terrible fire there arose a great movement for reform, real reform of the very conditions that made the loss of life so severe. The grisly details of the fire that dominated the news turned the deplorable lack of concern for the health and safety of the exploited workers into a great public issue; the sacrifice of so many who could have survived if only concern for their safety had created an enforceable requirement for fire protection in the workplace. The methodology of such protection was already known. Sprinkler systems, fire drills, occupancy limits, fireproof doors that could not be locked from the outside, adequate fire escapes, clearly marked exits, and regular fire safety inspections—all of which we have now become accustomed to in every place of public assembly—all these tried and true requirements were known in 1911, but they were not mandated.

The Triangle fire not only changed New York City forever; it also had a profound impact on reform legislation for decades to come, and as a result, American politics was transformed to an extent never before realized. Immediately after the fire, public outrage was sufficient enough for powerful interests to intersect and unify. In the city, a Committee on Public Safety was formed to identify and lobby for necessary improvements. Frances Perkins, a prominent social worker who had actually witnessed the fire, became secretary of the committee and volunteered full-time as did a number of respected experts on fire safety, sanitation, and engineering. (Two decades later, Perkins would become FDR's secretary of labor and the first woman to serve in a presidential cabinet.)

The committee sent representatives to Albany and got the attention of Assembly Majority Leader Al Smith and Senate Majority Leader Robert Wagner, legislators who were also among the best and most reliable Tammany Hall politicians. Wagner and Smith made things happen. By working closely with the reformers who were characterized as do-gooders by the politicians, who called them "goo goos," these Tammany stalwarts created an alliance that served their political careers, strengthened the Democratic Party, and determined its politics and programs for years to come.

Until the Triangle fire, Tammany Hall had frequently wielded its power to support the industrial interests that provided financing for the great political machine. But, the fire's tragic dimensions and the citizens' uprising that resulted made Charles F. Murphy, Tammany's brilliant chief, realize that by supporting the committee's demands and placing his powerful resources behind the effort for real change, he could both strengthen Tammany's role and enhance the public's perception of the organization. He accomplished this with his customary silent enthusiasm.

THE ALLIANCE GENERATES REFORM

The legislature then created the New York State Factory Investigating Commission on June 30, 1911, giving it a broad investigative mandate and full subpoena power to compel testimony. Public hearings were held throughout the state. The commission became Al Smith's priority, and it had a profound effect on the man who would eventually become Speaker of New York State's Assembly, a five-term governor, and, in 1928, the presidential nominee of his party.

A major legislative accomplishment in the first year of the commission's existence was a bill limiting women's work to fifty-four hours per week. The commission also proposed and passed laws that controlled the sanitary conditions of factories, regulated children's labor, provided fire-prevention measures and regular fire drills, and prohibited night work for women in factory buildings. Between 1911 And 1913, sixty-four bills were generated by the commission; sixty became law, and the commission's recommendations became a centerpiece of Governor William Sulzer's successful 1913 legislative program. Tammany Hall made sure that Sulzer's battles with Charles Murphy over patronage would not interfere with the legislature's commitment to the reforms emanating from the Factory Investigating Commission.

During his eighteen years in Congress, Sulzer had enjoyed a good reputation as a pro-labor Democrat, so as governor he was especially pleased to support the creation of the most enlightened labor code ever enacted in any state. The first factory bills that passed in the 1913 legislative session were signed by Sulzer on March 14; these regulated sanitary conditions in all workplaces. Another bill prohibited women from working between the hours of 10 p.m. and 6 a.m., followed by a law that established the State Industrial Board in the Labor Department with the power—after holding public hearings—to establish regulations over working conditions in dangerous trades. A bill was also enacted that prohibited smoking in all factory buildings and required them to install fire alarm signal systems, hold regular fire drills under official supervision, and enclose all elevator shafts; the bill also required physical examinations for all children who worked in factories. On May 10, Sulzer signed bills that prohibited factories from employing girls less than twenty-one years of age between 9 p.m. and 6 a.m., and prohibited employing children as operators of dangerous machinery or in trades injurious to their health. Another law required factories to have ample fire escapes and exits and safeguards against overcrowding. Yet another bill regulated working hours and vacations for railroad workers. During his congressional career, Sulzer had introduced legislation to create a U.S. Department of Labor. In 1913, this measure was adopted and signed by President Taft at a White House ceremony to which Governor Sulzer was invited.

On May 4, the *New York Times* said that the 1913 legislature had "put on the statute books more legislation for the benefit of labor than any legislature for the past twenty years."

THE HEIGHT OF PROGRESSIVISM

An illustrative story of "Silent" Charles Murphy's direct involvement in the reform movement in New York was told by Frances Perkins in her 1946 book, *The Roosevelt I Knew*. As a key volunteer for the Factory Investigating Commission in 1911, Perkins went to see Murphy at Tammany Hall to enlist his support for the commission's pending legislation. She wrote: "Mr. Murphy, solemn dignity itself, received me in a reserved but courteous way. He listened to my story and arguments. Then, leaning forward in his chair, he said quietly, 'You are the young lady, aren't you, who managed to get the 54-hour bill passed?' I admitted I was. 'Well, young lady, I was opposed to that bill.' 'Yes, I so gathered, Mr. Murphy.' He said: 'It is my observation that that bill made us many good votes. I will tell the boys to give all the help they can to this new bill. Good-by.'"

Murphy was a smart politician, and government reform was good politics in 1911. Besides, Murphy kept his fingers on the public pulse. He knew he could endorse reforms that did not undermine the power of the political machine, especially when such reforms pleased the machine's constituency.

This, then, was the practical epitome of the Progressive Era. Sulzer, who had been a genuine progressive since his service in Congress, along with Smith, Wagner, and Murphy, who came to progressivism as a result of the tragic fire, all worked together effectively to accomplish a major set of reforms that improved the lives of the working class for generations to come. They, and the laws they supported, set a standard that has been emulated across America for the past one hundred years.

Each phase of progressivism and each facet had its icons. William Jennings Bryan was considered to be an example of progressive leadership when he ran for president so unsuccessfully in 1896 and 1900. But, Theodore Roosevelt, who actually became president in 1901, was the first and probably the most dynamic progressive president, eventually splitting the Republican Party to create a progressive alternative in 1912, giving the presidency to Woodrow Wilson who could also lay claim to the progressive mantle.

In New York, Charles Evans Hughes, who served two terms as Republican governor from 1907 to 1910 was probably the most progressive New York governor. He regulated the insurance industry for the benefit of the insureds and the investors. Conservation projects, reforming banking laws, and the first measures to set safety and health standards and regulating working hours in factories, mines, tunnels, and railroads marked his term. Hughes was also the first to create a Public Utilities Commission, and give his support to child labor restrictions, and universal public education. The first workers' compensation law was one of Hughes's greatest accomplishments—although the original version was declared to be unconstitutional and was only corrected by a constitutional amendment a few years later.

While Governor Hughes's proposals for election reform, including a direct primary law, a simplified ballot law, and a more democratized party system, were not successful during his term in office, they certainly laid the groundwork for others to follow.

Governor Hughes was so highly regarded that in 1910 at the end of his term he was appointed to the U.S. Supreme Court where he served with great distinction until he resigned in 1916 to run, unsuccessfully, as the Republican candidate for president against Woodrow Wilson.

Sulzer's interests and his record made it quite apparent that, to a great extent, he sought to emulate much of former Governor Hughes's leadership. Though he would rarely mention this illustrious predecessor and never gave him any particular credit, there can be very little doubt that the Hughes administration was a fertile breeding ground for some of Sulzer's ideas.

11

Selecting Congressman Sulzer

In 1896, after completing his first term in Congress, thirty-three-year-old Representative Sulzer sought his party's nomination for governor, but he was rebuffed. The leadership did not consider him appropriate despite his obvious success as a popular vote-getter in his own district. Every two years thereafter—1898, 1900, 1902, 1904, 1906, 1908, 1910— he attended the state convention and tried again. As he grew as a successful progressive legislator, he was taken more seriously each time. Sulzer was constantly reelected by his very satisfied constituents, even in years when there were Republican landslides. He began to build a following upstate through his campaigning statewide for the national ticket when William Jennings Bryan was the Democratic candidate for president. By 1906, Sulzer had built a meaningful following and was taken seriously by a significant number of upstate Democrats, but was never Mr. Murphy's choice, although "Big Tim" Sullivan, the powerful Tammany leader of the Bowery district became a strong ally and urged his nomination for governor in 1906 and 1908.

The governor's files at Cornell provide considerable evidence of Sulzer's efforts to organize his friends around the state in the summer of 1912, intending to develop a groundswell for his nomination. Among the August correspondence were letters indicating that Chester Platt of Batavia was coordinating the organization of an upstate campaign. Sulzer was receiving a flow of letters from committed supporters who were attending meetings of Democratic organizations, and reporting back on who they met and their attitudes toward supporting Sulzer. Platt filed reports on his activities almost daily. He was making speeches at political meetings around the state advocating Sulzer's candidacy, distributing statements to the upstate press, and organizing mailing campaigns based on lists he was gathering, some Sulzer already had in his possession, or some that Sulzer's secretary, Louis Sarecky, was developing for him.

Sulzer's people throughout upstate New York reported that, while there were certain influential men who could be relied on by Sulzer if they became delegates, many others who wanted to support him reported that they were hesitant to do so until they saw how Charles Murphy was going to go. From reading these letters it is clear that wherever Sulzer's people went they found that upstate Democrats were generally very upset with Governor Dix, did not consider him reelectable, and were actually giving that message to Mr. Murphy. The correspondence reveals that even Sulzer's most ardent supporters understood that Mr. Murphy will decide who the candidate will be. They seemed respectful toward him, a few were actually affectionate, and some obviously fearful, depending on their relationship. It is also obvious from the correspondence that everyone seems aware of the fact that Mr. Murphy will make the decision, and several of Sulzer's correspondents tell him that they are also sending letters to Mr. Murphy. In mid-September, Platt reports that he is sending out a story to all of the countywide weeklies in the state entitled "Sulzer—A Man Who Is His Own Master." This was an obvious response to the widespread view of upstaters that Governor Dix had sold his soul to Murphy.

The variety of letters in the file reflects the same kind of activities that an intra-party candidate would be engaged in today. In early September, Samuel Gompers, president of the American Federation of Labor, wrote to Sulzer expressing his support. In September, Sulzer got a letter from the "Colored Democrats" organization in Brooklyn, announcing their endorsement. Congressman Sulzer had championed the cause of black veterans of the Civil War. A number of reports mentioned his popularity among Jewish voters. The overriding theme from his correspondence turns on the boast that he is independent and "never been bossed."

The upstate loyalists all complain about the domination of the state party from New York City. In my own extensive experience running statewide campaigns in upstate New York, this continues to be a widespread, but understandable, frustration among dedicated upstate Democrats, which still runs true a century later.

The year 1912 contained a set of circumstances that made Sulzer viable. Incumbent governor John Dix was broadly viewed unfavorably in the party, and among the public, because, although a non-Tammany man when nominated and elected only two years earlier, once in office he became visibly subservient to Mr. Murphy, a relationship that did not sit well with the press or the public. Traditional Democratic newspapers let it be known that they would not support him, and so had large numbers of active Democrats across the state. In one report, Platt claims to have a letter from Woodrow Wilson, the Democratic candidate for president of the United States, indicating that he will do all he can to prevent the re-nomination of Governor Dix.

Governor John Dix, a banker and upstate independent Democrat, had been elected in 1910. He had built his reputation as an independent Democrat who had served as chairman of the state Democratic committee. After his election, he allowed the Tammany organization to penetrate his office so deeply that by 1912, even Tammany considered him such a political liability in the public eye that he could not be re-nominated for a second term. One rumor had it that all the mail addressed to the Executive Chamber was sent to Tammany Hall for screening before the governor ever saw it. No evidence of the truth of that apocryphal story ever appeared, but the story clearly illustrates the governor's public image.

The leaders of Tammany decided they could not risk losing with him in 1912 because their most important concern was to keep Tammany's reputation clean enough to enable them to recapture the huge patronage and business potential inherent in electing their own man as mayor of the city of New York in 1913.[1]

There was nevertheless an unusual opportunity to elect a Democratic governor that year because the Republican Party had divided into two factions, the traditional Republicans on one hand and Teddy Roosevelt's progressives on the other. The progressives had nominated Oscar S. Strauss, a former U.S. ambassador to Turkey and Roosevelt cabinet member and a highly respected Jewish philanthropist. The regular Republican ticket was headed by Job E. Hedges, a prominent lawyer. New York City Democrats were afraid of losing their significant Jewish constituency to Strauss.[2]

Although Mr. Murphy had been hearing from all directions that Dix was not reelectable, loyalty required him to stick with the incumbent governor—at least for a decent interval. Presidential candidate

Woodrow Wilson had publicly demanded a free and open New York convention whose candidate would be on his ticket. When Dix dropped out at Murphy's order, after the third deadlocked ballot at the Syracuse convention on October 2nd, Murphy, clearly understanding the bossism issue, announced that he was not voting himself and he was going to instruct the delegates that it was truly a free and open convention, leaving them free to select among the several candidates who had survived the third ballot.[3] Every sign indicated he had picked former Albany congressman and former state comptroller Martin Glynn as his man. Mr. Murphy thought he was positioning his next choice as a man who would not find himself in Dix's position, and Murphy did not want to become an issue himself.

Many astute observers were not buying it. According to historian Kenneth S. Davis, the Syracuse state convention of 1912 "was in essence a rigged affair," characterized by carefully managed "freedom" calculated "spontaneity," and "openness," with Murphy holding out until the fourth ballot when Dix withdrew and Murphy released his delegates to vote as they saw fit.[4] State senator Robert F. Wagner, a Tammany man who led the New York County delegation, threw all of their votes to Sulzer, who was already the most popular with the upstate independent Democrats. Of greater importance, because of the Strauss candidacy, Sulzer was extremely popular with New York City Jews, an important portion of Tammany's support, with many residing in Sulzer's congressional district. Jewish voters certainly remembered Sulzer as the chairman of the House Foreign Affairs Committee, who led a successful movement to cancel the United States treaty with Russia because the czarist government was refusing to recognize the passports of American Jewish visitors who had emigrated from Russia. As Henry Morganthau said in his autobiography, Sulzer, as a congressman, had "consistently played up" to the Jewish element.[5] Morganthau described the ingratiating manner that Sulzer carefully cultivated to appeal to a "proud people who were accustomed to a lack of consideration from government officials."

According to Sulzer's own account and the *Times*, Sulzer was also the choice of a majority of the county Democratic chairmen, including the group of upstate independent Democrats who had been organized by Senator Franklin D. Roosevelt as the "Empire State Democracy."[6] Sulzer had supporters across the state, partly a residue of his eight previous efforts. Besides, his legislative accomplishments were genuine and

SEN. FRANKLIN D. ROOSEVELT
26TH DIST.

From *The New York Red Book* (Albany: J. B. Lyon Co., 1913).

progressive, his oratory impressive, and his energy seemed unlimited. In short, he had been on the right side of most issues and his popularity exceeded the boundaries of his congressional district, because, over the years, he had tirelessly made himself available to speak in other districts.

Friedman reports that many years later he interviewed George W. Blake, a political regular who was genuinely a close confidant of Sulzer, and Blake told him that Sulzer had received advance word of his nomination from Mr. Murphy himself. Nevertheless, when Sulzer was interviewed at his hotel, just after being nominated, he pretended to be surprised to have been nominated and said he had no intention of entering the campaign.[7] (Anyone who saw his correspondence in August of 1912, would have trouble believing that protest.)

The documents from Sulzer's own files also belie Sulzer's denial. Whether truthful or not, Sulzer's draft says that Dix was in close communication with Sulzer by telephone and when Murphy turned him down, "Dix telephoned his representatives and delegates in Syracuse to vote for Sulzer in accordance with the agreement between Dix and Sulzer. This brought about Sulzer's nomination." Although this revelation is the only time this version of the story has ever been told, it is not incongruous with the theory that Murphy really decided to nominate Sulzer and he had his man, Dix, tell some of the Tammany delegates. Sulzer's autobiographical draft goes on to say that Murphy always intended to nominate Martin Glynn. Sulzer's old friend, Jay W. Forrest, tells a similar story in *Tammany's Treason*.[8] Forrest attributes Murphy's last-minute turn from Glynn to Sulzer to the need to capture the Jewish voters they feared that Strauss would be likely to attract.

On the fourth ballot at Syracuse on October 2nd, Sulzer was nominated as the party's candidate for governor. Martin Glynn became the candidate for lieutenant governor. Sulzer made his independence the key issue of the campaign, and referred to the "free and unfettered combination of independent delegates" that had nominated him, repeatedly expressing the thought "I am free, without entanglements . . . William Sulzer never had a boss, and his only master is himself."[9] While the public considered Sulzer to be one of the most respectable of the Tammany men, he was also the only possible compromise between the upstate reformers and Tammany Hall, but it seemed to be the prevailing opinion that the free convention theme was only an illusion.

Despite accusations from many quarters, the Sulzer nomination was generally well received and presidential candidate Woodrow Wilson issued a statement expressing his pleasure and support, referring to "the freedom of action and of choice" at the Syracuse convention, and praising Sulzer as "a man of high principle" whose "reputation for integrity and independence is unquestionable."[10]

Sulzer's short personal campaign was organized out of his law office by his longtime secretary, Louis Sarecky, and a group of prominent friends who constituted a campaign committee. Of course, the Democratic state committee, Tammany Hall, and the Democratic Party organizations around the state were relied on. Sulzer wrote his own speeches and spoke at several meetings each night when he was in New York City, except for three campaign trips—a short one to Long Island, and a two-day trip up one side of the Hudson to Albany and back down the other side; there was a ten-day-long train trip with the lieutenant governor candidate and an entourage of clerks, secretaries, and press along. They headed across the state to Syracuse, Rochester, and Buffalo, and back to Albany and Troy along the Southern Tier,

Wherever he went, Sulzer drew enthusiastic crowds who wanted to say a word, touch his sleeve, or shake his hand. In many cases, people passed cash campaign contributions to him, and he thanked them graciously and put the cash in his pocket.

As a result of the Republican split, Sulzer's personal popularity, and his energetic campaign, which provided extensive exposure of his effective oratory, Sulzer carried the day with an impressive victory in a three-way race, even though the two opposing candidates combined drew significantly more votes. The totals were: Sulzer 649,559; Hedges 444,106; and Strauss 393,183. Sulzer could claim victory by a margin of 268,097, which enabled him to boast that he won by the largest majority in New York history. While that boast was legitimate, the truth was that Sulzer got fewer votes than Dix had only two years before and fewer votes than any Democrat in fourteen years.

12

Sulzer's Second Day as Governor

R ight after his inauguration, Sulzer initiated tremendous turmoil. By words and deeds he started two wars before his second day as governor was over. The first war was against Tammany's control of political patronage. The second was against corruption and inefficiencies in the state government. These incipient battles would have far-reaching consequences. A battle against the bosses was certainly out of character for a politician who had enjoyed the endorsement of the Tammany organization through the recent gubernatorial election and during most of his twenty-five years in Congress and the state legislature. On the other hand, such actions at the very inception of his gubernatorial term were consistent with his campaign rhetoric and the picture he brazenly sought to paint of himself as an independent progressive in the image of his distinguished recent predecessors, Charles Evans Hughes, who became a presidential candidate, and former-president Theodore Roosevelt. In those days, nearly every New York governor was generally considered to be a good prospect for the presidential nomination of his party, and several had been so honored. Until this day the more sophisticated leaders in the political organization had dismissed Sulzer's public statements as puffed up campaign oratory—not to be taken seriously. In fact, the body politic had been sharply divided for many years between reformers on the one hand and machine politicians on the other. A nationwide progressive movement was gaining attention as a significant factor in American politics. More recently under Charles Murphy's brilliant leadership, Tammany had demonstrated instances of its realization that the best way to maintain power was by supporting candidates who the people could take pride in.

Of course Tammany also expected loyalty from its candidates—absolute, unwavering, and total loyalty. Sulzer was sensitive to the public interest in progressive politics. While the repeated theme of Sulzer's statewide campaign for governor had been his proud pronouncement that he was totally free of boss control, based on the long history of his relationship with Tammany and especially with Richard Croker during his term in the assembly and his early years as a congressman, the political bosses accepted his campaign rhetoric as good politics for a candidate from New York City seeking statewide support. They were well aware of upstaters who considered the New York City machine to be anathema and accepted Sulzer's statements at face value because, despite years of Tammany endorsements, he had a superb record of standing for progressive legislation and he articulated his beliefs so eloquently. Besides, there had been times when he had prevailed without Tammany's help and he was always elected on his own merits and popularity.

The essence of what Sulzer was moving to accomplish was captured in the headline of the lead story in the *New York Times* on January 3rd: "Sulzer Invites Murphy to Fight for Leadership, Proclaims That He Is Democratic Chief in the State by Decree of the People."

Sulzer was well aware that his immediate predecessor, Democrat John Dix, was unable to run again due to the appropriate perception that he had sold out to the control of Tammany Hall. In eight years as the Chief of Tammany, Murphy had grasped unprecedented power as the leader of the Democratic Party in the state as well as the city. In November of 1912, Democrats had not only elected Sulzer, but also carried New York for Woodrow Wilson as president and a solid Democratic majority in both houses of the state legislature, the leaders of which were loyal Tammany men and very much beholden to Charles Murphy.

On inauguration day Sulzer had begun the process of ingratiating himself to the political reporters at the Capitol by skillfully telling them they were welcome to call him at any time and he would always be available. His immediate predecessor had been reticent about meeting reporters informally, so Sulzer's invitation was meaningful. This went hand in hand with the brand of populism he was trying to identify his administration with by calling the Executive Mansion "The People's House," abolishing the inaugural parade, walking to the Capitol, up the steps, and so forth. On the second day of his term, the new governor started acting on his promise of open government by inviting the reporters who covered him into the Executive Chamber for briefings twice a day.

His first regular morning meeting with reporters from the afternoon papers was scheduled for 11:30 a.m. About a dozen journalists arrived at the great Red Room, as the Executive Chamber is sometimes referred to because of its deep red plush carpet and red mahogany panels. The governor was occupied with a group of Democratic state committeemen, but he shooed them out, begging their leave to keep his appointment with the press representing the evening newspapers. He made a point by telling the politicians in a voice that could be heard that the reporters "were far more important than you." Even the hardened cynics among the newsmen had to be charmed by such unaccustomed deference. Not since the administration of Governor Charles Evans Hughes, which ended in 1910, had a governor made the press feel so important. As the reporters gathered around him, Sulzer endeared himself even further by calling on Mr. Platt, his secretary, to have chairs brought in to the chamber for the reporters who had always been expected to stand when interviewing previous governors. Theodore Roosevelt was the last governor to have offered them seats, and that was thirteen years ago. The correspondents were delighted with the governor's willingness and ability to answer any and all questions. Most were justifiably flattered by the governor's attention, especially when he started asking for their advice on issues.

While reporters on the political beat tend, with good reason, to be cynical about politicians, only a few of the most cynical were suspicious of Sulzer's skill and kindness. One of the cynics said, "He is going to play to the galleries to beat the band. It makes me sick."

During the late afternoon, Sulzer met with a second group of newspaper correspondents, twenty-four of them from the morning papers. It started out as a casual but informative, off-the-record, meeting. The governor's intention was to alert the press to his plans for instilling honestly, efficiency, and economy in his administration of state government. Sulzer's declaration of war came casually and did not seem to be planned according to one of the reporters present. A newspaperman asked, half in jest, "Have you received the O.K. of Charles F. Murphy, Tammany leader, on your plans?" At that point, the governor, who had been relaxing in a comfortable armchair in the center of the semicircle of newsmen seated around him in the far corner of the Executive Chamber, suddenly stood up.

"I knew that question would come up sooner or later and it's just as well that we have an understanding on this subject right now, and then we will never refer to it again," he said. Until that point, the governor had been talking on an off-the-record basis, that is, not for attribution, a clear understanding with the reporters in exchange for candor. The governor then asked that they go on the record—what he was about to say should be taken down verbatim and placed in quotation marks. "I am the Democratic leader of the State of New York. The people decreed it at the polls, and I stand on their verdict. I cannot succeed in doing what I want to do as Governor unless I am the leader. If any Democrat wants to challenge that, let him come out in the open and the people will decide."

Another reporter asked, "Does that mean that if Mr. Murphy wants to see you he will have to come to the Executive Chamber?"

"This is the place," the governor answered with a determined nod. "Mr. Murphy is the leader of the Democratic organization of New York County, and as such I will always receive him and listen to what he has to say, and if what he asks for is right he will get it, and if what he asks for is not proper in my opinion, I will tell him so and he will understand. The same applies to any other request, no matter by whom it is made." Sulzer went on to say, "But, Mr. Murphy will be most welcome here in the Executive Chamber, and his family will be welcome. They will all be welcome at the Executive Mansion. I will see anybody who comes here to see me. . . . But there will be no secrecy about anything I do. Everything in this Administration will be open and above board."

One of the reporters who was stunned by the governor's challenge to Murphy's leadership said, "Those are the most comforting words I have heard in this room since Governor Hughes left." To which Sulzer replied, "Well, you are likely to hear plenty like it if occasion should arise. I am not afraid of Murphy, I am afraid of no man. No political boss can make me do anything I don't think I ought to do. And, I may add, too, no newspaperman can drive me to do anything I think I shouldn't do; no matter how much they harass me. But I will always be amenable to just criticism."

The governor had succeeded in creating a big story for the morning papers.

While the press could not get any direct reaction to the governor's statement from Mr. Murphy himself, several Tammany district leaders who responded to calls from reporters who guaranteed that their names would not be used predicted that the "Chief" would take up the governor's gauntlet and make the challenge to his leadership the fight of his life. One Murphy confidant said that Murphy would spend every dollar he had to prevent the governor from beating him. Some Tammany lieutenants were already spreading the word that Murphy had already let it be known that he thought he had made a major mistake by failing to oppose Sulzer's nomination because had had assumed that Sulzer would be reasonable and would not start trouble if he got the party nomination. It was also revealed without any details that, at the end of December, before Sulzer took office, Murphy had tried to feel out Sulzer on certain new appointments that the governor had to make. Sulzer had refused, causing a break between them. Murphy subsequently let it be known to his leaders that he considered Sulzer to be an ingrate.

The second shot in Sulzer's war began later in the same afternoon. This one did not just occur casually. Sulzer had been preparing the details and had signaled his intention the day before in the inaugural address when he promised to review all of the departments of state government with an avowed purpose of eliminating useless expenditures, abolishing sinecures, and promoting honesty and efficiency for the taxpayers' benefit. Sulzer put these words into immediate action by announcing creation of a three-man Commission on Inquiry with the broad power to investigate all of the state's departments. The governor's intentions were evident from the names of the first two well-known citizens he selected. Both were known as men of integrity with no ties to the party machine. John Carlisle, who was designated as chairman of the Commission on Inquiry, was a well-known independent upstate Democrat whose reputation was based on his participation in several party movements designed to shake off the shackles of Tammany Hall. As the second commissioner, the governor named one of his longtime friends, John H. Delany of Brooklyn, who was a newspaperman. Delany was business manager for the *New York Morning Telegraph*. He had been a typographical union official who successfully fought the Kings County Democratic machine, which was a major ally of Tammany Hall and one of the foundations of its power.

The third member of the commission would be named later by agreement of the original two—and the governor let it be known that he expected the commission to hold public hearings that would lead to the punishment of crooks and grafters.[1]

Charles F. Murphy on the Atlantic City board-
walk. Bettmann/Corbis.

13

Mr. Murphy

Who was Mr. Murphy? It is not enough to know that in 1902 he succeeded Richard Croker as leader of Tammany Hall and kept that position until his sudden death in 1924 at the zenith of his power and influence. Nor is it enough to know that Mr. Murphy made the leadership of Tammany Hall a greater position of power and influence than ever before or ever since, and that he eventually became a positive influence on the most progressive social legislation, the extent of which would never again be achieved, or that a one-time adversary, President Franklin Roosevelt called him a "genius." For two decades after the turn of the century, Charles Francis Murphy was among the nation's most influential political figures.[1]

According to police estimates, fifty thousand people lined Fifth Avenue on Monday, April 28, 1924, to pay their respects to Mr. Murphy. The governor, the mayor, an ex-U.S. senator, and other dignitaries in high silk hats who served as honorary pall bearers filed out of St. Patrick's Cathedral with the other mourners, who had filled the great church to attend the solemn funeral Mass for "Mr. Murphy," as he was nearly always called. Thousands more followed the funeral cortege across the Queensboro Bridge to Calvary Cemetery where he was laid to rest.

Nobody was more personally devastated by Murphy's very sudden death than his protégé, Al Smith, who was then the governor of New York. Smith had lost a true and loyal friend. It was particularly tragic because at the time of his sudden death, Murphy was heavily engaged in a serious quest for delegates to the 1924 National Democratic Convention to support Smith's ambition to be president, and Murphy's ambition to be the one to make it happen.

Relatively little has been written about Murphy, who was known for his silence and who left no written records of his own, yet his impact on the direction of American politics was profound. It was an influence that changed for the better over the years in keeping with the political necessities of his times. In retrospect, it is very clear that the outcome of Boss Murphy's war with Governor Sulzer had a significant and positive influence on his personal development during the last decade of Murphy's life.

In 1858, the same year that the cornerstone for St. Patrick's Cathedral was laid on Fifth Avenue, Charles Francis Murphy was born. He was one of eight children of an Irish immigrant family who had settled in the Lower East Side of New York, where he was raised in a particularly tough area known as the "gas house" district, because of a proliferation of huge gas tanks that were built along the East River in 1842 to store the energy that then lit and powered the great city. The tanks leaked a foul smell that pervaded the entire neighborhood, which was heavily populated by poor Irish immigrant families. The district, which was also known as the home for many active gangs of young hooligans, ran from the East River to Park Avenue South between Fourteenth Street and Twenty-Seventh Street.

Leaving public school at age fourteen to help support his family, Murphy did a variety of manual work before becoming a horse-car driver in 1875 at age seventeen, on the crosstown Blue Line. Murphy organized the Sylvan Club, a social and athletic club with its own baseball team called the Senators, of which he was both captain and catcher. Murphy's team was a good one. The Senators were so successful that each week they won the $100 stakes playing sandlot ball on Sundays. With his share of these winnings and savings from his job on the horse car, Murphy saved $500 by 1892 at age twenty-four. It was enough to allow the young man to lease his own saloon at Avenue A and Nineteenth Street, which was to become the first of four Murphy saloons. "Charlie's Place" had the customary sawdust floor, the brass rail, a commercial bar towel, a large glass of beer and a bowl of soup for a nickel, with free crackers and cheese. The Sylvan Club maintained headquarters on the second floor, while Murphy tended bar on the first, catering to a mixture of stevedores, small businessmen, gas house workers, men who worked in the neighborhood lumberyards, local politicians, and even some white-collar workers—but no women. They were specifically excluded because Murphy believed that they did not belong in saloons. Charlie didn't like swearing either, so Charles' Place distinguished itself from more typical saloons by its ban on profanity and on women. Like most of the district leaders, Murphy drank only occasionally. As a bartender, Murphy excelled as a listener, but not as a talker. He always kept order, careful to offer his patrons support but not advice. For the immigrant Irish community, the saloon was a place of fellowship that provided a sense of social belonging. It was not unusual that the saloonkeeper would become a political force to be reckoned with, especially a man with Murphy's athletic ability, natural leadership qualities, obvious morality, and a great capacity to keep quiet. He was all these things.

At the same time Murphy's saloon was opening in the gas house district, the multitude of immigrants arriving in New York City had overgrown the capacity of Castle Garden, the old building on Battery Park at the tip of Manhattan where they were received and processed by immigration officials of the United States government, until the new recreation facility was opened in 1892 on Ellis Island in the city's great North Bay, where more than twenty million immigrants would be processed for entry into America over the next sixty-two years.

Murphy's brothers were already active in the local Tammany organization. William had become an alderman and John a councilman. The fourth saloon that Murphy bought also housed the Anawanda Club on the second floor. Anawanda was the district's local Tammany organization. Murphy joined and was elected as a member of the Tammany general committee. To the Murphys, like so many other Irish immigrant families, politics was a route to respectability in the new times and a way out of poverty.

Murphy did well enough from the proceeds of his saloons that he earned a reputation in the community as a charitable and moral man. He made meaningful charitable contributions, the most extravagant of which was a very well-remembered $4,000 contribution to the victims of the Great Blizzard of 1888, a tragedy for so many because the city had been ill-prepared to react.

He was a devout Catholic who rarely missed Sunday Mass and read only religious books. His personal habits were close to Puritan. He did not smoke, swear, or gamble; drank only rarely; and made it very clear that he did not tolerate off-color jokes. His most obvious attributes were his silence and his strength. He believed that he should never make himself conspicuous. Taciturnity was his hallmark.

Murphy was known for maintaining strong family attachments and he remained single until age forty-four when he married the former Margaret Graham in June 1902, a widow he knew from the gas house district with one daughter who Murphy treated as his own.

When Murphy joined the Anawanda Club, Edward Hagan was the Tammany district's state assemblyman and he became Murphy's political mentor. After a dispute with his district leader, Hagan was denied his re-nomination to the assembly in 1883. He consulted his popular friend, Murphy, who suggested that he run independent. Murphy managed Hagan's campaign and they beat the regular Tammany candidate, and became a force to be reckoned with. Soon Hagan and Murphy were welcomed back to Tammany Hall. When Hagan, who became the district leader in 1887, died in 1892, Murphy succeeded him as the Tammany district leader for the Anawanda Club and the gas house district.

Murphy was a quiet man of regular and reliable habits. As the district leader, he established routines to make sure he was responsible to the people who elected him. He made himself available to any of his constituents every evening by appearing under the lamppost at the northwest corner of Twentieth Street and Second Avenue, opposite the saloon where the Anawanda Club was located. His "office hours" leaning against the lamppost, beginning promptly at 7:30 p.m. and lasting until 10 p.m., were regular and people could rely on the fact that Mr. Murphy would be there listening and nodding to those seeking city jobs or favors, or help with their problems. The district's city aldermen and state assemblymen were always nearby, as well as a few of the club's ambitious lawyers, so Murphy could solve some of his constituents' problems by calling one of them over from the club across the street. It was in this milieu that Murphy established a technique, which would forever distinguish his style. He said very little, but he listened intently. His responses were direct and usually limited to "yes" or "no," if he had made a decision, or that he would "look into it" but never committing himself when he had not made a decision. Murphy's ability to keep his own counsel gave people the feeling that he always held something in reserve that was not revealed. That became his image. Murphy's silent style distinguished him as the "Silent Boss" and led to one story that is included in nearly every effort to describe Murphy's style.

While attending a Tammany Fourth of July celebration, a reporter noticed that Murphy had not joined in the singing of the "Star-Spangled Banner" by the assembled crowd. The reporter, suspecting that perhaps the Boss did not know the words, asked for an explanation from one of the well-known aides to the Tammany chieftain, who replied, "perhaps he didn't want to commit himself."

Murphy's personal brand of political leadership was distinguished by a determined effort to keep his district morally straight. True to his own moral compass, he opposed any form of graft in connection with saloons, gambling, or prostitution at a time when such corruption and police payoffs were rampant throughout the city of New York. Murphy's morality, however, did not extend to the forms of what was then understood to be honest graft, which was then practiced extensively by those political leaders who were getting rich on investment opportunities, contracts, and commercial favors that were available to them because of their access to powerful decision-makers.

On January 1, 1898, the newly consolidated city of Greater New York was created, when Brooklyn, Queens, and Staten Island were joined with the Bronx and Manhattan. Overnight, New York had become a city of 3.5 million people, the second largest at the time, after London. According to the *New York Tribune*, "the sun will rise this morning on the greatest experiment in municipal government that the times has ever known."[2]

On New Year's Eve 1897, one hundred thousand people crowded into City Hall Park in the rain to join together in celebration of the creation of the new city. The *Tribune* called it, "the biggest, noisiest celebration that Manhattan Island had ever known." Cannons were fired at midnight and the new city flag was unfurled. For many people, and for many different reasons, it was a time of expanded opportunities and Mr. Murphy had become one of the players. New York was growing and inside the expanded metropolis enormous opportunities were exploding in every direction.

As a result of Murphy's success in regularly and reliably getting out the Tammany vote in his district, he was rewarded with his first and only political job. The first elected mayor of the newly consolidated city, Robert Van Wyck, agreed to Richard Croker's recommendation to name Murphy as one of the city's four dock commissioners. The dock commissioners were important men because they decided who would have what access to the city's docks. Murphy was very proud of his public office and especially of the fact that he was now entitled to be addressed as "Commissioner." While it was rare for anyone to call him by his first name (he was usually "Mr. Murphy"), people in the know might ingratiate themselves just a bit for years to come by calling him "Commissioner."

It has been repeatedly reported by those who were familiar with the situation that when Murphy assumed his position on the docks board he was already comfortable financially, being worth about $400,000 by his own admission. Murphy's purse grew to a million dollars during his four-year term, which ended in 1901.[3]

As previously mentioned, one of the enrichments received by Dock Commissioner Murphy was in the form of shares of the American Ice Company, which had been granted the monopoly on the city docks.

During his last year in public office, 1901, Murphy created a new business entity called New York Contracting and Trucking Company. The other shareholders were his brother, City Councilman John J. Murphy; James E. "Big Jim" Gaffney, a city alderman; and Richard J. Crouch, a political ally. Murphy had 85 percent of the original shares, and his three colleagues had 5 percent each. Years later, when examined under oath by a legislative investigating committee, Murphy publicly denied owning any of the shares, but he provided no record of having transferred ownership. ("Big Jim" was the very same Gaffney who Governor Sulzer would refuse to appoint as his highway commissioner in 1913.)

During the administration of reform mayor Seth Low in 1902, the city commissioner of accounts reported that Murphy's company leased two piers from the city pursuant to a contract provided by the dock commissioners during Murphy's tenure at an annual rental of $4,800, and then re-leased the same facilities to another concern at $65,000 per year. Murphy saw nothing wrong with this transaction. The man who railed against vice and dirty jokes wallowed in honest graft.

By 1902, visible evidence of Murphy's expanding wealth began to emerge when he acquired his fifty-acre suburban estate at Good Ground on Long Island's Southampton Bay, which would later become known as Hampton Bays. Murphy built a nine-hole golf course on the property. He also maintained a small farm with a few horses and cows,

SULZER—Sulzer will have no boss but Sulzer!
MURPHY—When you finish your solo, Bill, just step upstairs.

Gubernatorial campaign cartoon, *New York Tribune*,
November 8, 1912.

and raised Great Danes. Good Ground and his golf game would become Murphy's only known indulgence for years to come.

New York Contracting and Trucking Company only exemplified how big money could be made in those days by people with the right political connections, especially those who allowed themselves to think big enough.

The Pennsylvania Railroad Company, which was in the process of building Penn Station on Thirty-Fourth Street and Eighth Avenue, had been stymied for some three years in its effort to obtain permission from the city to build the approaches to its major tunnels under the streets. The board of aldermen was holding it up. "Big Jim" Gaffney, Murphy's partner in New York Contracting was also a powerful city alderman. Very soon after New York Contracting won a two million dollar contract to excavate the station site the railroad got its franchise. Subsequently it was revealed that their bid was $400,000 higher than the nearest competitor. Neither New York Contracting nor any of its owners had any experience in the excavation business.

Very little about the transaction was surreptitious. The board of aldermen had been subject to a lot of criticism from the press and civic organizations, and reports had been circulated that the aldermen had demanded $300,000 in cash for the franchise to build the tunnels. It was also reported that "Big Jim" Gaffney had rallied the aldermen to vote for the franchise. It was only months after the franchise was granted that the excavation contract became known and people were able to put two and two together. But, the revelation had no impact.

The Penn Station deal became a model for similar subsequent transactions. In 1905, New York Contracting won a six million dollar contract to construct rail lines in the Bronx for the New York, New Haven and Hartford Railroad, after the company had won a three-year-long battle with the city for the rights to provide railway access to New York City from the north.

By 1905, the city experienced tremendous expansion. According to expert estimates and a number of investigations years afterward, New York Contracting or its affiliates had received $15 million worth of contracts with various entities that relied on the approval of city government or its various agencies.

There is no clear evidence of other specific deals that Murphy profited from, although accusations were made constantly throughout his career as Tammany's leader. None impeded his political success, despite continual allusions by journalists or political adversaries to the grasp and corruption of Tammany and Murphy personally. Political cartoonists frequently depicted Murphy in prison stripes, but powerful people continued to seek his friendship. As muckraker Lincoln Steffens once wrote, "Tammany was corruption with consent."[4]

When Murphy took over as the undisputed chief of the Tammany sachems in 1902, he brought with him the same moral compass that had guided him in his own assembly district. He eschewed gambling and prostitution and believed that paying off the police to condone such activities was not only immoral, it was bad politics. In this respect he was ahead of his time among the district leaders. At the first meeting of the district leaders that he presided over as their new chief, Murphy made his position clear. He wanted to take the district leaders out of the business of supporting bordellos and paying off policemen, and he made serious efforts to accomplish his goal—efforts that met with only partial success. However, graft from business relationships was not a moral issue in Mr. Murphy's perspective of right and wrong.

MURPHY'S STYLE

When Murphy moved into the chief's office at Tammany Hall, he gave his customarily terse interview to a reporter for the *New York Times* who inquired about what to expect from his new regime. "I won't do much talking. . . . I will be at Tammany Hall every day, and spend the hours between 3 and 5 o'clock in the afternoon at work. There is plenty of work to be done and the less talking the better."[5]

Murphy avoided flamboyance of any kind, even avoiding being conspicuous. Former mayor James J. Walker, himself a Murphy protégé, said: "Mr. Murphy once told me that most of the troubles of the times could be avoided if men opened their minds instead of their mouths." Good advice that Walker himself never took.

Those many who knew or observed him said that Mr. Murphy was naturally withdrawn and actually had little to say in social situations. People who sat next to him at dinner parties complained that they were not able to engage him in conversation. Fellow guests at a resort he frequented in Atlantic City, New Jersey observed that at mealtimes he would say nothing to his wife and daughter, and nothing more than "Good Morning" to his fellow guests, even though the womenfolk were most voluble.

Among his fellow members of the Tammany Executive Committee he was said to speak "in short, jerky, low sentences, seldom over twelve words long. Often a minute would elapse between sentences."[6]

Being close-mouthed, Murphy was an enigma to his peers. Silence generated the view that he was so politically shrewd that he obviously had some important knowledge that he was not revealing and deserved command of the situation at hand and time to handle it.

Murphy also impressed political colleagues with his thirst for every fact he might need to make a decision. He intensively interrogated whoever approached with a problem. One night each week was usually put aside to hear "confession" from his district leaders, one at a time. Without making any notes, he would rely on a superb memory to take care of their needs.

While his party business was usually taken care of at his office in Tammany Hall, Mr. Murphy took care of his public or commercial business in an entirely different atmosphere. Those with serious matters were usually invited to his red plush second-floor private dining suite at Delmonico's restaurant. At lunchtime a hansom cab would pick up Mr. Murphy at the wigwam and take him north to the famous and elegant restaurant then located at Fifth Avenue and Forty-Fourth Street. That was Delmonico's most recent location, having been originally established fifty years earlier at the bottom end of Manhattan Island at South William Street. It was the choice of the socially elect, with a reputation maintained by superb service, good food, a great wine list, and the most elegant surroundings. Over the Murphy years, every important businessman in New York City would find his way to Delmonico's at lunchtime for a special meeting with Charles F. Murphy. Occasionally, candidates for the most significant offices, important public officials, or prominent members of the judiciary would also be asked to come by for a meeting with the chief.

When the man so honored with an invitation arrived at Delmonico's he would first identify himself to the doorman who opened the door to his cab, and who would then pass his visitor's card to the elevator boy, who gave it to one of the liveried attendants who stood watch at the door to the second-floor anteroom, who then passed it to "Smiling Phil" Donohue, Mr. Murphy's most trusted aide and close friend, the only one authorized to enter the big red room to see if Mr. Murphy really wanted to see the supplicant. If Murphy consented, the massive paneled door would swing open just enough to admit the man to the inner sanctuary without permitting others waiting their turn in the anteroom to look in. There the guest would find Murphy seated at a very large mahogany table supported by carved mahogany legs with tiger paws, in a thick red–carpeted room with mahogany wainscoting, red plush armchairs, a huge gilt framed mirror, and scarlet fabric wall coverings. The room became known in the press as the "Scarlet Room of Mystery." Eventually, anyone who really counted in New York commerce or politics had been there.

The main impression that Murphy left with people who knew him best was that he was a man of his word, honest, frank, mild-mannered, considerate, intensely loyal, and extremely charitable to worthy causes. He was a man of impeccable personal character according to those who knew him best. People believed that once Murphy made up his mind, he was candid about telling you "exactly what he could do and what he would do for you if he could" according to the late James Farley, President Franklin D. Roosevelt's National Democratic chairman and postmaster general, who was once turned down early in his career when he sought Murphy's support for a Democratic nomination to the state senate for Rockland County.

Within two months of assuming the leadership in 1902, Murphy began to demonstrate his skills as a major political leader where they counted—at the ballot box. His first election campaign as the leader of Tammany Hall was the gubernatorial election of 1902. Murphy endorsed state comptroller Bird S. Coler to be the candidate of the Democratic Party. While Coler lost the statewide election to Republican Benjamin Odell, the press was tremendously impressed with Coler's plurality of 120,000 votes in New York City because Coler carried New York County by the greatest Democratic majority in history, thereby establishing Murphy's initial political credentials on the big stage.

In 1903 Murphy would have the opportunity to beat an incumbent mayor of New York City, Fusion Republican and avowed reformer, Mayor Seth Low, a former president of Columbia University, once mayor of the city of Brooklyn before he was elected mayor of New York. Low enjoyed an excellent reputation among the forces of municipal

reform. Unfortunately for Low, his high standards and principles conflicted with the needs of the city's business leaders who could not do
business with him. Murphy's candidate to win back City Hall for the
Democrats was George McClellan, a Princeton graduate, distinguished
and popular congressman, longtime member of Tammany, and son of
the Civil War general.

As his first move in the 1903 campaign, Murphy cleverly offered the
Democratic endorsement to two of Mayor Low's Fusion running mates,
city comptroller Edward M. Grout and president of the Board of Aldermen, Charles F. Fornes, both of whom were respected Republicans.
Both accepted the endorsement and were then promptly punished by
being dropped from Seth Low's Fusion ticket. By stealing two of the
reformer's candidates and adding McClellan's established respectability
to the Democratic ticket, Murphy's ticket won the election.

Expecting that he earned the opportunity to designate all of the
important appointees of the new administration, Murphy was soon disappointed when McClellan decided to select his own people for the
most significant positions. The mayor picked his own corporation counsel, secretary, tax board president, and commissioners of police, sanitation, and health, while leaving most of the others to Murphy. Mayor
McClellan said: "For other offices, I accepted the candidates of the
organization, Murphy's candidates, while almost all district leaders
seemed to be a very decent lot." Afterward the mayor discovered that
his chief assistants were suffering from "powerful mediocrity" and that
they were looking to Murphy instead of the mayor for their orders and
guidance.

McClellan created an ambitious program of public works and
expanded the development of the subway system, which opened in
1904 with the mayor himself driving the first train seven miles north at
forty-five miles per hour. The fare was 5¢.

Tammany supported Mayor McClellan's reelection in 1905, and
this time the campaign was for the four-year term that the state legislature had enacted for New York City's mayor. McClellan found himself
in a tough three-way race with publisher and former congressman
William Randolph Hearst as his major opponent. Hearst enjoyed the
support of the municipal reformers who used Tammany as their whip-
ping boy, claiming that corruption was rampant, but they were unable
to make their case with specifics. McClellan countered with a commitment to an independent administration, a promise that the Tammany

leadership did not take seriously, considering it to be just good campaign rhetoric.

Hearst's campaign was also based on a commitment to municipal ownership. He attacked McClellan for his support of private ownership of the city's new subway system, and he attacked Murphy for his investment in New York Contracting, showing cartoons of Murphy in prison stripes in the powerful Hearst newspapers, *The Morning Journal* and *The American.*

McClellan's first administration had not been blighted by the corruption and large-scale vice that the Republicans and Hearst had warned of. Murphy, for his part, was doing what he could to eliminate gambling and prostitution graft as a source of income for Tammany Hall.

With Murphy's support, McClellan won the newly adjusted four-year term by only 3,572 votes in a very close race in which Hearst got 224,925 to McClellan's 228,397, with Republican William Ivies getting only 137,193. Newspapers went to court to demand a recount, which did not change the results. In fact, McClellan's first term as mayor was free of any flagrant examples of Tammany corruption, graft, or large-scale vice.

McClellan gradually made good on his promise of independence and by the end of the first year of his second term, broke with Murphy. He replaced many of the Tammany appointees of his first administration. He refused to give Tammany any jobs on the new $100 million expansion of the city's Catskill Mountain water supply system, jobs which would have been helpful to Murphy's effort to control some of the votes of upstate Democrats in the legislature. McClellan also acted against the Bronx and Manhattan borough presidents who were Murphy allies, by having his commissioner of accounts, John Purroy Mitchel (who would later become mayor) investigate massive waste and fraud in their offices, leading to their removal by Republican governor Charles Evans Hughes. A third Murphy ally, borough president Joseph Bowel of Queens County, was embarrassed into resigning before he could be removed by the governor. A final and more permanent blow to Tammany was the fact that McClellan was turning more and more city jobs over to Civil Service and getting them out of the reach of the Tammany Tiger. It is not surprising that Murphy and his Tammany confidants considered McClellan to be an ingrate who would never have been elected in the first place without Murphy's support. But New Yorkers considered McClellan to have been an excellent mayor.

While McClellan certainly thought his anti-Tammany moves were the best politics for him in the prevailing climate that the progressive politics of the era required, and that the content of Hearst's campaign had reinforced, McClellan, who had ambitions of his own beyond the mayoralty, was also motivated by Murphy's most recent post-election maneuvering. Murphy decided to appease Hearst's ambition, and hopefully to get him off his back by supporting Hearst for governor.

By securing the gubernatorial nomination of the Democratic Party for Hearst, Murphy demonstrated that he had a significant say in the party statewide, he got some relief from the attention on himself in the Hearst papers and most significantly, by espousing Hearst's views on municipal ownership he took a giant first step toward having Tammany back social reform programs that earned respect for Tammany Hall to an extent it had rarely achieved up until that time.

Hearst eventually lost the 1906 gubernatorial election to Governor Hughes, who had been a superb governor and one of the leaders of the progressive movement in American politics that was capturing the imagination of lots of people across the nation.

McClellan then tried somewhat impulsively to get the Tammany Hall executive committee to oust Mr. Murphy. Murphy resisted and succeeded by finding a loophole in the Tammany bylaws, which allowed him to add some of his friends to the Executive Committee and defeat Mayor McClellan's effort.

Murphy had learned some lessons. By the time of the 1909 election he sought a candidate with a reputation for integrity and a posture of independence from the Democratic machine. Murphy thought that supporting such a candidate would enhance Tammany's image.

Since the 1897 incorporation of Brooklyn, Queens, and Richmond into Greater New York City, the leadership of Tammany had attempted from time to time to extend its power across the East River. In 1909, Murphy succeeded by promoting a very independent Brooklyn supreme court justice, William J. Gaynor, to run for mayor, and the Democratic leadership of Brooklyn and Queens accepted the idea. Gaynor was not the kind of person the public would ever have expected to have Tammany Hall support. Gaynor had a well-deserved reputation for independence and integrity, which is precisely why he was attractive to Murphy who needed that sort of man to oppose the elements of municipal reform that always assumed the worst about Tammany. As a supreme court judge, Gaynor, although known to be cantankerous, had demon-

strated that he would oppose political corruption, defend individual liberties, and support municipal ownership of the new subways. Gaynor was
enough of a pragmatist to appreciate that the support of Tammany Hall,
along with the other elements of support that he already enjoyed, could
make the difference in winning or losing, and Gaynor really wanted to
win. Murphy felt the same way, which made this alliance of strange bed-
fellows as successful as they had hoped it would be.

Once again, William Randolph Hearst ran a third-party candidacy
based on advocacy of municipal ownership. Gaynor won the election
with 42 percent of the citywide vote, against the 28.8 percent won by
the Republican Fusion candidate, with Hearst coming in third with 25.9
percent. Ironically, Gaynor wound up as the only Tammany candidate
on the city ticket to win. The anti-Tammany Fusion candidates for
comptroller and president of the board of aldermen were successful, as
were four of the five borough presidents. The fifth in Queens was a
Democrat who was anti-Tammany. Perhaps most important for the
future of the Democratic Party, Fusion candidate Charles S. Whitman
was elected district attorney in New York County and, by distinguishing
himself in that very visible office, he would go on to become governor
of New York in the future.

Gaynor turned out to be a formidable mayor, dedicating himself
and the people he appointed to economical government, honesty,
reform, and respectability. While Tammany got some public credit for
selecting such an upstanding man to run the city, the fact is that
Gaynor got rid of a lot of Tammany hacks who had nonproductive city
jobs, and did not appoint Tammany people to any key jobs, because the
mayor was dedicated to appointments based on merit and professional
qualifications, not on political contacts.

Although he had said some very kind and complimentary things
about Murphy after he was elected, publicly recognizing Murphy's
understanding of the importance of electing people with principles
and ideas, Gaynor had little patronage to provide for Murphy or his
men. When the press asked the newly elected Mayor Gaynor what he
was prepared to give Murphy, he replied, "Suppose that we give him a
few kind words."

Murphy was stymied for the time being during the first year of the
Gaynor administration of New York City, so he turned his sights on
Albany and the successful effort in 1910 to elect a Democrat as governor
of New York and a Democratic Party majority in the state legislature.

By the time Sulzer was elected governor of New York in November of 1912, Charles Francis Murphy had already been the established leader of Tammany Hall for a decade. The machine had weathered scandal and stormy seas, but still it prospered under his determination, wisdom, and forceful guidance in selecting some reputable candidates. Only two years before, on election night in November of 1910, Murphy's Democratic Party took virtual control of New York State. His candidate for governor, John A. Dix, was elected. As the Democrats took control over both houses of the state legislature, Murphy was able to designate his two most outstanding young men to the legislative leadership; thirty-seven-year-old Alfred E. Smith as the assembly majority leader, an Irish-American from the Lower East Side district that was adjacent to the one Sulzer had represented, and thirty-three-year-old Robert F. Wagner, a German-born Catholic state senator from the Upper East Side Yorkville neighborhood as the senate majority leader. Both of them were among the best and brightest of young and loyal Tammany stalwarts, both would eventually go on to much greater distinction.

In 1910 control of the state legislature gave the Democrats the power to name the state's United States senator. In those days senators were not directly elected. (A change in the U.S. Constitution to provide for direct election was finally enacted in 1913.) The Democratic Party caucus would make the recommendation and the legislature would elect the designee of the caucus, but the Democrats immediately got into a squabble. Murphy and the men of the legislative delegation that he controlled supported a Buffalo ally of Tammany, "Blue-Eyed Billy" Sheehan, a lawyer-lobbyist for the private streetcar interests who himself had once been Speaker of the assembly. Murphy thought that Blue Eyed Billy's Buffalo roots would make him acceptable to the upstate Democrats, most of whom were insurgents who were not part of Tammany, but upstaters, led by an attractive Hyde Park patrician named Franklin Delano Roosevelt who had just been elected to the state senate from Dutchess County on an anti-Tammany platform, strongly resisted. Roosevelt and his allies did not want to see a Murphy man in that position. To the upstaters, Tammany was an anathema. In one campaign speech, Roosevelt said, "I am pledged to no man, to no special interest, to no boss." To Roosevelt the deadlock over the nomination was not only a contest against Tammany and all it stood for, but a question of upstate versus downstate control, and the issue brought Roosevelt nationwide attention. The impasse went on for ten weeks and sixty-four ballots. Sheehan withdrew and a series of compromise candidates were rejected. Eventually a candidate acceptable to the upstate faction and the Tammany faction was nominated. His name was James O'Gorman, a reluctant and distinguished state supreme court judge from New York City. The upstaters were beginning to tire from the long fight and decided that they did not care about the fact that Judge O'Gorman was once the grand sachem of the Society of Tammany, the social arm of Tammany Hall, or that Murphy considered him to be a good friend. Having such a loyal alternative, Murphy was able to let the upstaters satisfy themselves that they had proven their point by blocking Murphy's choice of Sheehan. Murphy consoled himself with the knowledge that he would also be able to designate another loyal Tammany man to fill O'Gorman's seat on the bench.

By the time of the Democratic State Convention in Syracuse in 1912, it became evident that the party could not nominate Governor John Dix for reelection. There had been so many scandals or accusations of corruption during the Dix administration and the governor's close relationship with Murphy was a well-known ingredient of the governor's downfall. The only memorable thing Governor Dix ever did during his two-year term was to appear in public in an especially fancy uniform he designed for himself as the head of the state's National Guard, which he reluctantly gave up after the press ridiculed him. Democrats, led by the upstate faction including state senator Franklin D. Roosevelt's upstate organization called the "Empire State Democracy" to rival Tammany, turned to the popular congressman William Sulzer. Murphy eventually gave his silent nod of approval to Sulzer's nomination, a nod that he would live to regret as the biggest mistake of his life. Murphy's organization worked hard to elect Sulzer in 1912 and maintain a Democratic majority in the legislature as well.

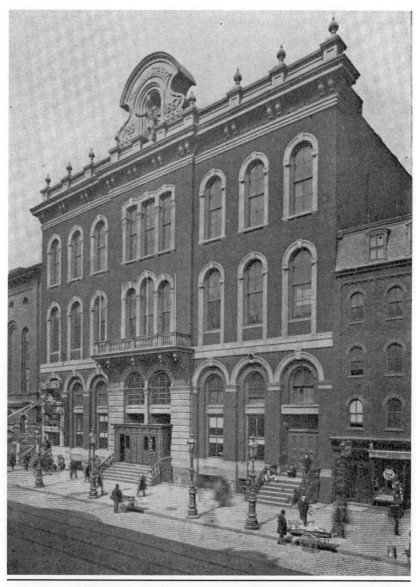

Tammany Hall, 14th Street, NYC, from Alfred Henry Lewis, *Richard Croker* (New York: Life Publishing Co., 1901).

14

The Secret of Tammany's Power
(And what was done with it)

When I began to tell the story of the elected governor of New York's clash with the leader of Tammany Hall, it became apparent in conversations with sophisticated people who were keenly interested in politics that few had a real understanding of what Tammany Hall was all about in 1913. Understanding Tammany is essential to understanding the high stakes that were the essence of the struggle between Mr. Murphy and Governor Sulzer.

Politics was a full-time business for the men who ran the Tammany organization. By building an efficient organization, managing it well, and making the right political decisions, the leaders of Tammany were able to derive their power from the people whose votes could be delivered to the candidates they blessed. The leaders used their power for their own benefit, sharing their spoils among themselves, and maintaining their position by giving something back to the voters who supported them in the form of jobs or valuable services and some very outstanding candidates.

Before the advent of television and open primaries, similar political machines existed in most major American cities, but nowhere was it more significant, as efficient, or as lucrative as it was in the rapidly growing city of New York at the turn of the century. Tammany relied on the votes of the immigrants and poor people who were struggling to survive in lower New York, while the city itself was expanding to the north. The success of the system at the turn of the century was a product of the times, the influx of immigrants, and the need to extend the residential areas of the city to accommodate them, combined with the political judgment and management skills that effective leaders like Croker and Murphy brought to the leadership.

From time to time Tammany decided who would be elected to almost every public office in the city, from mayor to sheriff, aldermen, congressmen, and state legislators. Based on loyalty, hard work, and financial contributions, the Tammany organization also decided which of its supporters got which jobs in the city government, who became a judge or a police captain, who might get a break from a friendly police-man or judge, who got to broker the business interests that were dependent on city regulations, contracts, and franchises, and whose business might either benefit from or be hurt by city or state action. Occasionally Tammany's franchised territory extended to state govern-ment, or at least the opportunity to negotiate a form of partnership with upstate Democrats or Republican Party leaders on matters of mutual interest. By controlling the nominations and elections of a suffi-cient number of state legislators whose votes could be delivered to a larger coalition, Tammany could influence the enactment of state legis-lation that favored its constituents or supplicants, or hurt its enemies, and it could also influence a legislator's committee assignments and leadership positions.

When Croker became the chief of Tammany in 1886, and Murphy was one of the district leaders, New York City still consisted of only Man-hattan and the Bronx. In Manhattan there were 180,000 voters. Croker could count on 110,000 of these people who were absolutely controlled by Tammany Hall, most of them poor immigrants who would cast their ballots for whichever candidate the Tammany leaders selected. They really were not interested in the issues.

Tammany Hall was at that time the most perfect political organiza-tion that ever existed, and, usually the most successful in achieving its goals. It was an organization where everyone knew his job. Each of the thirty-five New York County assembly districts elected several hundred members of the party's general committee in the primary. These gen-eral committee members, also known as "captains," elected one of their own as district leader and, by virtue of his office; he became a member of the Executive Committee of Tammany Hall. The district leader over-sees a few hundred captains who are responsible for maintaining direct contact with the voters. The captain is responsible for knowing the needs of each family in the district. There were just over a thousand captains in New York County, and about half of them were rewarded for their constant service with the voters with some kind of job with the city government. The operating organization was simple and well disciplined. Should the Boss's order require it, Tammany district captains could reach their people within a few hours, without the aid of radio or television, newspapers or other publicity. If they failed to reach them personally, they left them a note. The vote of loyal Tammany stalwarts, like the mail, could be delivered in rain, snow, sleet, or hail, without regard to how strongly public feelings had been aroused against the organization by various movements of political reformers.

When any problems arose among his constituents, the captain was expected to help the district leader solve it. In case of fire, the captain would find a place for the family to stay. If there were a problem paying the rent, the district leader could usually solve it, even if he had to pay it out of his own pocket. If a constituent were arrested, the family called the captain who arranged bail, and then sought out the complainant and tried to smooth things over. Frequently he was able to arrange for leniency with a Tammany-friendly policeman or judge. When necessary, the captain even arranged for passes for the family to visit their relatives at Blackwell's Island, the city jail, and he could usually arrange to have the district leader pay the family's rent while the breadwinner was incarcerated. If a lawyer were needed, one of the organization's lawyers would help because many young lawyers were hanging around the clubhouse looking for ways to ingratiate themselves with the district leader. Obviously such kindness at the time of need develops lasting loyalty.

Public works provided public employment for thousands of Tammany constituents. When someone in the family needed a job, the district leader could usually arrange something, either in city government or in one of the many businesses dependent on Tammany Hall's good will. If a city contractor were reluctant to help out, he was likely to find all kinds of stumbling blocks in his way when he sought a new contract or a change in the one he had.

Poor immigrant families, even those with jobs, always appreciated the extra food or the turkey provided by the district leader for the holiday. The district leader was expected to show up at wakes, funerals, weddings, bar mitzvahs, and first communions. He also provided recreation for his people. He gave big balls and small dances, summer night festivals, parties, parades, athletic contests, picnics, outings, and excursions—social events that had not yet been replaced by radio, movies, television, or the internet.

All he asked in return was the family's vote once a year and occasional attendance at a meeting when Tammany needed to produce a crowd.

Without fear of embarrassment, Charles F. Murphy participated in the "honest graft" system, at least at the beginning of his term as Tammany chieftain. Actually, there were no laws then prohibiting most of the schemes involving profits earned from inside knowledge of municipal plans. He received benefits as a dock commissioner, but we do not know for certain what he owned and profited from after his first few years as the chief of Tammany Hall. Unlike Croker who spoke rather openly to investigating committees, "Silent Charles" never admitted anything. He even denied any ongoing participation in New York Contracting and Trucking Company operations when the light of an effective legislative investigation was focused on it by the Lexow Committee in 1895. Regardless of the extent of Mr. Murphy's participation in anything after he took control of the Wigwam, there can be no doubt based in the ensuing investigations, that, at the very least, Murphy created tremendous opportunities for his friends and allies.

Clearly, Murphy's demand that his close friend and "ex" business partner, Jim Gaffney, be appointed to head the state highway program at a time when the automobile was coming into its own, and the state was busy building new highways, was not motivated by Gaffney's need for a good job, or Murphy's confidence that New York's roads would be better built due to his friend's experience in building railroad facilities. No, Gaffney was a very close associate of the Boss, and a wheeler-dealer who would benefit extensively from the ability to designate a lot of contractors and vendors of supplies.

This in essence is the other half of the secret of Tammany Hall. By maintaining a smooth-running political organization that could be counted on to deliver votes for its chosen candidates on Election Day, the Hall acquired considerable influence with elected officials who made important decisions. The significance of picking respectable candidates who can win allowed Tammany to control at least some aspects of the city, especially those that are most important to the contractors, industrialists, developers, and businessmen who have something to sell to the city or who merely need municipal approval for some aspect of their commercial objectives.

More than any previous leader, Murphy learned the importance of finding attractive horses to ride in election campaigns. By producing such an exemplary leader and government official as Al Smith, for example, Murphy saw how important it was to the success of his machine and to his own power that the Democratic Party must stand for the kind of progressive social legislation that Al Smith promulgated because it was the governor's popular programs and his platform that attracted voters.

Even today, a century later, while we are witnessing the great effort to eliminate millions of dollars of soft money from American politics, nobody can say with certainty exactly how much money went from businessmen to politicians, but several public investigations documented evidence of a lot of it. It was the sheer enormity of the deals and the vast amounts of money that we know business leaders parted with and politicians collected that is so shocking to us today. Equally appalling to those who live in the new millennium is the fact that the public that lived in Murphy's days, and even more so in Croker's, was relatively tolerant of these thieves who were raising the cost of their government by allowing competence to yield to corruption, rather than protecting the interests of honest businessmen who could not compete with that corruption. It was the public that eventually paid the price of the government overpaying for everything it needed to serve the people.

The amounts of money that various investigations by city, state, and federal officials, and some newspapers, exposed in turn-of-the-century dollars—amounts that in today's terms would be worth at least twenty times as much—are enormous. The opportunities for corruption at the turn of the century were enhanced by the fact that New York City was growing enormously and quickly. The great population explosion created by the influx of millions of immigrants meant that the city had to add services and facilities to absorb them. The population grew northward. Housing had to be constructed. Transportation facilities had to be extended and the availability of new sources of immigrant labor meant that all kinds of businesses could be started or further developed. Every one of these and other examples of municipal expansion created economic opportunities for lots of people and Tammany was nearly always on hand to cash in. Occasionally the upstate Republican machine got a share.

When Robert Van Wyck was elected as the first mayor of the newly expanded city of three and a half million people in 1897, the city's budget was approximately $90 million, and the army of city employees had reached sixty thousand. Today, just over one hundred years later, the city claims over eight million residents, and a similar number of suburban dwellers whose lives are centered in the city, an annual budget of over $30 billion and an army of 350,000 employees, 90 percent of whom are civil service union members.

The Tammany organization financed its own operations by assessing municipal jobholders a percentage of their salaries, reportedly at least 5 percent, and by assessing candidates for elective and political offices a flat sum ranging up to $25,000, depending upon the job, and by accepting political contributions from businesses it could do favors for, a practice that survives to this day when political contributors get "access" to municipal, state, and federal officials whose campaigns they continue to contribute to.

Some examples of the tips of icebergs of corruption that have emerged to quantify the extent of "honest graft" at the beginning of the nineteenth century allow us to appreciate the extent of the problem.

A report of a State Legislative Insurance Committee in 1906 revealed that the major insurance companies disguised their contributions to both Republican and Democratic parties to buy influence in the state legislature in 1904 alone, as legal expenses. In just one year, the Mutual Life Insurance Company disbursed $364,254.95, the Equitable Life Assurance Society, $172,698.42, and the New York Life Insurance Company, $204,019.25. Multiply these numbers by twenty to measure them in today's dollar values. Charles Evans Hughes was the counsel to this legislative committee whose revelations led to his election as governor of New York in 1906.[1]

In 1914, the U.S. Interstate Commerce Commission held hearings in Washington that revealed that the directors of the New York, New Haven and Hartford Railroad had set aside a fund of $1.2 million to be distributed among "people of influence" in the politics of New York City to procure needed changes in the charter of the New York, Westchester and Boston Railroad Company that eventually went bankrupt. The railroad's stakes were very high.[2]

According to Myers's *History of Tammany Hall,* by 1905 it was estimated that Murphy's company, New York Contracting and Trucking Company, or its offshoots, had received contracts totaling $15 million from various corporations and interests dependent upon New York City favors.[3] Myers also reported that the Metropolitan Street Railroad Company had laid out a total of $90 million to "enrich the insiders." Among the leading purchasers of influence at the turn of the century were the various transportation interests engaged in building their subways, streetcar lines, and elevated railroads to provide the transportation necessary to allow New Yorkers to move northward to upper Manhattan and the Bronx, and to the Brooklyn and Queens suburbs.

While all these things were going on in New York City, money was also changing hands in Albany when Tammany frequently allied itself with its Republican counterparts from upstate New York in order to pass or defeat legislation, which impacted on the interests of the business community. Many, but not all, of the legislator's votes were for sale. Legislation helpful to particular business interests could be enacted and "ripper bills," introduced to hurt particular business interests, who were expected to pay to have them withdrawn, were rampant.

15

War Clouds on the Horizon

Sulzer embarked on an ambitious legislative program at a time when the population of the state was growing rapidly. The social needs and infrastructure requirements generated by the tremendous influx of new immigrants and the expanding industrial society were enormous. The Triangle Shirtwaist Fire and the work of the state's Factory Investigation Commission had made an enormous impression and highlighted the need for labor and industrial reforms. The new Democratic-controlled legislature began the year by considering the progressive proposals of the new Democratic governor—which were outlined in Governor Sulzer's Annual Message, the document delivered to them on Inauguration Day. Most of these initial proposals emanated from the platform that the Democrats had endorsed at their Syracuse convention reflecting long-standing party positions that were reiterated during the statewide campaign that elected Sulzer to a two-year term and his Democratic running mates for state senate and assembly for two- and one-year terms. The details of the governor's initial program provide a significant picture of the important issues of 1913. Sulzer began his message by pointing out that in 1913, New York had more than a twelfth part of all the wealth of the nation and one-tenth of its population. The next one hundred years were destined to alter the Empire State's relative standing in America.

Legislation was required in a number of key areas and the governor set his priorities. The governor's first request was to ask the legislature to have New York ratify the Seventeenth Amendment to the U.S.

Constitution providing for the direct election of U.S. senators instead of the then-existing constitutional requirement that they be appointed by their state legislatures. The legislature responded promptly and, after ratification by two-thirds of the states, on May 31, 1913, the U.S. Constitution was so amended.

By asking the legislature to submit to the voters of New York "as soon as possible" the constitutional amendment to give women the right to vote, the governor fulfilled another important pledge he made during the campaign

This first annual message was the governor's opportunity to lay out his personal priorities in general without specific action he was asking for. Sulzer clearly addressed the issues that were his greatest concern— starting with conservation of the state's natural resources, recapturing from private commercial interests the state's authority to develop the St. Lawrence Seaway as a source of electric power.

Sulzer's next priority was to ask the legislature to amend the election laws wherever necessary to improve their effectiveness and facilitate independent nominations. Without more specificity, the governor asked the legislature to "simplify the procedure and make complete and more effective the direct primary system of the state." This particular request would very soon prove critical to the governor's future.

Among the most important social issues of the day, members of the legislature were already deeply affected by the public shock and reaction to the young lives lost in the 1911 Triangle Shirtwaist Fire. Sulzer spoke in eloquent terms to a most receptive legislature. He asked the legislature to address the need for safety standards to protect life and health, and prevention of occupational diseases. "I hold it to be self-evident that no industry has the right to sacrifice human life for its profit. . . ." He sought legislation to provide for statewide compulsory education and restrictions on child labor, saying that "no industry that depends on child labor for its success has a right to exist."

Sulzer called for enactment of workers' compensation or insurance laws, which were especially necessary to protect women and children, and addressed the need to fix living wages and industrial standards; enactment of a workers' compensation law was needed to replace the one that had been passed under Governor Hughes's leadership and then declared unconstitutional by the state's highest court.

Sulzer, whose own federal legislation as a congressman actually led to the creation of the U.S. Department of Labor in 1913, urged a reorganization of the state's department of labor to enhance the range of its authority.

The governor pointed out that the rapid growth of the use of automobiles generated considerable attention to statewide expansion of good roads, generating a need to reorganize the state department of highways to improve the efficiency and economy of road building and maintenance, thus laying the groundwork for soon-to-be-revealed scandalous contracts that existed under previous administrations.

Like so many new governors before and since, Sulzer pledged his administration would keep expenditures down to a minimum to avoid tax increases and to stop extravagance and waste.

At the end of his message came the governor's proposal that would turn out to be the one that justifiably grabbed the headlines of the day—and would very soon have a monumental impact on his administration. It was a broad new idea and not anticipated as were most of the others. The governor told the legislature that a Committee of Inquiry had been suggested to him to inquire into every department of state government, to "ascertain where expenditures can be checked and the money of the taxpayers saved," and empowered to recommend administrative reorganization and consolidation of state bureaus and commissions.[1] Five days later, Sulzer appointed his own Committee of Inquiry and empowered them with a power of subpoena authorizing them to take testimony under oath.

At the outset there was every reason to believe that the newly organized legislature, dominated by a Democratic majority elected with Sulzer, and led by two genuinely talented young men, Wagner and Smith, would see the state's major problems from the same perspective as the governor did. Optimism prevailed among those who favored the legislation that Sulzer sought. The legislature supported most of the governor's requests. Senate majority leader Robert Wagner had been the leader of the investigative committee created in reaction to the 1911 Triangle Shirtwaist Factory tragedy, which shocked the city and the nation because 146 lives were lost in a factory fire when no safety rules existed. Along with assembly Speaker Al Smith, Wagner had spent a great deal of time seriously studying the conditions of industrial facilities across the state, holding hearings, and getting a firsthand perspective of the extent to the dangerous conditions and practices that threatened the health and safety of workers in cities around the state. The valuable lessons they learned made it both realistic and politically correct for them to address the variety of related needs that the governor called attention to, and which by 1913 had become familiar issues to their constituents.

Obviously, a great deal of preparatory work had been invested in the governor's message prior to his inauguration. He knew what action was needed and he incorporated a great deal of it in his first opportunity to let the legislature and the people have a very carefully developed picture of what he proposed to accomplish.

Most of the governor's progressive proposals to address the key issues of the day, supported by Speaker Al Smith and senate majority leader Robert Wagner, were promptly adopted by the Democratic majority in both houses with frequent Progressive Party and occasional Republican support. These included bills that enhanced the civil service system and responded to the need to improve factory safety drafted by the Triangle Shirtwaist Fire Investigating Commission headed by Senator Wagner. Legislation was adopted to strengthen minimum wage and workers' compensation laws, exclude child labor, regulate working conditions for women, and reorganization of the New York State Labor Department to make it far more effective on matters of industrial safety.

By the end of the third day of the Sulzer administration, neither Silent Charles Murphy nor anyone else had responded to the governor's challenge to Murphy's leadership. During his daily Executive Chamber press conference, Sulzer was asked if he had heard from any of the Democratic Party leaders about his assertions of party leadership. "No," the governor said quietly, "I don't know what they think of my assertion, but if their thoughts on the subject run contrary to mine, this is the place where they should come and make their kick."[2]

Actually, the public reaction to Sulzer's challenge was impressive. The governor's office had been flooded with messages of good will, praising his position and encouraging him to stand firm. Sulzer had good reason to be pleased with himself.[3] Among the messages of support from outside of New York, was a telegram from president-elect Woodrow Wilson, still unhappy with Tammany's lack of enthusiasm for him at the 1912 nominating convention. Woodrow Wilson had turned against the New Jersey Democratic organization that had plucked him from the presidency of Princeton and elected him governor of his state, where he created an impressive record of independence and leadership that propelled him to the presidency. His telegram stated that he agreed with Sulzer's proclamation that as governor he was the leader of the Democratic Party in New York State. Newspapers reported that there were numerous congratulatory messages to the governor from around the country and abroad, some even encouraging him to seek the presidency of the United States.[4]

Anti-Tammany upstate Democrats had expressed their enthusiasm to Lieutenant Governor Martin Glynn, who had opened the state senate's proceedings by rejecting Tammany's efforts to dictate his senate committee assignments, a power that was then enjoyed by the lieutenant governor, although his predecessor usually made these designations only after receiving instructions from the party.

Among his visitors that third day in office, the governor openly entertained Democratic Party leaders from two factions in Buffalo, one pro-Tammany who had been allied with Murphy and the other, the head of Erie County's anti-Tammany faction.

The governor told the press about his agenda for implementing the previously announced graft hunt. He let it be known that his own executive department would be "the place to begin" and if the commissioners asked, he would testify himself in order to set a good example. Sulzer announced that the next target of the inquiry would be the adjutant general's department where irregularities during the Dix administration had been brought to the governor's attention. On his first day as governor, Sulzer had replaced the general whom Governor Dix appointed to head New York's National Guard.

Because charges were already circulating about corruption in building and maintaining state roads, Sulzer also revealed that the state highway department would be the next target for investigation. The governor told the newspapermen that public officials enriching themselves at the expense of the state through the process for handing out contracts were participating in a form of graft that he was particularly determined to eliminate. "We want to get at the truth. At the same time we must proceed according to law and protect the rights of all concerned," the governor told the reporters gathered for his afternoon conference. "If any official hasn't done his duty, I will get after him."[5]

On January 13th Governor Sulzer made a major legislative proposal—he asked the legislature to repeal the charter of the Long Sault Development Company enacted during the gubernatorial administration of Republican governor Charles Evans Hughes. (In 1907, under tremendous pressure from lobbyists, a law was enacted giving the Long Sault Development Company the right to develop the water power of the state at what later became the site of the St. Lawrence Seaway power development.) Sulzer claimed that the state's water resources could never be legally turned over to private developers, citing an opinion of the attorney general, and demanded that the private corporate developer return its charter rights to the people of New York State.[6]

Contrary to what happened when John Dix was elected governor and Murphy attended his inauguration, staying in an Albany hotel for a couple of weeks, talking patronage and appointments, Murphy deliberately avoided Sulzer's inauguration and did not appear until January 12 when he came to Albany for the first time that year to attend the required meeting at the state Capitol of the electors to elect Woodrow Wilson president of the United States. When it came his turn at the receiving line at the governor's Executive Chamber reception for the electors, Mr. Murphy said, "I wish you a happy New Year, governor." The governor replied, "I thank you, Mr. Murphy."[7]

That is all that was said between Murphy and Sulzer. Afterward, the electors were invited to lunch with the governor at the Executive Mansion (The People's House). Accounts of that luncheon did not indicate that Murphy and the governor had any further discussion.

On January 6th, he filled the vacancy on his new Commission of Inquiry with H. Gordon Lynn, a highly credentialed accountant and investigator who was working in the office of New York City's commissioner of accounts, the organization charged with auditing city agencies and rooting out corruption. Lynn was also a loyal Tammany Hall man.[8]

The investigation team went right to work. On Sunday night, the governor called his three commissioners to a meeting at the Executive Mansion—where he turned over a slew of significant documents and correspondence he had already accumulated to provide leads for various investigative avenues. During that meeting he informed his commissioners that he had considerable resources to put at their disposal—a lawyer from the attorney general's staff, support from the state comptroller, the New York City commissioner of accounts, and the city's bureau of municipal research. In addition, the governor had arranged for the introduction of a bill to appropriate the first $50,000 toward the commission's expenses. They were off to a good start.

Sulzer's initial public relations were effective. By the beginning of the third week of his administration, Sulzer had succeeded in positioning himself almost precisely where he wanted to be. The governor was genuinely delighted to read the *New York Times Sunday Magazine* section on January 19—a cover story of two full pages of in-depth analysis of the new governor, his goals, and his potential place in history. Some of the words in that newspaper article would be prescient, as they set the scene for the new administration: "Not since Charles Evans Hughes sat down in the governor's chair six years ago has public attention been focused on Capitol Hill to the extent it is today. Mr. Hughes, as all men know, performed his difficult task with vim and vigor, with intelligence and independence. With William Sulzer, another rugged, picturesque, perhaps unique figure has forged to the center of the stage at the Capitol."

Sulzer had to love any analogy with Governor Hughes, who had earned national attention of a heroic nature by virtue of his Progressive programs during two terms as governor from 1907 to 1910. Hughes left the governor's office with the people's greatest respect as a progressive reformer who fought successfully against the powerful and corrupt Republican machine that dominated upstate New York politics, much the way Tammany dominated the city of New York. Hughes had to be one of Sulzer's heroes and role models—although his partisan instinct never permitted him to say so publicly or even privately. According to the *Times* magazine article, Hughes was an idealist with a practical bent and "the zeal of an iconoclast." The article said that Hughes responded when people were waiting for a "voice in the wilderness of politics to point to new and more perfect paths in public life." The *Times* credited Governor Hughes with providing a new set of ethics to govern the conduct of public officials on a moral basis and looked to William Sulzer to take hold where Charles Evans Hughes left off.

Sulzer took great satisfaction with the *Times* that day as it compared him with the last New York governor who made the nation sit up and take notice.

As the *Times* finished its long newspaper analysis—it picked up on the special role of the new legislative leadership and the involvement of Tammany Hall—recognizing publicly and quite accurately the revitalized position that Tammany had placed itself in as a result of the pressures placed on it by the people's reaction to the Triangle Shirtwaist Factory Fire. The article said that "Both Senate Leader Wagner and Speaker Smith are young men. They represent in a measure the new spirit that some have discovered in Tammany Hall, and declare that the organization has turned its back on the practice of the past."

Sulzer's challenge to Tammany's leadership had achieved one of its goals already if the *Times* commentary was reflecting what its readers understood. Readers were full of hope because they believed that "Mr. Sulzer would not be the important factor he is had he not unheeding and unafraid, flaunted in the face of Tammany a declaration of independence."

The real truth was that Sulzer's success would depend upon the legislature—and the legislature was controlled by Tammany. Mr. Murphy also read that prophetic *Times* magazine when he came home from Mass on Sunday morning. Whether the story caused him concern or he considered it to be just great public relations for the new governor could not be ascertained. For Sulzer, the article was a personal success. Clearly he had made his point. The *Times* magazine concluded:

> The ultimate attitude of Gov. Sulzer and of Tammany with regard to the important questions with which the Sulzer administration will be compelled to deal—as yet is a matter of conjecture largely. Only the next two years will tell.
>
> There is plenty of work for Gov. Sulzer to do. How he does it will depend if—like Mr. Hughes—he is to emerge from his administration, a National figure, or, like his Democratic predecessor, come out of it tagged and doomed to the deeper shadows of political oblivion.

Sulzer could not have wished for anything better than this important newspaper. On January 20, the day after the *Times* magazine article appeared, another issue to face the new governor came to the public's attention when John Purroy Mitchel, then the president of New York City's Board of Aldermen, rose at a Public Service Commission (PSC) hearing in New York City to challenge the terms of a major contractual arrangement pending between the city and two of the private companies that provided subway services. Mitchel was outraged at some of the proposed contractual terms that would bestow new advantages to the private companies and hurt the city in the future. The contracts required the PSC's approval and its then-chairman, William H. Willcox, who was known to favor the contracts with the private owners, was due to be replaced by a gubernatorial appointment when his term expired on February 1st. Those favoring the much-needed expansion of subway services covered by the contracts included financier J. P. Morgan and many prominent men on Wall Street. The *New York Times* and a number of elected officials wanted the contracts signed before Chairman Willcox left office. The public opposition of Mr. Mitchel, an independent Democrat who had been elected to his important public office as a result of his success as a special investigator of municipal corruption, was stunning in the ferocity of his public attacks and the extent of his detailed disclosures about the disadvantages to the city that the private operators had negotiated.

William Randolph Hearst, the publisher of two of New York City's major newspapers, a former congressman (1903–1907), unsuccessful candidate against Tammany Hall's choice for mayor in 1905, and then in 1906, when Murphy tried to ingratiate himself, unsuccessful Democratic candidate for governor with Tammany support, had always stood against private ownership of the subways and actually made this issue a cornerstone of his political platforms. Sulzer advocated municipal ownership of all public transportation in his first assembly campaign in 1889. Hearst, who had frequently fought against Tammany Hall and publicly derided Murphy, especially by regularly featuring him in prison stripes atop a tiger in newspaper cartoons in the Hearst papers, had a long and good relationship with Sulzer, who his newspapers supported in 1912. At about the same time as Mitchel was criticizing the PSC in New York City, Hearst was meeting with Sulzer in Albany and pressing him to replace Willcox with one of Hearst's allies from the Independence League, the political organization standing for municipal ownership that supported Hearst's campaigns for mayor and governor.[9]

Tremendous pressure was brought to bear on Governor Sulzer from both sides of the issue, which was one for which much merit could be asserted on either side. Great sums of money were at stake for the city and for the private subway operators. There was a desperate need to see that expansion of the subway system was not delayed. Among the allegedly important arguments presented to Sulzer—who had made much of his commitment to "home rule" as one of his basic political philosophies—was that by changing the chairman of the Public Service Commission at this time, it was alleged that he would be violating the principle of home rule because a new chairman would be likely to thwart the efforts of the representatives of New York City who were negotiating the complex arrangements with the private owners.

On January 29, just two days before Willcox's term was to expire, Sulzer met with former New York City mayor Seth Low who came to

Albany to persuade him to let Willcox hold over and finish the subway contracts. While Sulzer had never stated what he was going to do, despite all the pressure, the next morning's *New York Times* headline story claimed that Sulzer had changed his mind and now seemed to be favoring a contract with the private operators, and that he denied being influenced by Hearst. But, Sulzer remained publicly uncommitted. On January 30, the governor allowed himself to be interviewed on this subject:

> "Shall you send any appointment for the Public Service Commission to the Senate prior to February 1," the governor was asked.
>
> "I do not see how I can do it, and I cannot make any appointment on Feb 1 because the Senate will not then be in session," he replied.
>
> "In other words, you will have to send it in on Friday or Monday?"
>
> "Yes, but I shall not send it on Friday."
>
> "You have also said that you would not remove Mr. Willcox."
>
> "I did not say that."
>
> "Does this apply to all Public Service Commission vacancies on both commissions?"[10]
>
> "I should say so."
>
> "That is, you will send no nomination in prior to the convening of the Senate on February 3?"
>
> "Well, as I view the situation this morning, my judgment is that I cannot make an appointment until there is a vacancy." . . .
>
> "Have you been asked to make an appointment this week?"
>
> "I have been asked a great many things."
>
> "Has Mr. Hearst asked you to send in an appointment this week?"
>
> "I am asked to do a great many things, but I do what I think is right. And as I am responsible I am very careful in doing anything to be sure so far as my own conscience is concerned, that it is for the best interests of the State's general welfare."
>
> "Has Mr. Hearst asked you to make an appointment in advance of the expiration of Mr. Willcox's term?"

"I do not care to discuss the matter further. I think I have put my position clearly to all of you now, and I hope that you will put it clearly before the people of New York."

"You do not want to say that you will send in a nomination on Monday night?"

"No."

"Then that question is left entirely open?"

"Yes."[11]

At the time, the public was unaware of anyone who the governor was actually considering for the post. Long afterward, Sulzer told the whole story, but this may be the first time it has ever been published. According to Sulzer's account in his draft autobiography in the Cornell files:

I saw Murphy . . . at Judge McCall's house, in New York City, on the night of the second of February. I talked from Albany with Mr. McCall over the telephone about the Public Service Commissionership. We made an appointment to meet at his house that might.

I left Albany for New York that afternoon, and Judge McCall met me with his automobile at the 125th Street station.

He told me Mr. Murphy was at his house waiting for us. We talked going down to his house. He said he would accept the Public Service Commissionership if I would insist on it. But he wanted Mr. Murphy's consent, so there would be no difficulty about his confirmation.

When we reached Judge McCall's house I went upstairs and met Mr. Murphy in the front room. We talked over several matters. Judge McCall was present part of the time. Then we had dinner.

After dinner Mr. Murphy and I discussed matters at considerable length regarding appointments. Mr. Murphy urged me to appoint his friend, John Galvin, Public Service Commissioner, in place of Mr. Willcox, whose term had expired.

The subway question was very acute in New York, and great pressure had been brought to bear on me by prominent citizens to reappoint Mr. Willcox, or to let him remain in office until the subway contracts were disposed of.

I urged the appointment of Henry Morgenthau, or George Foster Peabody, or Col. John Temple Graves. Mr. Murphy would not hear of these men. He talked long and earnestly on behalf of Mr. Galvin.

Finally I suggested as a compromise Judge McCall. The Judge said he would accept, provided it was agreeable to Mr. Murphy.

We discussed the subway question, the proposed contracts, and various other matters. The hour was getting late and I finally said that unless Judge McCall was agreeable to Mr. Murphy I would send in the name of Henry Morgenthau to the Senate the following Monday night, and if he was not confirmed, of course, Mr. Willcox would hold over, and that that would be agreeable to a great many citizens in the city.

Mr. Murphy finally agreed to the appointment of Judge McCall, and it was understood that the Judge should send me his resignation by messenger the following Monday afternoon.

On February 3, Sulzer sent to the Senate the nomination of supreme court justice Edward E. McCall to succeed Willcox as chairman of the PSC. The press said that Governor Sulzer had personally persuaded McCall to step down from the Supreme Court bench to take the job. The justice was confirmed by the senate that night on a straight party vote. McCall announced that he would not approve the subway contracts. McCall was known to be friendly with Charles Murphy. Murphy was interviewed about the McCall appointment and he vigorously denied having anything to do with it. The reporters said Murphy was smiling. (Later in the year, McCall would wind up as the Tammany candidate for mayor.) The governor was pressed by reporters the next day as to whether Murphy had recommended McCall or had anything to do with his nomination. The governor responded by saying that "he had as much to do with it as the man in the moon."[12]

In his 1922, autobiography *All in a Lifetime*, Henry Morganthau said that Sulzer had asked him to come to his room at the Waldorf Astoria one day prior to his decision to support McCall. According to Morganthau's account, Sulzer told him that "the powers," meaning Tammany Hall, "are trying to force me to support a certain man for chairman of the PSC, and I was refusing to do it because I don't think it's a proper appointment. But, they are getting very angry about it, and I don't know what to do." "I told him there was only one thing he could do and that was to continue to refuse to support him." "But, complained Sulzer, it means my political death if I don't name him." Morganthau's story has a serious flaw in that the record is pretty clear that Sulzer came to New York City from Albany for the first time since his inauguration on February 8, five days after the McCall appointment.

The governor's action in nominating Judge McCall was a great disappointment to those who were counting on his promise of independence from Tammany Hall—including at least two of the major newspapers that had been encouraged by Sulzer's promise of independence. On February 4, the *New York World*, the Joseph Pulitzer paper that was among the governor's most steady supporters, said in an editorial that "at a time when he should have shown his strength and his leadership, he has surrendered to Fourteenth Street. . . . Governor Sulzer has shaken the fine promise of independence that he built up after his inauguration."

When the *New York Times* editorial analyzed the governor's allegedly independent choice of Judge McCall to replace public securities commissioner Willcox, and the senate's quick approval of the appointment, it concluded that "Mr. Sulzer's leadership has vanished with the first occasion he had to show it," and Mr. Murphy modestly declared himself "pleased."

Sulzer reassured his Progressive friends that he was still free of boss control. On February 8, in his first trip to New York City since his inauguration, the governor addressed a high-class audience at a Lotos Club dinner in his honor. It was the first public affair that he attended since taking office and he reiterated his vow "no influence would control me but the dictates of my conscience. . . . Have no fear, I will stick to that."[13] Public service commissioner McCall also addressed the audience that night.

Governor Sulzer then sought improvements in the civil service merit system by standardizing procedural examinations, by maintaining efficient records, and uniform classification of positions. As the second month of his administration began, the new governor's initial legislative proposals were still being well received and acted on favorably by the new Democratic legislature as most of his constructive proposals were already adopted party positions.

The incipient battle between Governor Sulzer and Tammany Hall would be fought on three fronts: legislation (will the Tammany-controlled senate and assembly adopt the governor's proposals), patronage (who controls the appointment of state officials), and investigations (the governor exposing scandals in government attributable to Tammany Hall).

16

The Patronage Battle

The first signs of war were revealed in disputes over political patronage between Governor Sulzer and Tammany chief Charles Murphy about the appointment of important public officials. The governor's bold pledge to make independent patronage decisions had been challenged by his appointment of Judge McCall to the important Public Service Commission post and raised serious doubts about his sincerity—but Sulzer conceded nothing and continued to maintain his independence, including his initial claim that Mr. Murphy was not consulted or otherwise involved in the selection of Judge McCall, a "fact" that Mr. Murphy confirmed.[1]

But this would not be the last time Sulzer would be able to demonstrate his independence. The very next day, after the unfavorable editorials appeared, a dispute was reported in the Senate Finance Committee that had reported favorably on the nomination of Devon P. Hodson, a Murphy man from Erie County, to the Public Service Commission's upstate region, while at the same time the senate committee withheld approval of the governor's nomination for state commissioner of health, a Rochester lawyer named Milton R. Gibbs who was allied with the anti-Murphy faction of the party in Monroe County.

On February 5th, the *Times* also reported that another nomination battle was brewing over the re-nomination of Colonel Joseph F. Scott as superintendent of prisons because Scott had refused Sulzer's request that he fire a Republican who was serving as warden of the state prison at Auburn, New York, to make a place for Charles F. Rottigan, a close aide to Thomas Mott Osborne, who was a prominent anti-Murphy

169

supporter of Sulzer from that part of the state. While this appointment had not yet reached the senate where approval was required—the governor's Committee on Inquiry had publicly announced it was to begin its review of the state's prisons on February 11th.

Speculators also reported that the reappointment of Gordon Reel, the state highway commissioner, an appointee of Governor Dix, was also in jeopardy because the governor's graft investigation commission had already found serious deficiencies in this department. Commissioner Reel carried Murphy's blessing.

Governors designate significant numbers of people to powerful positions. The commissioners who headed the departments and those who lead other state agencies, manage the state's business, and employ large numbers of state employees, some of whom are civil service and some political appointees. Their work affects the lives and taxes of many people. They administer big budgets for employees, offices, equipment contractors, and services. In most cases the experience in these important and frequently interesting executive positions will impact the officials' career because they gain a valuable long-term credential in whatever industry they are involved with. These people are frequently sought after by major corporations they regulate. Because of the influence a department head wields, his favor is often highly sought after by those who can benefit from it. In 1913, unethical state officials without scruples could line their own pockets generously. Governor Sulzer knew all this and sought to avoid filling his key positions with people whose primary goal was to save themselves instead of the people.

While Tammany was a New York City–based organization, a significant portion of its power over state government came from its alliances within the Democratic Party organizations in most of the upstate cities. The upstate democracy was divided between pro- and anti-Tammany factions in upstate New York. Dutchess County senator Franklin D. Roosevelt and Auburn, New York, leader Thomas Mott Osborne were leaders of the upstate independent democracy. When the pro-Tammany factions in Buffalo, Rochester, Syracuse, and Albany got together with the Tammany powers in New York City, Tammany was generally able to control the party's statewide decisions. Congressman Sulzer in his frequent previous quests for the gubernatorial nomination of his party had created alliances with some of the anti-Tammany upstate Democrats, an opportunity that he exploited effectively when organizing the statewide presidential campaigns for William Jennings Bryan, which gave him the opportunity to meet with active Democrats upstate who were interested in Bryan's candidacy, even though Tammany disliked him.

Accordingly, Sulzer appeared to be adopting a policy of only accepting Tammany Hall recommendations of loyal Tammany men for those state positions that would not put them in a position to plunder the public trust, while maintaining a different perspective for those men who the governor needed to rely on because he was confident of their integrity and their loyalty to him. The governor walked a fine line, and this conflicted with the views of some of those Sulzer supporters who really believed that the governor's public commitment to good government should mean that he should take no recommendations at all from Tammany and thereby let everyone know that Sulzer meant everything he said about being the real leader of the Democratic Party.

It is fair to assume that the governor took his middle position because he knew that Tammany controlled both houses of the legislature, which he needed to enact the progressive legislation he was advocating. By law the Tammany controlled senate had to approve his most significant appointments. On the one hand, both houses had to approve the budgetary appropriations for the programs that the governor wanted to implement. On the other hand, it was also clearly understood by the governor and everybody else that Tammany was under greater public scrutiny and had weakened its own position with the public by overplaying its hand through the administration of Governor Dix.

The press and politicians were watching closely to see how Sulzer's relationship with Murphy and Tammany Hall was going to work in light of the specific public challenge that Sulzer had so immediately laid down by publicly proclaiming that he was now the leader of the Democratic Party and was not taking direction from Tammany Hall.

On Saturday March 1st, while staying at the Waldorf Astoria in New York City, where he had come to address a Friday night dinner of the state's allied real estate interests, it was reported that Governor and Mrs. Sulzer were leaving for Washington on Sunday to attend the ceremonies for the inauguration of President Wilson. The *Times* of March 2nd reported that the governor seemed "greatly pleased" to go to Washington and especially about the prospect of riding a horse at the head of the New York delegation in the inaugural parade. He told the press, "in the Inaugural parade on Tuesday I shall ride a horse, but it will be no new experience for me." The governor said he expected to have a conference with President Wilson on Wednesday and return to Albany on Thursday. Sure enough, the *Times* published a photograph of Governor Sulzer riding a horse in the inaugural parade on Tuesday, March 4th, tipping the famous battered slouch hat that he wore during the campaign and on at his inauguration instead of the silk high hat customary for such formal occasions. No other governor received such a cordial welcome from the parade spectators as did Sulzer, who was already a popular national figure. The New York section of the parade included the band of the 369th Fighting Irish Regiment of the New York National Guard, playing Irish tunes in front of a delegation of 1,200 Tammany Braves, each wearing a silk top hat and gray gloves. There was nothing surreptitious that day about the boys from Tammany Hall.

The issue of federal political patronage was the lead political story in the *Times* that week because the press paid a lot of attention to the fact that while in Washington the governor had attended a conference at the Shoreham Hotel with New York senator James A. O'Gorman, Mr. Murphy himself, and Thomas F. Smith, the secretary of Tammany Hall, as well as John H. McCooey, the Brooklyn Tammany leader. At that conference, the governor was straightened out about federal patronage. The group of powerful Irish-Americans, all-important Tammany men, let him know the rules of the game, that federal patronage was customarily funneled through the state's U.S. senator and that the governor's presentation of petitions of New York applicants for federal offices that were forwarded to President Wilson were not appropriate. Senator O'Gorman informed him, practice and precedent required that such petitions had to be presented by a U.S. senator to get anywhere.

At the national convention that nominated Wilson and during the presidential campaign, Sulzer had been a Wilson supporter and Tammany was not. When the governor got back to Albany, he was asked if there was any final determination as to who was the dispenser of federal patronage in New York during the Wilson administration. "That is a very interesting question, isn't it?" the governor replied, "but I will not say anything about it just now." He was then asked about whether he would say anything about the conference with Senator O'Gorman in Washington. The governor said, "The talk we had was of little moment and I was there for only a brief time. I had to catch a train to New York. There was some talk about that," he replied, "but not to any great extent. I spoke up in favor of a few friends myself and I think they will all get their jobs too." This last sentence was spoken with considerable emphasis.

The governor was asked about his visit to President Wilson. "I had a very pleasant talk with him," the governor replied. "It is a very old rule with me never to repeat what the president tells me or what I tell the president, so, of course, I cannot discuss this matter any further."

By mid-March the newspapers began to reveal some of the bitterness that was breaking out between Tammany Hall and the governor. On March 11, the *New York Times* broke the story of the dispute over the vacancy of highway commissioner. "Silent Charlie" Murphy made his first statement since the governor's public announcement on his second day in office that he was now the party's leader. In response to a report from Albany that Murphy had told the governor that if he did not appoint his business associate, James Gaffney, to replace Governor Dix's highway superintendent, C. Gordon Reel (whom the governor had already fired), Tammany would begin to fight him. Rumor had it that the report from Albany had emanated from the governor himself and if Murphy found that to be the case there would certainly be a break between them. Murphy's public statement was: "I never heard of the proposal to appoint Mr. Gaffney to the place of superintendent of highways until I saw it in the afternoon newspapers today. If I knew that Governor Sulzer had offered the place to Mr. Gaffney, I would advise Mr. Gaffney to decline it. I am certain that if Governor Sulzer is questioned about this he will answer as I have answered, that I have never asked him to appoint Mr. Gaffney as superintendent of highways nor to any other place at his disposal."

It was pointed out that the governor had already appointed Mr. Gaffney chairman of the advisory board to study the highway situation, but Mr. Murphy's friends said that the "Chief" had nothing whatever to do with the appointment, that he had not suggested it, and, in fact, knew nothing of it until the appointment was made.

While the legislature had acted swiftly on much of the governor's constructive legislation in January, it had fallen behind in February and the governor had reason to be concerned about whether or not Tammany was deliberately using its influence to hold his program hostage—yet that concern could not be clearly established. On the other hand, the senate had been holding up some of Sulzer's nominations for offices that needed senate approval.

On March 13, the assembly passed the governor's bill to reorganize the state's highway department. At the same time, the senate, by a unanimous vote, rejected Sulzer's nomination of Milton Gibbs, the

Rochester anti-Murphy lawyer to head the health department. The senate finance committee revealed that, since holding up his nomination, they had discovered some embarrassing charges of unprofessional conduct about Gibbs's handling of a plaintiff's personal injury case.

On the other hand, the ides of March brought the governor the good news that the first of his legislation arising out of the work of the special Factory Investigatory Commission had passed both houses of the legislature and could be ready to be signed by the governor. One of these bills required cleanliness in factories. The other prohibited employment of women before 5 a.m. or after 10 p.m.

The *New York Times* headline on March 17th said: "MURPHY TO BOYCOTT THE SULZER DINNER." An elegant nonpartisan fiftieth birthday celebration at the Café Boulevard in New York City, backed by a committee of prominent public figures, long scheduled for March 18th, became serious news when Charles F. Murphy (who had already accepted the invitation) revealed that he would not attend the Sulzer tribute due to a previous conflicting engagement. When the 758 names on the seating list were released, other, but not all, major Tammany leaders, were discovered to be staying away, including U.S. senator O'Gorman and assembly Speaker Al Smith.

St. Patrick's Day, March 17, 1913, was a major day of public revelation that open war was on between the Boss and the governor. The *Times* headline made it very clear: "SULZER IN OPEN WAR WITH TAMMANY BOSS—TELLS FRIENDS HOW HE DREW HIS FIRE WITH GAFFNEY AND THAT HE EXPECTS REPRISALS. READY TO GO TO THE PEOPLE. GAFFNEY SAYS HE DOESN'T WANT ROADS JOB, BUT PICTURES AN 'IDEAL COMMISSIONER RESEMBLING HIMSELF.'"

James Gaffney reportedly called on the governor for a fifteen-minute visit at the Waldorf Astoria. The press reported that he wanted to let Sulzer know why his business interests prohibited him from consideration as highway commissioner.

At the 120th Anniversary Dinner of the Friendly Sons of St. Patrick at New York's Hotel Astor, a major celebration, over seven hundred of the mostly Irish guests heard an address from Sulzer. He avoided state issues—and spoke with his usual flowery elegance about the significance of St. Patrick's Day and paid tribute to the Irish people. The big news of the event, however, was the fact that Sulzer ignored Mr. Murphy completely. The *New York Times* headline was "SULZER IGNORES

MURPHY—BOTH GUESTS OF THE FRIENDLY SONS OF ST. PATRICK—NO GREETING." The *New York Times* description of the governor's appearance was reminiscent of so many similar political events and its near universality deserves repetition here:

> It was just 9:30 o'clock when Governor Sulzer and the members of his military staff entered the ballroom and the band in the gallery, which had been playing Irish ballads, struck up, "Here Comes the Chief."
>
> All the diners, including Mr. Murphy, who was seated at table 14 with Thomas F. Smith, Secretary of Tammany Hall; Philip F. Donohue, John F. Malone, John F. Galvin and other Tammany followers rose to their feet. The procession, with the governor at its head, made slow progress through the crowded room. As the governor stopped to shake hands, Mr. Murphy stood silently, with his hands resting on the back of his chair. Mr. Smith, however, pushed his way to the head of the speakers' table and greeted the governor cordially, shaking his hand and pointing out his seat to the right of Judge McCall.[2]

On the day after St. Patrick's Day, the war between the governor and Murphy was of necessity a significant topic at the governor's big, supposedly nonpartisan birthday celebration. Contrary to the pre-dinner coverage of the seating list—most of the major Tammany officials and party officials did attend—except for Murphy himself. The governor's fiftieth birthday celebration was a huge success—so much so that the line of people without tickets for whom there no room was extended half way down the block from the Café Boulevard.

The now well-publicized war between the governor and Mr. Murphy's Tammany Hall was certainly on every political mind. Some of the dinner speakers at the governor's birthday dinner publicly urged the governor to defy Tammany. The governor finessed the entire underlying political power struggle with his own flamboyant but eloquent address:

> You know me as I am; and as I ever hope to be. I would not be different if I could, and I could not if I would. You know that I have no race, no political, and no religious prejudice. The only

possible prejudice I have is against entrenched wrong to remedy which I have struggled with all my life. I am broad-minded in my views. I believe in my fellow man, in the good of society generally, and I know that the times are growing better. My face is to the dawning of the better and the brighter day that heralds the coming of the Brotherhood of Man. New York is the greatest state in the Union. It should always be an exemplar of economical, efficient and progressive administration. As its Governor, I shall in so far as I can give the people of the state an honest and efficient, an economical, and a businesslike administration of public affairs. I say businesslike advisedly, because I assure the businessmen in every part of our state that they can rely on me at all times to do my utmost to promote the commercial interests of our Commonwealth. I realize how important they are, and shall always be exceedingly careful to take no step that will jeopardize the financial and the commercial supremacy of the first State in the Republic?

Long ago I made a vow to the people that in the performance of my duty no influence would control me but the dictates of my conscience and any determination to do the right—as I see the right day in and day out regardless of the political future or personal consequences, Have no fear—I will stick at that.[3]

Henry Morganthau, President Wilson's chief fundraiser as chairman of the National Democratic Committee's Finance Committee, a well-known Sulzer supporter, addressed the testimonial audience. Morganthau, delivering a major address to the celebration, spoke to the governor directly:

You have wished, and have been in training all your life to be a leader of the people. You have wished it so long that now it has become true, and we wish to see your wishbone converted into backbone, for you will need much of it. Backbone is in truth a mighty resource for one who would fight Murphy and Tammany. Without it failure and defeat are certain, and if victory is to be won the backbone on which all depends must be an inflexible structure.

> We look to you to be the governor of the Empire State and not to be the agent of undisclosed principals who hide themselves from public view. They can no longer govern this country, State or city, and no office holders need be responsible to or afraid of them.[4]

The newspapers maintained their close observation of the war at hand. Morganthau's speech generated a favorable editorial in the *New York Times* the next day under the headline "Backbone," calling Mr. Morganthau's advice "sane and helpful." On March 19th news stories appeared, apparently emanating from Tammany Hall, saying that there had been a secret meeting in New York between Sulzer and Murphy at which they had buried the hatchet. Both men specifically denied that they had met. Murphy even denied that they were at war with each other.

When the governor returned to Albany, he continued to deny that he had met with Murphy during his sojourn in New York to celebrate St. Patrick's Day and his own birthday party. He attempted to avoid further discussion of the war with Murphy that had dominated the political headlines for the past few days. Murphy continued to respond to constant press inquiries that he had not met with the governor and he had not recommended Gaffney for highway commissioner.

Insiders said the governor, who frequently advocated "home rule," would only recognize Murphy's recommendations for filling offices within New York County but would resist any interference with the governor's prerogatives elsewhere in the state.

For those who really believed in Governor Sulzer's avowed efforts to separate himself from the leadership of Tammany Hall, his mere statements were not enough. Independent Democrats, primarily from upstate New York, were urging him to sever all relations with Tammany Hall and to say so publicly. The governor was getting this message from a number of independent Democrats who had come to visit him at the capital to tell him that his plan to distribute patronage by county was not strong enough. They argued that, if the governor really hoped to cut Tammany out of participation in government, he could not leave them in control of patronage emanating from their big-city jurisdictions. They argued that, with Tammany controlling a united New York City, the county leaders in the boroughs outside of Manhattan were unlikely to make recommendations that Mr. Murphy did not approve of. According to reports that reached the press, some sixteen independent Democratic leaders held a long meeting with Sulzer in Albany attempting to persuade him that the time had come for a combined attack on Tammany at the state and federal level. Henry Morganthau had stayed overnight at the Executive Mansion, or the People's House as the governor called it, and because of his splendid relationship with President Wilson and his friendship with the governor, he was considered to be especially influential.

On March 25th, Governor Sulzer addressed the annual dinner in Albany of the Democratic Editorial Association, encompassing one hundred Democratic editors from upstate New York. He told his audience that he was the Democratic leader of the state of New York. Previously, he had only made such claims during interviews, so by making it before a public audience, he was elevating his case. The governor said, "As the governor, I knew from the experiences of the past that, in order to succeed, I had to be the governor in fact as well as in name . . . no man, no party, no organization can make me a rubber stamp. I am the governor. Let no man doubt that."[5]

The governor was cheered when he rose to speak and again when he finished his speech, during which he was frequently interrupted with bursts of applause. The governor's public statements before such an enthusiastic audience certainly elevated his political disagreements by putting them beyond denial.

During the governor's speech he addressed his principles of home rule, a phrase which usually refers to the concept of letting municipalities make their own decisions. With respect to state legislation, home rule requires that a bill affecting a specific municipality requires a message from the governing body of the city, town, or village requesting the bill. Sulzer extended it into the political as well, using this good government principle to justify his political concept of letting each county govern their own politics, or more accurately a justification of the governor's recognition of Tammany Hall when it came to political appointments and political issues relative to New York City.

As the end of March approached, Sulzer's battle with Murphy had become regular front-page news across the state. Tammany warriors and anti-Tammany soldiers began to realize that their own interests were affected and possibly or potentially damaged. The governor was especially eager to break the deadlock in the senate over his appointments as he had a number of important places to fill. The governor's friends and close associates wanted to see the war expanded and expected that the people would rally behind Governor Sulzer's effort just as they had behind Governor Charles Evans Hughes only a few years before when he defied the Republican organization and appointed independents and Democrats he trusted. Despite the possibility of a threat of a Tammany-inspired holdup to the governor's proposed legislation, the truth was that both the senate and the assembly had been working overtime to put through the progressive bills recommended by the governor. Senator Wagner and Speaker Smith, the Tammany leaders of both houses, were identifying themselves with reform and civic improvements, and they were not going to let Tammany or the governor put them in a position of acting contrary to the best interests of the people of the state in order to make a political power point.

On Thursday, March 27, 1913, the *Times* headline was "SULZER AND MURPHY GET TOGETHER." The story from Albany was that U.S. senator James A. O'Gorman had been busily trying to reach a working agreement between the governor and Murphy. According to the *Times*, Sulzer "does not relish the idea of a fight with Tammany Hall." The *Times* report said there was a distinct prospect of peace between the warring parties and, if the senate confirmed the governor's appointees for state highway commissioner, commissioner for efficiency and economy, commissioner of health, and state labor commissioner, as well as his choice for chairman of the upstate division of the Public Service Commission, the governor was willing to work with Democratic state chairman George Palmer, a Tammany man, on certain patronage, beginning with the appointment of three New York supreme court judges to vacancies coveted by Tammany Hall.

The legislature was indeed doing its job and doing it well. On March 29, Governor Sulzer signed two bills proposed by Senator Wagner; one reorganizing the state labor department, extending its jurisdiction and creating an industrial board to oversee factory safety rules. The other Wagner bill that the governor signed that day created protective rules regarding the employment of minors.

By Monday, March 31st, the press revealed a lot of inside information leaking out of the "14th Street Wigwam." The organization "braves" who hung out at the hall were growing increasingly concerned about the patronage battle emanating from Albany.

During the first week of April the governor approved ten bills that had been submitted on behalf of the factory investigating commission. Among the achievements of this legislation were requirements that factory owners maintain employee living quarters in a thoroughly sanitary condition, prohibiting smoking in factories, and authorizing the newly created industrial board in the labor department to make rules and regulations regarding ventilation and seating. Other bills in the package required cleanliness in factories, special regulations for dangerous employment, physical examinations of children employed in factories, basic assurances of wash rooms and lockers for employees, the enclosure of elevators and hoisting shafts in factory buildings, fire alarms, and supervised fire drills. As it turned out, one of the amazing facets of the war between Sulzer and Tammany Hall was that, despite the heat of the political battle and the weapons employed, the progressive legislation generated by the Triangle Shirtwaist Fire and other subsequent revelations emanating from the Factory Investigating Commission, everyone was able to work together to achieve monumental legislative progress to remedy some of the serious dangers to civil society. The legislative retribution that had Sulzer so concerned was not realized and the Democratic governor and legislature amassed a wonderful progressive record in the people's interest.

As April began, the fourth month of Sulzer's administration and the last full month of the term of the new Democratic legislature, it became apparent to sophisticated observers of the Albany scene, that, despite his public pronouncement of political leadership and his open efforts to generate enthusiasm among his significant anti-Tammany friends in the Democratic Party—particularly upstate—the governor's repeated courtship of the independent faction had not really paid off in the kind of support the governor needed. These longtime political enemies of Tammany were not convinced that Sulzer could accomplish his avowed purpose because he had so obviously elected to compromise by giving the Murphy followers a share of his important appointments rather than follow the advice of the independent Democrats who advocated a total freeze-out of Tammany. By virtue of his selection of major Tammany men for certain offices, beginning with the appointment of Judge McCall to the important Public Service Commission chairmanship, he had undermined the confidence his public statements should have inspired. The list of recommendations now bottled up in the senate left too many significant vacancies to be filled by Tammany, leaving many of those who would naturally provide the general support the governor needed feeling that perhaps Sulzer was not really qualified to lead the battle against Murphy that they had envisioned. In an extremely erudite front-page analysis on April 7th, the *New York Times* headline said: "SULZER AS LEADER HAS NO FOLLOWERS—THREE MONTHS IN OFFICE, HE IS DESERTED BY INDEPENDENTS AND CAN'T CONTROL LEGISLATURE—NOW TIRED OF THE CONTEST REJECTS ADVICE TO FIGHT MACHINE AS HUGHES DID AND IS INCLINED TO MAKE PEACE WITH MURPHY."

The headline summarized the long story that followed, concluding that the senate, including independent Democrats, was not as subservient to Tammany as one might anticipate because the organization men were more concerned about public reaction among voters when they had to run for office again than anything else, and independents had

> a lack of confidence in the governor's qualifications for leadership and in his intentions. Today there is virtually a deadlock between the Democratic governor and the Democratic senate over appointments. As a result of this the governor, rather than risk defeat for his nominees in the senate, is allowing half a dozen important posts to remain vacant or be filled by men whose terms have expired but whose places the governor would like to give to men of his own selection. The officers waiting to be named are two public service commissioners, both up-State, the head of the new Labor Department, the Commissioner of Efficiency and Economy, the Health Commissioner, and the Labor Commissioner. A place on the Hospital Commission and the office of State Architect are yet to be filled. The governor's plan regarding these appointments, according to one of his friends, is to send them in one by one as the senate takes action, and to hold out the hope of one public service commissionership and one other appointment going to Tammany in order that the senate may confirm the governor's nominees for other places.

Meanwhile, as the tug-of-war continued over the governor's key appointments, a small group of "mediators," as the press called them, were meeting on behalf of the governor and Mr. Murphy. Toward the end of April, just before the legislature was scheduled to adjourn, progress was reported. Governor Sulzer's key appointees would be approved. John N. Carlisle of Watertown, New York, would become highway commissioner; John H. Delany, a Tammany friend, embraced by Sulzer, would head the newly created Commission of Efficiency and Economy; and John Mitchell was nominated by the governor as commissioner of labor. Two men, Eugene Philben and Bartow Weeks, favored by Tammany, would be appointed to fill vacancies on the supreme court, New York County. Two upstate Tammany supporters, state Democratic chairman George Palmer and W. E. Leffingwell of Watkins Glen, would be named as the upstate members of the Public Service Commission. The job of state health commissioner would go to a Sulzer nominee, Dr. Herman Biggs, a longtime employee of the state health department who had participated in drafting the legislation that reorganized the department.

As the session drew to a close near the last week of April, the governor's nominee for the labor department was still not assured and his proposal to nominate John Riley for superintendent of prisons to replace Colonel Joseph Scott, a Tammany appointee who had been terminated by Sulzer when he defied the governor after he was publicly accused of serious malfeasance by the governor, who had begun to hear about the deplorable conditions at Sing Sing and Auburn state prisons.

Although Mitchell was nominated by Sulzer, his appointment was subsequently nullified by the courts after a lengthy battle that was eventually decided against Sulzer by the court of appeals, the state's highest court, because the governor had no authority to fill the vacancy with Mitchell when he did because Mitchell had been previously rejected by the senate.

17

Government by Investigation

The first shot in this phase of the war was fired almost immediately after the inauguration. It was a stealth shot—for a short while it was hidden from all except the most sophisticated observers. In his January 1st annual message to the legislature, the governor indicated an interest in the creation of a new committee on efficiency and economy to delve into the state government and analyze its efficiency and effectiveness. His message did not ask the legislature to create the committee. Within days the governor appointed three men to his committee. Pursuant to his authority under the Moreland Act provisions of the state's executive law, he gave them the power to subpoena witnesses and take testimony under oath. The legislature quickly appropriated $50,000 for the committee's expenses and they were assigned offices in the Capitol where they began their work on January 6th. The power to issue subpoenas and take testimony was most significant. The makeup of the three-party "committee" was also significant. It was headed by John N. Carlisle of Watertown, New York, a long-standing independent Democrat, with a reputation as an aggressive opponent of Tammany Hall. The other two members were both Tammany men—H. Gordon Lyons of New York County and John H. Delaney of Brooklyn. Delaney was the business manager for the *Morning Telegraph* and Lyons was an accountant employed by the city of New York. Both were reportedly on excellent personal terms with Charles F. Murphy and each of them had a good reputation. To some observers, the fact that Tammany loyalists could outvote the independent chairman created understandable suspicion, which was never to be justified by the committee's work. The attorney general assigned an attorney to assist them, and the state comptroller and the New York City Board of Estimate contributed auditors and investigators to facilitate the committee's work.

The new commissioners were required to make their first report within sixty days. Soon newspapers began to reveal reports of waste in state contracting for highway construction and maintenance, prison conditions, and contracting for repairs at the state Capitol building.

By Wednesday, January 8th, the press started to refer to the governor's Committee on Inquiry as "Governor Sulzer's Graft Investigating Commission." By the end of the first day's hearings on January 8th, the commission zeroed in on its first target. It turned out to be General William Verbeck, adjunct general of the state under Sulzer's three predecessors, Governor Charles Evans Hughes, Governor Horace White,[1] and Governor Dix, who kept the general in place when he took office. The graft investigators had taken testimony that a $45,000 purchase of land for a state National Guard arsenal was illegal and contrary to two opinions of the attorney general because the land purchase had not been approved by the state armory commission. In addition, the committee criticized Adjunct General Verbeck's publication of the *Militia Journal* in his office with the state's money. Verbeck had been promoted to a major general in command of the state's National Guard by Governor John Dix in the closing days of his administration. On his first day in office, Governor Sulzer had replaced General Verbeck and Verbeck had resigned. Bad blood was obviously flowing in the National Guard.

It turned out that the property, which was sold to the state, was owned by the First National Bank of Albany where Governor Dix was employed as vice president until he took office as governor.[2]

It should not be forgotten that this was the age of honest graft, but many hoped it might be the beginning of the end of that age.

The need for reform was understood to be a national problem in 1913—and New York was not unique. On Sunday, January 9th, the *New York Times* headline on its lead story was: "GRAFT UNDER FIRE ALL OVER NATION." The story began:

> Never in the history of the United States have so many investigations been underway as at present. In almost every department of human activities, from one end of the country to the other, some kind of a committee or other is trying to unearth graft or wrongdoing. . . .

In all of the union there are not more than a half dozen states which are not investigating in some form or other. New York State is having its share. Governor William Sulzer had not been in office two days before he appointed a committee to investigate all of the state's departments and this committee is now head over heels in work.

In addition, the governor was already engaged in the process of arranging an independent investigation to discover ways and means to lower the death rate in the state and prevent the spread of epidemics. He had also ordered the investigation of fire insurance conditions with a view toward creating a new policy. In New York City, investigations of police corruption and vice were grabbing headlines for several months.

While details were not immediately available, it was generally known that the committee had begun to look at the state prison system and the governor was unhappy with Colonel Joseph F. Scott, a holdover from the Dix administration as state superintended of prisons who was reputed to be an accomplished penologist.

In February, the *Times* reported on a city alderman investigation, and an investigation by District Attorney Whitman of gambling houses in New York City that paid regular stipends of $50 a week to Charles Murphy's brother John and another $50 a week to Murphy's brother-in-law, Police Captain Patrick Cray, for police protection.[3] As the month of March began, New York County district attorney Whitman was busy investigating the political connections between Tammany and the Liquor Dealers Association. Leaks from the district attorney's office said that the liquor dealers had contributed a total of $150,000 to Tammany's state campaign three years before, according to a *Times* story of March 2nd that contained lots of details.

On March 7th, Governor Sulzer issued a public statement to the effect that there must be no more "waste, graft, or incompetency in building or repairing highways." This remark prefaced the announcement that he had removed another Dix holdover, C. Gordon Reel, from his job as state highway commissioner. The governor's statement said:

The Highway Department is in a deplorable condition. To speak moderately, there has been great waste and much incompetency in the construction and maintenance of roads. I am determined in the future to go slow and make no mistakes, and see to it that the taxpayers get a dollar's worth of good roads for every dollar expended of the people's money. There will be no more contracts let until we know more about them. We want to get all the facts and sooner or later we will get them. I know, and every other man knows, who has common sense, that we can build and maintain just as good roads in the State of New York as they can construct anywhere. We must do it, and we must do it honestly and efficiently, and provide every agency for economical maintenance.

There must be no more waste, no more graft, and no more incompetency in building and maintaining good roads in the State. The people expect this and I have made up my mind to do all in my power not to disappoint their expectations.

Details of the investigation about waste had not yet been revealed although it was known that the governor's graft investigation commission was probing the state highway and building maintenance program.

On March 21st the governor's Commission on Inquiry released its final report.[4] It was undeniably a superb job and reflected a thoughtful analysis of the organization of government in New York and was as thorough as anyone could expect in the allotted sixty days that the committee had been given to do its work. The investigation had actually provided a constructive blueprint for the road to enhanced efficiency and economy by explaining the organizational deficiencies in the way that government was set up, inevitably leading to huge waste and unnecessary expense. One basic problem they identified was the disorganization with so many departments operating rather independently and without uniform rules. Each department established its own accounting system and gubernatorial control was prohibited. The committee's 123-page report began with the prophetic summary: "The business of the State can reasonably be said to be run without any systematic plan whatever. Each department is conducted as an independent enterprise, and there is no effort at cooperation, no point or place where the various activities of the state government concentrate. The governor appoints heads of departments, generally, with the advice and consent of the Senate, and there his real power practically ends."

The committee recommended enactment of thirty-five bills designed to make state government more efficient and more responsible. The first five bills the committee recommended were designed to provide a new structure to get things under control, beginning with a recommendation to create a permanent state commission of efficiency and economy to continue the committee's work on a permanent basis. The other bills created a state Board of Estimate to coordinate and control all appropriations, to give the state comptroller absolute power to audit and examine every state expenditure, and another bill to create a state Board of Contract and Supply to control all purchasing for every state agency. All of these proposals, constituting a much needed and very constructive major modernization of state government, were promptly enacted by the legislature and signed by the governor.

While their report addressed real issues in different departments and described specific problems at numerous hospitals, prisons, schools, among others, the commissioners had insufficient time and resources to go into enough specifics in each area, but they nevertheless were able to apply accepted principles of management and show how millions of dollars could be saved.

In a few cases they were able to illuminate and document scandalous examples of waste and corruption—these usually made headlines and were embarrassments to Tammany.

Most of this legislation was enacted. The governor's committee had proven its worth and its contributions to better government were real and long lasting. During the spring of 1913 the governor's graft investigators—as the Committee of Inquiry became better known to the press—was actually pursuing major investigations of graft and incompetence in the state prison system and the highway construction and maintenance program. Other major investigations related to money being squandered in the repair and reconstruction of the Capitol building itself. All the investigations were initially swift and somewhat superficial due to restraints of time imposed by the governor and resources limited by the legislature. Nevertheless, the extent of fraud was so apparent that the auditors and investigators were quickly able to hit enough pay dirt that they could readily point to sufficient evidence of malfeasance that further work by district attorneys could reasonably be expected to lead to indictments or guilty pleas. In a relatively short time, Sulzer called tremendous attention to the vast corruption in state government, and the extensive involvement of Tammany politicians across the state.

By the close of the 1913 legislative session at the beginning of May, the embarrassment of so many political colleagues of Mr. Murphy did more than anything else to create the irreparable break in his relationship with the governor and meaningful damage to the Democratic Party organization.

THE THAW CASE

In February the three members of the Committee of Inquiry, accompanied by their counsel, John Norton, went to the Matteawan State Hospital for the Criminally Insane to interview Harry K. Thaw, the eccentric railroad and coal baron who was imprisoned there for the dramatic 1906 murder of Stanford White, the famous architect, in front of hundreds of witnesses at a public dinner. Thaw considered White a rival for the affections of beautiful showgirl, Evelyn Nesbit. The governor's graft commission was investigating an allegation that Dr. John Russell, the superintendent of the hospital, had sought a $20,000 bribe from Thaw's attorney to release Thaw from the prison hospital. Thaw was brought to a room at the hospital where the commissioners had gathered to hear his testimony, but Thaw refused to testify on the grounds that he would only testify if he was brought to Albany to testify in the same hearing room as other witnesses testified in—a rather unusual legal theory intended to be similar to a Fifth Amendment claim. Refusing to create a legal excuse for having the prisoner released from Matteawan, even temporarily, the commissioners let him go back to his hospital room and referred his case to Manhattan district attorney Whitman to investigate with a view toward indicting Dr. Russell or Thaw's lawyer. They then instigated a call to Colonel Joseph Scott, superintendent of prisons, to fire Dr. Russell, only to find that he had just resigned by telephone. Thaw's lawyer was eventually convicted. Thaw himself was eventually declared to be sane and released in 1915.

TAMMANY PROTECTING SALOON KEEPERS

At the end of February news reports revealed that Manhattan district attorney Charles Whitman was heavily engaged in an investigation of public graft totaling over a million dollars a year in $10-a-month payments to the police from over ten thousand New York City saloons. This investigation broke when New York City mayor Gaynor issued an order to the police department that uniformed officers must keep out of saloons in the city, which led to the confession of a precinct captain. "I collected twice as much from my precinct before the excise payments were taken away from me. I was told to let the saloons alone, that they were being looked after by bigger men than me."

As the story unfolded over the next few days, it was revealed that in some districts there were Tammany district leaders collecting 25 percent of the profits from taverns in their districts, and the police were getting monthly payments on top. There was also a citywide liquor dealers association making legal campaign contributions to Tammany Hall at election time. (All this was a precursor, albeit more sophisticated, to the Knapp Commission hearings during the administration of Mayor John Lindsay, which revealed the extent of the local precinct pad that was common at that time and made Detective Serpico a movie hero.)[5]

THE CAPITOL REPAIRS

The governor's graft investigators were widening the scope of their activities. On the first of March a small story appeared in the *Times* about the investigator's interest in the extensive work being done at the State Capitol to repair the serious damage done by a major fire in 1911. Over $1.6 million had already been spent on the repairs and additional millions in future expenditures were anticipated. The governor had just fired Herman W. Hoefer, the longtime state architect who supervised the work. Sulzer's executive auditor John Hennessy had reported irregularities in the administration of the electrical and other capitol repair contracts that led to the termination of Hoefer—a loyal Tammany man who was another leftover from the Dix administration.

Hennessy's detailed report was issued on April 8, 1913, addressed to the Trustees of Public Buildings—the state agency that Sulzer properly turned over responsibility to for finishing the Capitol building repair job properly. Hennessy's report was a detailed blueprint to how to rip off the state and enrich friends of Tammany to the eternal detriment of the taxpayers.

The story began with the recommendation that the two top people involved—the state architect Mr. Hoefer and his deputy, J. P. Powers—were not competent to fulfill the duties of their offices. The auditors discovered that they had two companies on percentage contracts rewiring the Capitol. After the state architect had engaged the New York Construction Company under a private no-bid contract, Governor Dix had requested that he add the Tucker Electric Construction Company as well. As a result, the state architect was paying double overhead charges for supervision, foremen, and extra timekeepers. The investigators discovered that over the protest of the state superintendent of construction, the state architect had removed the state inspectors who kept the time records on the two electrical jobs and designated two other men to keep time records. These two were put on the contractor's payroll. The state architect had also asked Tucker Electric to remove its foreman and replace him with somebody designated by the state architect. The timekeepers who worked for the contractors—not for the state—were unqualified and either selected by the architect in the one case or designated by a political leader in the other.

Hennessy's report described a padded payroll—with labor charges "entirely out of proportion to the cost of materials," which is an appropriate test. The auditors reported that "many of the men drawing per diem wages had only a payroll connection with the work." When confronted, the manager admitted that the labor was "largely unnecessary."

"It was clear that the payrolls had been padded, not only as to actual time worked, but also as to men on the job," the Hennessy report concluded and backed up its conclusion with preposterous figures submitted by the contractors and approved by the state architect. For example, a mason's union officer testified that only one of the eight men who were down for $5.50 per day, and who had allegedly worked overtime, were even known to him and had actually worked on the job. The job records proved to be fraudulent in several respects. The audit report detailed one offense after another.[6]

THE STATE PRISONS

Because he was well known to be a Tammany man favored by Charles Murphy, Colonel Joseph Scott, superintendent of prisons and a holdover from the Dix administration, aroused the suspicions of Governor Sulzer regarding his competence and qualifications. When indications of misconduct or incompetence reached the new governor from friends in Auburn, New York, Sulzer asked Colonel Scott to replace the warden at Auburn State Prison with Charles Rattigan. Rattigan was recommended by Thomas Mott Osborne, the longtime Sulzer supporter from Auburn who was a prestigious anti-Tammany independent Democrat. Osborne had earned impressive credentials in penology. Scott considered Sulzer's request to be an interference with his administration of the prison system and refused the governor's request—a decision that earned the governor's enmity.

On March 17th, Governor Sulzer released a preliminary report of the Committee of Inquiry charging Colonel Joseph F. Scott with a series of bad judgments and implications of serious malfeasance.

The following week—the governor sent Colonel Scott a letter enclosing some of the specifications of the charges outlined by his Committee of Inquiry, asking Colonel Scott to attend a hearing in his office the next day or submit a written response.

When Scott refused to respond, he was removed from office. Sulzer's order of removal charged Scott with inefficiency, incompetence, dereliction and neglect of duty based on ten specific findings of the Committee of Inquiry. The charges included mismanagement of serious problems with unqualified subordinates, and conferring favors to an inmate of the Matteawan State Hospital for the Criminally Insane, Henry Thaw, who was allowed to have large sums of money in his possession at the hospital with which he was purchasing favors and special privileges, including his own attempt to be released.

Reportedly, Tammany chief Charles Murphy had made several pleas to the governor to try to get him to retain Scott who Murphy called a "good friend," but Sulzer ignored the chief's request. The *Times* headline was "SCOTT IS OUSTED, SENATE REVOLTS." Tammany elements in the state senate had already made it clear that their sympathy was with Colonel Scott. Senator Murtaugh, an independent Democrat unaffiliated with Tammany and the representative for Colonel Scott's hometown of Elmira, charged the governor with playing political fastball over the superintendent's job and he sought a hearing independent of the governor. The senator actually got the senate to unanimously adopt a resolution of conscience against Sulzer. The governor ignored Murtaugh and fired Scott who had refused to attend the governor's hearing and sent a rather insubordinate letter instead. Sulzer sent the senate the name of Judge John Riley of upstate Clinton, New York, to fill Colonel Scott's vacancy.

The day after he terminated Scott, Sulzer appointed George Blake, a very old friend, political supporter, and well-respected newspaperman as special commissioner to examine and investigate the state prisons, giving Blake subpoena power, but no salary.

Blake issued three detailed reports in April covering his examination of conditions at Great Meadow (April 9, 1913), Auburn (April 27, 1913), and Sing Sing (April 21, 1913), all released May 11, 1913.

The state of the prison system in New York was so disgraceful and inhumane that Blake's report became a gigantic revelation of the dirty details. In 1913, New York, like most other states, had a prison factory system in which prisoners produced furniture and the supplies for state institutions and municipal facilities.

Auburn

The story of the status of conditions at Auburn prison is far more shocking because of the situation that existed there for prisoners. As Blake said with some eloquence and great importance:

> I have found in Auburn prison brutality, violation of the law, waste and general incompetency. Twenty-eight prisoners have become insane during the last twelve months. The testimony of trustworthy witnesses indicates that cruel punishment deprived some of these prisoners of their reason, that the prison doctor is careless and unfeeling, and that he has repeatedly refused to attend upon women during confinement.
>
> More than three thousand pounds of food is thrown into the swill barrel every week. . .
>
> The State has been supporting a number of fine horses and vehicles for the pleasure of the warden . . .
>
> There is no real supervision, every one of the officials appearing to do as he pleases. . . .
>
> The physician of the prison has held that place since May 8, 1898. He is an autocrat. Abundance of evidence shows that he is brutal in his treatment of the sick, neglectful of their needs and that he flagrantly violates that section of the Prison Law which defines his duties. No effort has ever been made by any of his superiors to compel him to moderate his severity or stop him from compelling sick men to expose their persons for examination before their associates or to curb his intolerant and incompetent administration. . . .

This doctor has absolute control over the sick. At a time when men should receive humane treatment they go under the control of this physician who treats them in a more brutal manner than they are ever treated when they are well.

Every nook and cranny of the prison reeks with tales of the cruelty of this man. . . . Once under this doctor's care the men are in a desperate plight.

If he desires, he has the power of ordering into an isolation cell any sick man he pleases and the unfortunate prisoner immediately falls under the suspicion that his mind is unbalanced. Here is some of the testimony:

Q. What would happen if a man became insane? A. Why, there are so many men that are put in that condition we have to send them up to Dannemora for being insane.

Q. When the men came here were they apparently sane? A. Yes, sir. . .

Q. Do you think punishment of this character is necessary? A. I would say that it was not; I should say they should have enough water to drink and enough bread to eat; and I think they should have bedding to lie on.

Q. They are punished in a three-fold manner; by depriving them of water, light, and by creating physical discomfort? A. I consider it a more crying shame to have them square-chalked,[7] which leads to insanity. I have seen boys break down completely, and beg to me to get them relief.

Q. Is it your opinion that a man might remain normal throughout his life, and become insane through this treatment? A. Yes, through being square-chalked. Yes, I know it to be so.

Q. How often was the superintendent here? A. Well, I do not know; he was here three months ago.[8]

Great Meadow

Blake's report on the condition of the new prison at Great Meadow was only a lead into the forthcoming report on the old Auburn and Sing Sing prisons that were functional. Great Meadow was under construction and only partially operational. According to Blake's initial report:

For more than two years this prison building job has been used to rob the State. . . . It has been frequently said that there is a "prison ring," forged for the purpose of stealing the people's money. I believe this statement to be true because the dishonesty of this particular job has so many ramifications. The bills for inferior work and for work not done at all passed through the hands of the State Architect, his representatives at the prison, the Comptroller and the Superintendent of Prisons. All of these persons, with the exception of the Comptroller, must have known that the bills were dishonest and should not have been paid. Yet they passed smoothly along and the money found its way into the pockets of the contractor. A careful investigation might show how much of it remained there. This was only part of the ring. The other parts were the subcontractors, who provided what labor and material they pleased without interference. . . . This project was conceived in graft. The State paid $92,000 for property worth not more than $30,000. The excuse for this initial crime was the alleged need of a hospital building in the health-giving air of the Adirondack region. This was a mere subterfuge. The fact was that the owner of this property induced his political friends to help him unload it upon the State at more than three times its value. . . . The first draft of prisoners arrived at this prison on February 8, 1911. There are only a few more than 400 prisoners located in the cell house now; while there are cells for more than 600. This is another specimen of the methods used in managing the prisons of the State. These 200 cells each lighted and equipped with toilet and running water, have been left vacant while men are sleeping two in a cell in other prisons and on cots strung along the corridors.[9]

This last mentioned information about the new cells became prophetic in light of what Blake found at Sing Sing.

Sing Sing

Sing Sing is probably the oldest and most infamous of the state prisons in New York and in 1913 it was already the oldest and in desperate need of rehabilitation. Blake's report was released on May 11, saved by Sulzer for a time that he needed a blockbuster in accordance with the governor's highly tuned sense of public relations.

The heading in the *Times* story of May 11: "Calls Life Torture in Sing Sing—Lack of Sunshine and Dripping Moisture Cripple Convicts Says Report."

> The prison is remarkable because of the lack of any cohesive or well-poised plan of government. It is so slipshod and incompetent as to breed the suspicion at the first glance that the purpose is to cover up dishonest methods by a brazen show of innocent carelessness.
>
> I found no one man in the prison who appeared to know the slightest thing about the work he was expected to do, with the exception of the prison doctors, who are, without doubt, conscientious men striving to do their duty in the face of manifold difficulties.

While using very harsh language to criticize Warden John S. Kennedy, accusing him of violating the law and causing the state to "lose thousands of dollars in a way that points directly to graft," Blake does not really justify this accusation sufficiently to have made it so strongly. Blake went on to pin most of the problems he found on former-superintendent Joseph Scott. The Blake investigation gets specifically sharp on Scott's credentials.

Blake's report dramatically describes the horror of keeping two men in an antiquated cell designed for one and dripping with moisture by extracting testimony of Dr. Mareness, the assistant prison physician:

> The cells are primarily responsible for the large number of cases of rheumatism that occur in the prison. A number of these cases have been severe enough to incapacitate a man so that upon his discharge he was partially, if not wholly, unfit to follow his usual work. At the present time there are a large number of chronic rheumatism cases. Two hundred of the cells are occupied by two men. These cells are intended only for one. No care is taken in selecting the two men who have to occupy a single cell. A man sentenced to prison for assault and undergoing his first term of imprisonment is sometimes compelled to occupy a cell with a habitual criminal. The cells are infected with vermin. It is impossible to fumigate or disinfect them. . . .

The low thief, stricken with disease, with no mental capacity and with the lowest possible instincts has often been locked into a cell with a man of education, of some ideals and of clean personal habits. This would be bad enough if the cells were light, or large, or clean, instead of being dark, and small and filthy. Also they are unsanitary and those on the ground floor drip with moisture so that the inmates of them have striven to protect themselves from the chill and dampness by hanging sheets and blankets over the walls. In these cells men contract rheumatism. In many cases they become victims of chronic rheumatism and go out crippled for life. . . . The cramped and unhealthy conditions are made worse by the presence of vermin in the cells. . . . Life in these cells is torture to every grade of man who has a spark of imagination, or who ever lived in a decent home. Even the lowest and most degraded man must undergo cruel and unusual punishment when confined in these cells during the horrors of the ordinary night.

Blake added another dimension to his report when he alleged, again without providing any basis for his charge,

There is only one other thing that could add to the misery of these men and that one thing was not overlooked by Colonel Scott or Warden Kennedy. This was the knowledge that certain men through political influence, or by the payment of money, or by some other reason, received favors.

I shall also make a separate report along these lines which will require a special investigation in an effort to expose men in this State, some of them public officials, who banded themselves together to wring money from these prisoners. I have evidence showing that because of influence, exerted by men well known in various walks of life, money has been wrung from persons seeking clemency for prisoners.

If the commutations and pardons bought were always delivered there would have been a glint of fairness in the transaction, but in some cases the "goods were not delivered."

I have evidence showing that by the payment of money men have been accorded the privilege of seeing their friends alone in a room adjacent to the warden's office. I strongly suspect, and I believe I will be able to prove it, that certain men throughout the State have used employees within the prison to ferret out for them prisoners with means in order that they might, by promises of clemency and of privilege, wring some money from them.

A quote from Warden Kennedy, in the Blake report, explained the underlying cause of the problem with doubling up prisoners in cells designed for one: "At the present time the cell block contains 1,200 cells and we have over 1,500 prisoners. This necessitates doubling up, which is a crime pure and simple. On the lower gallery it is impossible to keep the cells dry. The moisture on the walls on a day like this is awful. You can scrape the water off the walls. I never saw anything in the prison reports coming from Colonel Scott that was of any value."

The report concludes with analyses of a series of the prison's purchases, all containing implications of graft, but insufficient evidence. The final paragraph of the report is worth repeating: "The commissary department of the prison is run along incompetent if not dishonest lines. There is criminal carelessness if not downright grafting. Signs that this is the case stick out as plentifully as quills on the back of a frightened porcupine."[10]

The very day after the Blake report was issued, Sing Sing warden John S. Kennedy sent a copy to the Westchester County Grand Jury. He denied any wrongdoing on his part vehemently and refuted portions of Blake's report, while asking the grand jury to investigate. Kennedy specifically denied receiving any graft and denied the entire story of prisoners receiving favors in exchange for money.[11]

HIGHWAYS—CONSTRUCTION AND MAINTENANCE

March 7, 1913, turned out to be the beginning of two major departmental issues. Governor Sulzer had quickly demanded that the removal of C. Gordon Reel, Governor Dix's highway superintendent, based on preliminary information from his Committee of Inquiry, that there was a great deal of incompetence and waste in the construction and maintenance of good roads.

In their final report filed on March 16th, the governor's Committee of Inquiry scanned the entire range of executive departments for its initial impressions. The commissioners concluded their sixty-day survey with the finding that "the investigation of the highway department we regard as the most difficult. . . ." The obvious problems had to do with the vast amounts of money being spent on construction and repair of highways.

The commissioners had a preliminary look at the department's budget and saw that in 1912 appropriations of $4.5 million were made for the department, which was now seeking $4.8 million for 1913. This did not include design and construction of new highways—which were financed with a bond issue. More than half of the budget was for maintenance. The auditors decided that the previous year's budget cost $1.4 million more than it should and that the forthcoming 1913 budget should be cut to $2 million based on the excess costs caught by the committee's auditors due to obvious overpayments for labor and materials in the repair program and the need to build to better specs and enforce them on the new construction program, while requiring the department to only award contracts on a competitive bid basis.

These findings led Governor Sulzer to appoint John A. Hennessy on March 25th as a special commissioner to examine and investigate the state highway department, with full power to issue subpoenas and take testimony under oath.

Hennessy's initial report revealed extensive waste and apparent corruption in the contracting of road maintenance, the cost of which was only partially revealed in the highway department budget as a significant portion of road maintenance expenses were financed through municipal budgets and special bills. The far larger expense was for new road construction financed by a $50 million bond issue. That expense was the major target for the favored Tammany Hall supporters, which made Murphy's concern about who would head the highway department under Governor Sulzer so important to both men.

The Commission of Inquiry auditors pieced together a powerful story by comparing three years' expenditures for road repair. The comparison yielded some basic information. For example, in 1909 one-third of the cost consisted of supplemental contracts modifying the originally contracted cost. In 1910 and 1912, the supplemental contract cost was insignificant, indicating that somebody paid attention to the opportunity to hold contractors to their bids.

A general conclusion reached by the auditors, based on information from the comptroller and the chief engineer of the highway department, was that the true cost of highway repairs had been excessive—averaging about 20 percent more than the real economic cost. This analysis covered the last year of the Hughes administration and the two years of the Dix administration. Throughout the analysis, both Tammany and Republican political influences and patronage were playing the same game of awarding contracts to favorite political supporters of the party in power.

The auditors were able to establish and report on the significant additional expenditures in excess of the real cost of oil, stone, and earth excavation in source material. While reporting on a number of wasteful and non-useful methods of contracting and estimating that were nearly always employed to the contractor's advantage—the Hennessy report concluded that "The most vicious feature of the method of letting contracts appears to have been the practice of awarding contracts for repairs without asking for competitive bids." The report showed that in 1912, 75 percent of these road contracts were assigned to contractors chosen by highway department officials without competitive bids.

Within weeks after Hennessy's appointment as a Moreland Act commissioner, corruption cases arising from the highway maintenance and contracting programs were being referred to district attorneys in twenty-two counties all over the state for prosecution—and eventually people started going to jail. For example, Hennessy reported in August of 1918 that Tammany-affiliated Democratic leaders in Rockland County were indicted. He said that roadwork in Rockland was 70 percent fraudulent and the state got the benefit of only thirty cents on each dollar spent. Hennessy said of "the more than forty roads examined in twenty-two counties, we found only three that pass muster, and only one that is clear all the way."

He described in detail exactly how the corrupt contractors were ripping off the state by building roads that did not meet the specifications—making them narrower than required, using old rather than new materials, making the road surfaces half or even less than half as thick as called for, and other perversions of specifications—which would be approved by inspectors who were paid off.[12]

Hennessy said that "as these cases develop the electors of New York will learn that the political organization . . . captained by Charles F. Murphy in New York City . . . is organized to loot the treasury and regards every honest man as its enemy."

But, the legislative leadership eventually cut off the funds for Hennessy's investigation and left him with a gubernatorial mandate that was unfunded. A private appeal was made to a dozen men who contributed and volunteers were engaged—but Hennessy was soon unable to maintain the necessary staff to provide well-prepared and foolproof cases for referral to prosecutors.

Certainly the extent of and attention to these investigations of corruption in a variety of major state facilities and organizations—all of which led back to regular Tammany Hall vendors as the beneficiaries of illegal advantages—made a mortal enemy of the man who could have put a halt to the corruption but instead was limited to bringing it to public attention. Sulzer had to be stopped. It was a matter of survival for some very important people.

DESCRIPTIVE INCIDENTS

We have a natural tendency to look at the past from the perspective of the present. That perspective can be misleading because the passage of time and accumulation of experience changes some things and not others. The significance of the Sulzer story lies in the fact that, on the one hand, so many of its lessons are relevant to today's political times, and on the other hand, our conditions today are very different due to what we learned from the experiences of the past (provided we remember the lessons); combined with changes in our communications and the differences brought on by the advent, first of radio, then television, and recently the internet, and the modernization of the methods of publishing books, newspapers, and magazines. For the most part, these changes have meant improvements, although we are frequently given reasons to long for the past. While powerful and impregnable city and state political machines no longer exist, political clubs and special interest organizations of varying degrees of importance and motivation certainly do. The influence of party machines, whether Tammany or otherwise, has been eliminated or defused relatively recently, but some of their power remains in the hands of the wealthy who can more easily acquire and maintain political power by paying for advertising, campaign consultants, and workers. So, the concept of "pay to play" is exploited by special interests that are only occasionally compatible with the greater good. Some of the best political leaders picked by the political bosses would never have been elected if they had to compete with better financed people for campaign funds.

Here are a couple of good stories to illustrate the atmosphere in Albany in 1913 that invite comparison with modern times.

Senator Stilwell

One of my favorites is the story of Governor Sulzer and Senator Stephen J. Stilwell, a state senator from the 21st district of the Bronx. Senator Stilwell, a lawyer with offices in Manhattan, was a proud descendant of one of Westchester County's oldest colonial families. He was born on a farm known as the Stilwell Homestead, was educated in the Yonkers public schools, and graduated from New York University Law School. Seeking a larger field of practice, he moved to the Williamsbridge area of the Bronx in 1897 and became "an ardent worker in the ranks of Tammany," according to his own official biography in the *New York State Redbook* of 1913. He had first been elected to the state senate in 1908 and was twice reelected to consecutive two-year terms. When the senate convened in January of 1913, Stilwell was named chairman of the senate committee on codes.

Sometime in early 1913, Governor Sulzer, who worked hard to be available to constituents, received a man in his office named George H. Kendall, president of the New York Banknote Company, one of the two banknote companies in the state. Kendall came to the governor complaining that his firm was disadvantaged because his competitor had a monopoly on New York State business. He asked the governor if a bill could be introduced in the legislature to prohibit such a monopoly. The new governor advised him to go and see Senator Stilwell, because such legislation was in the jurisdiction of Stilwell's committee.

The legislation Kendall sought would have made it a misdemeanor for the stock exchange to refuse certificates engraved by the New York Banknote Company. Then existing law required the stock exchange to deal only with certificates of a quality approved by the state.

Shortly afterward, Mr. Kendall wired the governor charging that Senator Stilwell had threatened to hold the bill in his committee unless he was paid a sum of money that, on further inquiry, turned out to be $3,500. According to Kendall, the price was determined by the number

From *The New York Red Book* (Albany: J. B. Lyon Co., 1913).

of senators who Stilwell would be obligated to share the bounty with. Sulzer responded by sending a telegram to Kendall asking him to come to Albany at once, which he did. According to Sulzer, "the story of Kendall's experience with Stilwell was a story of as brazen an attempt to steal as I have ever heard." Sulzer later described it as "a story that was interesting . . . because it shows how legislation is bought and sold by men who introduce legislation for their own personal gain."

Sulzer heard the details of Mr. Kendall's encounter with Senator Stilwell:

He used the fact that I had sent Mr. Kendall to him as an evidence of his importance and his power. His very first act in connection with the bill was graft, inasmuch as he took Mr. Kendall in tow and told him it would cost him $250 to have the bill drafted, a bit of petty grafting in itself. Shortly after the bill was drafted Stilwell had Kendall come to his office and there told him that it would cost $500 for each of the four code committeemen in order for him to get the bill out of the committee. Kendall, who had had some experience in legislation, immediately protested that this would mean that the bill would get out of the senate committee, whereas there was still the assembly committee to think of. Stilwell said he would look up the assembly committee, and that the next day he would let Kendall know how much it would cost to get the bill out of that committee. It was there he fell, for strange as it may seem that a man as crafty as Stilwell should have been so foolish, for he actually wired to Kendall "fifteen is the right number," meaning that $1,500 would have to be paid in addition to the $2,000 that he had already demanded for the senate committee.

Mr. Kendall had accumulated undoubtedly strong evidence and he had brought most of it in documentary form with him to Albany. I listened to his story in amazement. I heard also to my surprise that several days before, he had taken the matter to Senator Wagner and that Senator Wagner, the Democratic leader, had forced the clerk whom Stilwell had used in the bill drafting room to resign, but that otherwise nothing had been done.

I immediately sent upstairs for Stilwell to come down—the legislative halls being on the third floor of the capitol, whereas the Executive Chamber is on the second floor. The moment Stilwell entered the room and saw me talking to Mr. Kendall the expression on his face was sufficient to have convicted him of the charge. He braced himself, however, and walked toward my desk with an ugly expression on his face but ill-concealing his guilt.

"'Senator,' I said, 'you know Mr. Kendall?'

"'I do," he replied.

"Then," I said, "you probably know what Mr. Kendall has told me, and if what he says is true, you had better go upstairs and hand in your resignation."

"'I can explain," he said, "the matter he complains of to my satisfaction."

"'You may be able to explain it to your own satisfaction,' I said, "but you cannot explain it to my satisfaction. You are a disgrace to the State.'"[13]

After the Senate Judiciary Committee refused to discipline Stilwell by a vote of 28 to 21, Sulzer took the senate committee report and referred it to District Attorney Whitman of New York County who promptly had Stilwell indicted and convicted, after which he was sentenced by Justice Samuel Seabury to serve a sentence of four to eight years in state prison for seeking a $3,500 bribe.

Stilwell died in Grasslands Hospital in Westchester County in 1942 where he was receiving medical treatment as a prisoner in the nearby county jail where he had been incarcerated for nearly a year awaiting sentencing after pleading guilty to a new charge of attempted bribery. Apparently Stilwell had not learned a lesson from his earlier imprisonment because in 1940 he was convicted in Westchester County of attempted bribery involving an offer of $1,000 to a Mamaroneck Village trustee to obtain the appointment of a friend to the village police force.

Gubernatorial Security—1913

Some aspects of the story of the Sulzer administration are striking because of the similarity to the way things are done in Albany today. Other aspects of the Sulzer governorship illustrate how different 1913 was from today. It was reported in 2010, that the New York governor's security detail consists of two hundred state troopers. In 1913, New York did not have any state troopers. (The state police were created in 1917 with 257 mounted troopers and there was no security detail for the governor. Today there are approximately 4,600 troopers statewide with helicopters, laboratories, and boats at their disposal.)

On February 23, 1913, the *New York Times* reported that Governor Sulzer revealed a story about a plot to assassinate him. According to the governor, a man arrived at the Executive Chamber on the previous Friday morning asking to see the governor. He was informed by the governor's staff that Mr. Sulzer was too busy to see him, so the man told one of the governor's assistants that he was there to warn the governor of a plot to kill him. The stranger was turned over to Owen L. Potter, Esq., an assistant counsel and the governor's pardon clerk, the lawyer on the governor's legal staff who dealt with applications for pardons and extraditions that regularly reached the governor's office.

The visitor told Mr. Potter that the previous day he was searching for highway machinery in one of the villages in Albany County and, as he approached an unused cider mill, he heard voices. He claimed he had overheard the details of a plan to kill the governor. He said two men were talking and they also discussed a plan to visit Schenectady and kill a man there. At that point, the informant said he was discovered by the plotters who assaulted and robbed him. After first going to a doctor, he decided to come to Albany to warn the governor. The governor's assistant counsel directed the man to the Albany police department headquarters and gave him a letter on Executive Chamber stationery addressed to the city's deputy commissioner. The man returned to the Executive Chamber shortly and told Mr. Potter that he could not find police headquarters. He left the letter with Mr. Potter, saying he must leave the city at once.

Governor Sulzer told the press that although he was receiving some threatening letters he had received them all through his public life and paid no attention to them. However, the *Times* reported that letters threatening the life of the governor had actually reached Mrs. Sulzer, who took the threat much more seriously. Reportedly she arranged for a guard to protect him on the way to and from the Capitol, but the governor told the reporters that "if I have a body guard, I am not aware of it."

18

The Direct Primary Battle

The initial combat in the Sulzer/Murphy war was fought on three battlefields, patronage, investigations, and legislation. The patronage battle ended in a stalemate. There was a compromise. Sulzer placed some of his key men in important positions but Mr. Murphy got most, but not all, of his choices. In the investigations battle Sulzer was clearly the winner, having exposed some of the worst corruption in years, putting the light of publicity on several serious situations where the taxpayers were being exploited for the financial benefit of the selfish few who were closely related to the leadership of the organization that Governor Sulzer called the "Invisible Government." Some of the perpetrators of corruption would eventually face justice when and where even the chief of the Society of Tammany could not protect them.

The anticipated legislative battle never materialized. Despite the war over patronage and the governor's success in the war on corruption, the Democratic legislators, even the organization men, were eager to act responsibly and create a good progressive record for themselves—and they did so. Those from New York City were especially concerned because a major mayoral election would face them in the fall and Tammany's legislative record in Albany could be used for them or against them. Besides, the legislature was led by Smith and Wagner. These two Tammany men were leaders whose reputations and power were based on their substantive achievements in good government. For that reason, most of the governor's program was enacted, and both the legislature and the governor could take perpetual pride in their achievements during the first quarter of 1913. Some of the structural reforms to state government were monumental and everlasting.

Sulzer could boast of the fact that almost all of the legislation contained in his original program, and significant compatible programmatic legislation, was adopted by the Democratic, Tammany-controlled, assembly and senate. His gubernatorial record would be positive for posterity when it came to enacting Progressive laws that were good for New York. The proposals of his Commission of Inquiry would provide a basis for a long-lasting modernization of state government. Sulzer was victor in this battle, but only because the Democratic legislators—Tammany and anti-Tammany—stood with him for Progressive legislation and reform. Warriors on both sides of the battle had enhanced their own records and the Tammany bosses had wisely refrained from abusing their power to control legislation as a tool in the fight with the governor. At least that was the case as the time approached for the legislature to adjourn.

This is not to say that matters always ran smoothly. There are always bumps in the road to good bills and sincere substantive differences among men of good will and appropriate criticism to be levied. In crafting legislation, needing the consent and cooperation of so many elected representatives, there is always room for different or slightly different ways to do it—which takes time, persuasion, and compromise.

The governor was severely criticized for his support of the full crew law that was enacted during that session at the behest of organized labor. The new law required minimum numbers of crewmen on certain trains. Railroad management considered it to be a sellout to organized labor. This law prevailed in the railroad industry for many years to come and actually survived in New York through the late 1950s when it was finally repealed at the demand of that industry, whose members had been burdened with the expense of unnecessary firemen on diesel locomotives. Governor Rockefeller signed the repeal.[1]

The Republicans and some of Sulzer's Democratic enemies made hay out of the allegation that Sulzer had committed himself to the railroad labor unions by promising to sign a full crew bill during his campaign for governor in 1912. The opposition claimed it was illegal and unconstitutional for someone to promise gubernatorial action in order to get elected. The issue received a lot of newspaper attention. After a few weeks, the matter blew over except to the extent that, for those who believed the charge and ignored the governor's denial, it left a stain on the governor's shirt—even though legislative and gubernatorial candidates are obviously expected to tell the voters what legislation they will advocate or oppose if elected.

By early April it had become quite apparent that Governor Sulzer's relationship with Mr. Murphy had reached an irretrievable breaking point. Sulzer's refusal to appoint Murphy's choice for highway commissioner was key to Murphy's limit of tolerance with the recalcitrant and truculent governor who he considered to be an "ingrate" for all that Tammany had done for him over the years. The investigations that were by that time regularly releasing scandalous information proving to be an embarrassment to grafters and profiteers associated with Tammany were combining to confirm Murphy's lack of confidence in Sulzer's relationship with the party Murphy controlled. Sulzer had every reason to believe that his legislative success and the image of a fighter against corruption would stand him well with the voters in the next election. Nevertheless, Sulzer's extensive political difficulties with Tammany forced him to the realization that if his re-nomination at a state convention in 1914 was going to be dependent on the good will of Tammany Hall, his career might already be over. No Democratic governor could get re-nominated by his own party unless he could rely on a state convention not controlled by Mr. Murphy.

Sulzer chose his direct primary bill as the means of accomplishing his objective—freedom from Tammany—relying on the voters to assure his re-nomination and reelection in 1914. If Sulzer could enact a bill that eliminated the state convention, and the power of party leaders to nominate statewide candidates, his survival would be in his own hands.

Elimination of the state convention was an issue that was previously put on the table by two-term Republican governor Charles Evans Hughes (1907–1910), a committed Progressive reformer who had tangled with the Republican Party organization. Hughes prided himself on his independence from the party and a general instinct to keep politics out of his decisions as much as he could. Reform had been an effective effort in his administration and indeed he had practically eliminated the scandalous influence of the infamous "Black Horse Cavalry," the name given to a group of Republican and Democratic legislators who wielded undue influence on behalf of major corporate interests. These men had made a fortune enacting or killing their own bills at the behest of influential businessmen whose influence was usually expressed in cash. However, Hughes had failed to get the kind of campaign reform that he sought and his own Republican legislature rejected his direct primary proposal in 1909 and again in 1910.

When Sulzer sent his annual message to the legislature in January, he had called for legislation to simplify the election laws relative to the direct primary system to make it more effective. At that time he was no more specific. Nor did he comment on the Democrat's direct primary bill when it was introduced by Senator George A. Blauvelt on February 17th or since. A similar bill had been introduced in the assembly. The Blauvelt bill was a direct response to the governor's annual message on that subject. It was drafted with the guidance of the legislative leaders as a fulfillment of the long-standing party platform position. The Blauvelt bill was never intended to be a landmark of reform—and there had been no clamor for such reform. The bill eased up on the number of signatures needed to nominate, and generally made independent nominations easier, but it certainly did not extend the application of the direct primary concept beyond the existing areas. Most importantly, it left the state convention in the law. During the ensuing legislative debate and committee discussion of the bill, no word was ever sent by the governor, nor had he commented on it.

Simultaneous with Governor Sulzer's falling out with Mr. Murphy, the governor developed a keen interest in the direct primary bill he had virtually ignored until then. On April 10th, like a wounded lion jolted to awareness, Sulzer created anew the battle. His general message to the legislature asserted that it was his duty to call attention to "the insistent demand of the people of the State for a reform of the election laws . . . and shorter ballot; and for direct state-wide primaries."

The governor's message of April 10, 1913, recited language from the platforms of all three parties represented in the legislature—Democrats, Republicans, and Progressives—each of whose platforms called for laws for "direct primaries" with no mention of any particular public position on the extent to which primaries should apply, except that both the Progressive and Republican platforms did specifically mention "delegates" to the state convention. The governor's message encompassed all these party platforms and used their supportive arguments to make the case for giving up the existing system of electing delegates to a state convention, replacing it with a new legal structure that would have the registered voters of each party nominate their candidates for statewide public offices (governor, lieutenant governor, attorney general, and state comptroller) by a vote of all members of their party—and then create a platform committee comprised of those who were nominated as statewide candidates and the state committeemen from each district.

The governor's case was based on easily understood principles. He argued that people were just as capable of nominating candidates as they were of electing them.

Governor Sulzer concluded his message with the phrases that came closest to revealing his purpose. He said his proposed changes in the law aimed to "restore to the people rights and privileges which have been usurped by the few, for the benefit of invisible interests which aim to control government officials, to pass laws, to prevent the passage of other laws, and to violate laws with impunity."[2]

Governor Sulzer had fired the equivalent of another "shot heard round the world" in this new battle with Mr. Murphy. He had to know that by doing so he would reaffirm their conflict. He believed that he would win this battle by pressuring the legislators through their constituents to get his bill enacted, putting him in a position to get re-nominated without the support of Tammany Hall—and beyond that, if he achieved his objective, like President Wilson he would be perceived as a great reformer who beat the bosses and thus made himself eligible for the next presidential nomination. The stakes were high, very high, and from Sulzer's perspective his approach seemed to be both logical and realistic considering that his three months of fights with Mr. Murphy had already rendered him unable to be re-nominated no matter how popular he was with the electorate.

By pursuing this position, Sulzer had also precluded any compromise with Murphy unless he would also accept humiliation in the form of defeat or rejection of the bill he was proposing so publicly. This was most likely a fight to the finish, leaving the big question—could he convince Mr. Murphy's men in the legislature to enact his bill by persuading the public to demand that they do so.

The next day the governor presided over a meeting in the Executive Chamber with about thirty Democrats who were well-known independents and familiar dissidents, one Republican, and two or three leading Progressives. Out of this group, the governor created a committee to draft his bill. The newspapers reported that the real legislative leaders were not concerned about the governor's bill. They were confident that the Blauvelt bill would be passed and sent to the governor. They also opined that most of the voters opposed the governor's suggested changes. There was no apparent evidence of public clamor for the governor's position on state conventions.

On April 16th—the senate passed the Blauvelt bill—adding a few amendments that had been included in the governor's message, but there was no support for the governor's concept of doing away with the state conventions to nominate statewide officials. The senate also decided to adjourn on May 2nd. Sulzer's direct primary bill was ready for introduction on the 21st of April.

On the 24th of April, the governor vetoed the Blauvelt bill with particularly harsh words. In his unusually vituperative veto message, the governor unfairly attacked the integrity of several genuinely reform-minded and Progressive legislators, saying that the bill "must be branded as enacted in bad faith; wholly fraudulent; and a glaring breach of the pledged faith of every member of the legislature. . . . This measure is a fraud on the electors of our state . . . a betrayal of the people."

Sulzer then called a meeting of all of the state's Democratic county chairmen and asked them to decide if they were for him or against him in his fight for direct primaries. He told them, "If any man is against me or my party, in efforts to keep faith and party pledges, I am against him. He is no Democrat, and I will do everything in my power to drag him out of the Democratic Party. There will be no compromise between the executive controlled by the people and the legislature controlled by the political bosses." He specifically challenged each county chairman in the Democratic Party.

"I want every Democratic chairman in the state to decide whether or not he is with me or against me. If he is with me, I'll be with him, but if he is against me, I'll be against him, and he will be a party to driving me out of public life, or I'll be a party to driving him out." Sulzer pulled no punches and concluded with a threat to every county chairman: "Rest assured that in this struggle, those who help me will win my gratitude; that those who oppose me will merit condemnation."[3]

The governor let the party chairman know he would go to work to defeat any of their legislators who refused to support him. It was a "either you are with me or against me" case. If you are with me, you will have my favor and my enthusiastic support, was the message the governor publicly delivered to the members of both houses. If you are not with me, you will have to explain why and expect me to challenge you

From *The New York Red Book*
(Albany: J. B. Lyon Co., 1913).

in your own districts, to refuse to sign any legislation you are able to
pass, and to come to your neighborhood and denounce you.[4] He could
not have been more direct, or more confrontational. There was no justification for anyone to be confused. Each member of the legislature

would have to make a choice. This was designed to be the bloodiest battle of the small war and a battle fought in the open.

Sulzer proudly released a telegram he had received from Colonel Theodore Roosevelt supporting his efforts to reform New York's electoral law. The former president told Sulzer that he agreed that "only by direct primary legislation can we make the people really masters of their own party organization, and unless they can thus master their own party organization they have no real control of the government."

The governor's vicious veto message turned out to do unnecessary harm to his own cause. Senator Wagner spoke rather eloquently on behalf of his colleagues. More in sorrow than in anger, he rose above the governor to say, "I say that it hurt me as it hurt other senators to meet with such an experience after we had done the best we could for the people, after we had done the best we could for the governor in the advocacy of his reforms, merely because we disagreed with the details and not with the principles of one of those reforms."[5]

Staying on the high road while appealing to his own legislative constituency, Wagner went on to reach out to his newest adversary: "I hope that I shall never so far forget myself as to accuse another who in thinking for himself differs with me, of being a fraud and a dishonorable man, I am sure that upon mature reflection the governor of this state, for whom I have the greatest personal regard and friendship, whom I have defended day after day upon the Senate floor when he was attacked by senators of the minority, would not use the language he did with reference to the conduct of this legislature."

Nevertheless, elegantly putting his personal pique aside and proving his own fairness, Senator Wagner then said that he thought the efficiency and economy department proposed by the governor would benefit the state and urged that the governor's nomination of John Delaney to head the new department should be confirmed.[6]

By now the break within Murphy was an open and oozing wound. Despite continuing efforts of emissaries of both men, there was no way to put Humpty Dumpty back together again. This would be the fight to the finish that many of Sulzer's friends and advisors from the independent group of Democrats had long anticipated and encouraged, confident that good Sulzer would prevail over evil Murphy. Sulzer really believed that this issue would resonate with the public and, by taking this cause directly to the people, he would prevail. Otherwise, there was

no practical reason to join this battle over the issue of eliminating state conventions—which was the issue Sulzer created for himself knowing that Governor Charles Evans Hughes had lost the same battle with the legislature only five years earlier.

The governor's threat to call the legislature back in special session if his bill was not passed did not impress the members. On April 30th they defeated his bill overwhelmingly by a vote of 42 to 8 in the senate and later by a straight party vote in the assembly. According to the *Times* story of May 1st, the senate bill was "beaten beyond the hope of resuscitation." During the debate the governor was denounced for his dictatorial methods and the substance of his proposal was virtually ignored as the members denounced Sulzer's campaign of intimidation. Member after member arose to announce their refusal to be politically excommunicated for refusing to succumb to the arguments of one man, even if he was the governor. Senator Wagner chastised the governor for failing to raise the convention issue during the formulation of the original Blauvelt bill and accused him of "ingratitude" to the party that made him, and he implored his colleagues to stand up to the governor's threats and not let him browbeat them.

The governor let out word that he would start his campaign for a direct primary bill on the Fourth of July and he would use the bosses' weapons of patronage power against them—by ousting from state service any of the protégés of those political leaders who opposed him and seeking new appointments only for those who took his side against the Tammany organization.[7]

Those who were objective political observers seemed to be in agreement that the governor could not succeed in ever getting the legislature to support his direct primary plan to eliminate the state convention. Thoughtful men with some expertise believed that his plan was doomed because the organization was strongly opposed to the elimination of the state convention, and many believed that the governor could not rely on Republican support either when their most recent history revealed that the Republican party had rejected Governor Charles Evans Hughes's effort to achieve the same reform in 1909 and 1910.

The governor called for the anticipated special session of the legislature to consider his direct primary bill on June 16th after he met with his newly organized direct primary campaign committee in the

Executive Chamber, which was so fully attended that many who wanted to be there had to line up in the hall outside the Executive Chamber on the second floor of the Capitol. A committee of one hundred was appointed to launch the campaign. Included in the leadership group were such prominent men as William Randolph Hearst, Herbert Lehman, District Attorney Charles S. Whitman, John Purroy Mitchel, Ralph Pulitzer, Vincent Astor, Henry Morganthau (who agreed to head the Committee on Ways and Means, to raise the necessary campaign funds), and Colonel Theodore Roosevelt, the former president of the United States who sent word that he would speak on behalf of Sulzer's proposal and called on all Progressives to join in the effort.[8]

On May 16, the governor began to carry out his promised retributions. He announced that he had designated Dan Dugan, a member of his direct primary committee, to replace Patrick McCabe as Albany County Democratic leader. McCabe was a well-known Murphy man. At the same time he issued orders to all of the department heads he controlled to start to weed out the organization men so they could be replaced with job candidates who were recommended by the party leaders who supported him. He also let it be known that certain of Patty McCabe's recommendations for contracts at the Capitol would be replaced. He took similar action with his people in charge of the highway department, and the public works department who controlled jobs on the barge canal. Hundreds of state jobs and contracts were involved—and applicants to replace them soon started to appear at the Executive Chamber. The governor was serious.[9]

Sulzer also used his veto power on numerous thirty-day bills that had been left with him when the legislature adjourned on May 2nd. Bills introduced by Tammany men that were not considered vital by the governor were rejected, including some $3 million worth of appropriations, while he also vetoed bills creating new jobs in certain state agencies.

On May 18 Sulzer commenced his long-promised swing around the state by railroad—believing that with speeches to crowds of people he would have a dynamic impact on enough voters who would then appeal to their legislative representatives to support his bill at the forthcoming special session. Sulzer was confident of his ability to rally the supporters he would need. The entourage on his special train involved staff, stenographers, secretaries, and newspapermen as well as prominent members of his campaign committee, some of whom also spoke to the crowds that gathered to support him.

Governor Sulzer campaigning. From Jay W. Forrest and James
Malcolm, *Tammany's Treason, Impeachment of Governor Sulzer:
The Complete Story Written from behind the Scenes, Showing How
Tammany Plays the Game, How Men Are Bought, Sold and Delivered*
(Albany: The Fort Orange Press, 1913).

The *Times* headline on May 18, 1913, summarized the situation: "SULZER CONFIDENT OF PRIMARY VICTORY—ON EVE OF SPEAKING TOUR HE PREDICTS TRIUMPH, BUT POLITICIANS DOUBT IT."

Sulzer's initial campaign trip to western New York began in Buffalo. Mayor Fuhrmann and former Erie County Democratic chairman and former state chairman William J. Conners, who had been deposed by the Murphy alliance, were once the dominant force in Erie County and they did a superb job of planning and promoting the governor's trip to western New York. These anti-Tammany Democrats were using the governor's appearance to recover their own leadership in Erie County. Nobody met the governor's entourage at the Buffalo railroad station because it did not arrive until 11 p.m., having stopped at key cities around the state like Syracuse and Rochester, where Sulzer supporters came aboard to confer briefly with the governor. The next day, however, the governor reached crowds totaling twelve thousand people, at three different venues in Buffalo, according to reporters traveling with the governor's entourage.

While the people were excited to see their governor, there was very little enthusiasm for his direct primary bill. While his audiences were generally supportive of Sulzer's opposition to boss rule, his case for the direct primary bill as the basis for his campaign against bossism was not readily understood by some. His first meeting was held at the Old Convention Hall that had recently been rehabilitated by the city as an economic attraction. Eight thousand people there, gathered to dedicate the new facility, caught sight of their governor at a rally, but only half of them remained until the end of the governor's speech, which was also remarkable because 25 percent of the audience were women and children who, the *Times* reporter said, "had come to see, not hear . . ." According to the *Times* headline of May 20th: "BUFFALO LUKEWARM TO SULZER APPEALS"; "TWELVE THOUSAND PERSONS HEAR HIM SPEAK TO HIS PRIMARY BILL—LITTLE ENTHUSIASM." The governor employed threats to cut off patronage in Erie County unless the county's legislative delegates were supportive of him.

Most importantly, the *Times* story captured the governor's mood when it described three specific confrontations the governor had at a reception in his Buffalo hotel suite. These incidents were uniquely revealing of aspects of his personality and attitude at the time that were most unlike the "Plain Bill" Sulzer the people had elected less than a year before. The detailed report reflected the reporter's surprise, if not shock, at what he observed about the governor.

He served flat notice that no patronage would be given to Erie County until the lawmakers from here were whipped into line for his direct nomination bill. The threat was made with all the pugnacity of an old-time boss, and in the hearing of a score of persons.

Dr. Frederick T. Koyle, recently an army surgeon who has known Mr. Sulzer for many years, called on him to ask him to appoint a friend to a place in the reorganized State Health Department. The governor stepped back sharply and raised his hand and his voice so that every one of the suite could hear him:

"Not another job will go to Erie County from the Executive Chamber until the Legislators from Erie County see fit to vote for my direct nomination bill. This is final and I want you to tell your leaders so unless the Erie Legislators come to the support of my bill, Erie will not get a look in on patronage."

Dr. Koyle was dumfounded and drew back in amazement. He told the governor he could bring endorsement for his request from veterans associations in various sections of the State.

"I don't care!" The governor exclaimed. "Tell those people that if they want their endorsements to count for anything with me they must get out and hustle for my bill."

Dr. Koyle said afterwards that he felt thoroughly humiliated as a result of his experience.

A moment later Gen. George C. Fox, the retired commander of the Seventy-fourth Regiment accompanied by Lieut. Thomas N. Harris, commander of the Naval Militia here, called on Gov. Sulzer to thank him for approving substantial appropriations for the benefit of the local militia.

"I don't care for verbal thanks from you nor anybody else," the governor told them. "The only kind of gratitude that is acceptable to me is gratitude translated into action. Tell your leaders to get the legislators to redeem their party pledges and vote for the Direct Nominations bill. I have been most generous, not only with you but with this city in general."

When the representatives of the newspaper published by Norman E. Mack, former Democratic Chairman and member of the Democratic National Committee, came up to interview the governor, Mr. Sulzer turned on him sharply. Mr. Mack is not with the governor in his fight.

"Huh!" said the governor, "your boss is Norman E. Mack. Why he should send anybody to ask me if I am going to compromise I don't know. He knows where I stand. There will be no compromise. You go back and tell Mack that he is only a dreamer if he is thinking of compromise. This is a man's fight, and will be a fight to the finish. Mr. Mack got a big appropriation for his commission and a nice trip to Panama at the State's expense. He ought to be with us in this right out of gratitude if nothing else."[10]

The governor's campaign headed back east along the state's Southern Tier, heading for Elmira and making stops in Attica, Warsaw, Saratoga Springs, Hornell, and Corning, after which it returned to Albany with last stops at Elmira and Schenectady. According to the *Times* account of the trip, the governor received his first really enthusiastic reception since starting the tour from the audience of six hundred people at Hornell. In Elmira, he had a significant confrontation on the platform where he gave his speech on the direct primary bill before an audience of five thousand people. One of his major opponents, Elmira senator John F. Murtaugh, who was respected as an independent Democrat, sat on the stage during Sulzer's speech and then spoke against the bill after Sulzer finished his presentation. Both speakers were civil to one another and acknowledged a genuine difference of opinion. However, Sulzer told the *Times* reporter covering the trip that he would drive Senator Murtaugh from public life unless he voted for his proposals at the forthcoming extra session.[11]

While Sulzer was capturing the attention of the press on this campaign trip, senate majority leader Robert Wagner answered his claims by soberly explaining that the Democratic legislators favored direct primary reform, but not the elimination of the state convention because it was essential to have open discussion of party positions among delegates from all over the state. He pointed out that at the 1912 state convention where the platform was drafted by a committee he headed, there was no mention of eliminating the state convention as Governor Sulzer had been wrongly and repeatedly saying across the state.[12]

At the inception of his campaign to abolish the state convention as the way to end boss control of politics in New York, some who lauded the objective expressed the view that he could not succeed in making a moral issue out of direct primaries. Some objective analysts of the week's campaign who were supporting the governor's effort raised legitimate questions. Many of those supporters of the governor's proposal came to it out of their own quest for patronage and political power that a governor could bestow on them, some of them were on the other side when Governor Charles Evans Hughes proposed similar direct primary bills eliminating the state convention when it went down to defeat in 1909 and 1910. While the Tammany-led legislative Democrats opposed the abolition of the state convention, they had genuine good government policy arguments for doing so, and they favored about all of the other reforms the governor proposed and were ready to do business with him in that regard. The governor's objective was based on his firm belief that he would not have a chance of re-nomination if he had to rely on the next state convention to nominate him.

Soon after returning to Albany, the tired but pleased governor announced plans to spend the end of May campaigning for his direct primary bill in New York City. He professed pleasure at his upstate reception and claimed assurances of support for his bill. However, according to the *Times* of May 23, friends who had been on the Buffalo tour and supported his appeal from the platform did not share his optimism. The general consensus of his own friends, and the press who followed him, was that the governor had been warmly received by the thousands who heard him speak and he was personally very popular. People supported his appeal for independence from Tammany, but did not seem interested in his direct primary bill and did not consider it to be so vitally connected to the issue of boss control. Several prominent legislators indicated publicly or privately that he had not swayed their vote and they intended to vote against Sulzer's bill.

The planned Memorial Day weekend speaking tour of the city would include appearances in Brooklyn, Manhattan, the Bronx, Queens, and Staten Island, and a number of prominent New Yorkers were solicited to share his platform. As preparation for the next week's campaign were being arranged, bickering among the members of the campaign committee, which had become known in the press as the War Board, resulted in disputes about who would be invited to speak and where the different events would be held.

In his three days and nights of city appearances the governor deployed tremendous energy. He also continued to display an uncharacteristic degree of feistiness and bad taste. The *Times* account of the final evening of his weekend tour of the city captured the moment:

SULZER THREATENS AS HIS TOUR ENDS
CALLS HIMSELF MAN OF PEACE BUT WOULD FLAY OPPONENTS
ADDRESSES THREE MEETINGS IN BEHALF OF HIS DIRECT
PRIMARY PLAN—HINTS AT ALBANY SCANDALS

Governor Sulzer, in the course of a sixty-mile automobile ride, taken within the confines of New York City last night to promote sentiment in favor of his Direct Primary bill, said in three speeches along his route that first of all he was a man of peace. He insisted that he loved peace. Then he said that he ". . . would strip any man who fought against him of his hide and tack the hide to the ceiling of the Capitol at Albany."

Gov. Sulzer did not content himself with this threat. He warned his hearers that, while he was too busy just at present to tell them all he knew about Albany, he might be compelled to come back and tell them things that would make them want to join in lynching bees.[13]

The governor had actively addressed more than a dozen crowded meetings during his three-day visit to the city, some political and some civic groups, even a group of clergy men of all faiths, reaching an estimated fifteen thousand voters. At each encounter the governor denounced the influence of Charles F. Murphy, the leader of Tammany Hall and William Barnes, Jr., Republican state chairman. As was the case throughout most of his upstate tour, the governor was warmly received. His attacks on the bosses were cheered, but there was little visible enthusiasm for the bill to eliminate state conventions and most people remained ignorant of the bill's provisions despite Sulzer's efforts. No members of the New York City delegation to either house of the legislature acknowledged a change of heart toward the governor's bill as a result of his three-day tour. The press reported that the Tammany leadership was much relieved by the lack of any public conversions of senators or assemblymen who had voted against the governor's proposal during the regular session in Albany. On June 1st, the *Times* reported that the view from Tammany Hall was that unless the governor won this battle for the elimination of the state convention, Mr. Murphy would "lose no time in forcing his retirement from public life."

Back in Albany, Governor Sulzer announced vetoes of thirty-day bills left by the legislature, vetoes which detrimentally affected funding for projects sponsored by legislators who voted against his direct primary proposal during the regular session. Sulzer found some encouragement in rumors of a few upstate members who were pressing to vote for the bill at the following special session.[14]

In early June, senate majority leader Robert Wagner spoke out against the governor's behavior—denouncing him for his reckless rhetoric about lynchings of recalcitrant legislators and his accusation of lawmakers' corruption, as well as his vindictive abuse of his veto power. No state senator in the Democratic caucus was reported to be considering support for the governor's bill, including upstate independents as well as Tammany men. Only a few assemblymen from Brooklyn told the press that they were open to consideration of support for the governor.[15]

The following week the governor drove to the Catskills mountain area in pursuit of his campaign for the direct primary bill, which was about to be considered at the special session called for June 16th. Once again Sulzer was well received by especially large and enthusiastic crowds—one thousand in Catskill Village alone—but again, garnered very little interest in or support for his legislation.[16]

About ten days before the date for the special session, every legislator, every county Democratic chairman, and each member of the Democratic State Committee received a fourteen-page pamphlet from Norman Mack, the state's National Democratic committeeman, entitled "The Truth About Direct Primaries," providing a detailed analysis of the governor's bill and detailing the reasons why it should be defeated, emphasizing the fact that by virtue of the overwhelming number of Democrats registered in New York City—compared to the number of Democrats upstate—New York City would be able to name the state ticket. While the pamphlet notably refrained from personal attacks on the governor, it did point out that the governor had not discovered that his party was committed to abolishing the state convention until April 1913—more than three months after his initial annual message to the legislature, which failed to mention the abolishment of state conventions.

Meanwhile, the governor announced his own plan for the last week of campaigning prior to the special session. He confirmed engagements on Wednesday in Rochester; Friday in New Rochelle, Yonkers, and White Plains; and four speeches in New York City on Saturday.

At the same time—the Progressive Party announced that Colonel Theodore Roosevelt would speak in Buffalo and Rochester and then in New York City, at Cooper Union with Governor Sulzer. Roosevelt addressed a crowd of six thousand in Buffalo, and just like Sulzer, he was received enthusiastically and warmly, but without enthusiasm for the bill he came to discuss.[17]

At Sulzer's appearance in Yonkers on Friday night, June 13th, the Warburton Theatre was jammed to the doors with more than five hundred people waiting outside.[18] The governor denounced Yonkers senator John F. Healy as an enemy of the people. Senator Healey had previously announced that he would never support the governor's bill because the governor had been insulting and threatened to veto his legislation. Yonkers assemblyman Tracy F. Madden had also been denounced by the governor. Both were fiercely hissed and booed off the stage in a near riot that also prevented others who came to support Sulzer from taking the stage.

Before leaving the theater, the governor asked for a show of hands of those who supported his bill—and he got unanimous support. However, the audience at the event sponsored by the Westchester Civic League was largely composed of members of Roosevelt's Bull Moose faction. None of Westchester's legislative delegates were supporting Sulzer's bill and there were no conversions in spite of his personal popularity.

Despite the fact that Colonel Roosevelt withdrew from his promised appearance at Cooper Union with the governor, Sulzer concluded his campaign there on Saturday night, June 14th, at a meeting presided over by Henry Morganthau with addresses by Sulzer and William Randolph Hearst. Hearst's appearance turned out to be significant because he had previously been aligned with Mr. Murphy in New York City politics and he had been Murphy's unsuccessful candidate for governor against Hughes in 1908. Hearst told the Cooper Union meeting that he would bolt the Democratic ticket in the fall municipal election if Sulzer's bill was not enacted. That was an important and prophetic warning because Tammany was banking on recapturing control of the city mayoralty—and Hearst's newspapers were very important to them.[19]

Two days later, June 16th, the special session of the legislature convened. The *Times* headline summarized the moment: "SULZER CONFIDENT; TAMMANY DEFIANT." The press reported that the governor was positive that the members of the legislature, Democratic and Republican, had seen the light and even those who opposed his proposal at the regular session would respond to their constituents' desire to have those members support his bill. It was also reported that Mr. Murphy was convinced that there could be no possibility of reaching any understanding with the governor and that his people should not retreat from their position against the governor's bill. Senator Wagner said that the governor's effort to stir up the people's support for the bill had failed.

The night before the special session was to begin on June 16th, Patrick E. McCabe, clerk of the senate and close ally of Mr. Murphy, having just weeks before been displaced by Governor Sulzer as the Albany County dispenser of state patronage, issued a public statement charging the governor with dishonesty and duplicity. Mr. McCabe revealed Governor Sulzer seeking and obtaining secret conferences with Murphy while posing as his enemy in public speeches and statements. McCabe listed four specific meetings for which he supplied detailed accounts, giving the dates, places, and participants. According to the account published in the *New York Sun* on June 17th, McCabe's release was a notice to Sulzer that Murphy and other party leaders who were attacked by Sulzer in his campaign would no longer keep quiet. Mr. Murphy's side was not going to take it anymore.

The session opened with referral of the governor's bill to the judiciary committee in each house—where no public hearing was contemplated. As reporters interviewed the legislative leadership, it rapidly became apparent that the predictions of the day before were correct. Very few votes were changed and the bill was doomed, "DOA" in today's language. Senator Wagner said that he doubted if the governor would gain a single vote in the senate. Assembly majority leader Aaron J. Levy said that the governor would get no more than ten additional votes in the assembly—and defeat of his bill was assured.[20]

On June 18th, the third day of the special session, the *Times* editorial, entitled "THE GOVERNOR'S LOSING FIGHT," said that defeating the governor's bill "faithfully represents and reflects the prevailing sentiment of the people of New York."

On June 24th the bill reached the assembly floor where it was defeated by a vote of 92 to 54. Only four members who voted against it at the regular session converted to the governor's support, one Republican and three Democrats. Two of the Democrats had benefited from extensive highway appropriations to their districts in bills approved by the governor.[21] The next day, June 25th, the senate voted 38 to 10 to defeat the governor's bill, and then passed the Blauvelt Bill again by a party vote of 32 to 16, as the assembly had already passed it 77 to 59.

Campaign cartoon, by Victor Ralph Lambdin, May 29, 1913.

The coup de grâce was administered by the senate on the day they defeated the governor's direct primary bill.[22] Another battle of the war was over and it ended in defeat for Governor Sulzer.

When the speechmaking ended, the editorial writers on the major papers that followed the story of the governor's campaign to eliminate the state convention seemed to reflect a consensus of differing perspectives of the governor's tactics. While crowds had rallied to his support when he spoke to "Boss Rule" and the "Invisible Government," it certainly appeared that, despite an immense and deliberate effort and the well-organized campaign that exposed him to thousands of people in just two weeks, the governor seemed to be incapable of arousing a public uprising to the cause of new legislation, probably because the citizenry questioned his fundamental sincerity even when his cause was quite obviously in the public interest. Because Sulzer's own long and well-known public career was rife with examples of popular causes that he had loudly espoused, most likely to advance his public image and his career, while maintaining his well-known long-lasting ties to Tammany Hall, his sincerity was questionable in the eyes of some observers even among those who supported his cause. To them he appeared demagogic regardless of whether they were on his side or against him. However, the fact of an entire career in which his allegiance to Tammany was crucial to who he was made it hard to take him seriously, when his delivery was so near perfect, always powerful and exceptionally articulate even if bombastic. "Character is, after all, the one essential in a public man," wrote the editor of *Times Work* in August 1913. He said "bombastic championing of the 'people's cause;' spectacular assaults upon bosses, even energetic work on behalf of necessary reforms will not avail; what the people demand above all, is a real, honest, sincere, devoted man. . . . The popular mind seems unerringly to detect the true from the false in its leaders."[23]

According to the *New York Post* editorial of July 26th, "the people did not rally to the governor because he did not talk or act like a governor. He lacked dignity and self-respect. He was loose-tongued and loud-mouthed, constantly boasting of what he had done and what he was going to do. Constant violence of speech and tumultuousness of action had no success against a vicious or perverse legislature." All these conclusions, along with the previously described views of the *Times* writers, combined to give the reader of these accounts a good and logical picture of what happened in this large and very transparent war over political power. It certainly raises an interesting question of how the public would have reacted to the same sort of campaign today, with our enhancement in communications and the extent of exposure of the players in today's television times. Would the players have had to play their role differently and would the outcome have been different?

Senators Wagner and Frawley. From Jay W. Forrest and James
Malcolm, *Tammany's Treason, Impeachment of Governor Sulzer: The
Complete Story Written from behind the Scenes, Showing How Tammany
Plays the Game, How Men Are Bought, Sold and Delivered* (Albany:
The Fort Orange Press, 1913).

19

Murphy's Revenge

On June 11th, just a few days before the legislature assembled for the special session on June 16th, the *New York Times* carried a front-page story about a pending legislative investigation of Governor Sulzer's administration. Legislators were forming a new joint legislative committee, comprised of senators and assemblymen, intending to examine the governor's use of his veto power and promises of patronage to secure votes for his bill to eliminate party conventions for selecting statewide candidates. The proposed investigation was a retaliatory effort suggested by the leaders of the Democratic organization, which the governor had so bitterly denounced in campaigning for his direct primary bill. With amazing foresight, Tammany's legislators quietly set the stage for this joint legislative committee during the very closing moments of the regular session in early May, anticipating exactly the kind of case that Governor Sulzer would make for his direct primary bill, as well as the threats he had made so publicly.

The investigation would be headed by Senator James J. Frawley of New York County as its chairman and staffed by loyal Tammany lawyers. Frawley was a handsome, bespectacled man who was serving his sixth two-year term in the senate. A reliable Tammany warrior, he was chairman of the powerful senate finance committee, who took pleasure in his participation in organized athletics. The intent of the legislative leadership was ominous. The initiation of such an investigation would turn out to mean much more to Governor Sulzer than the defeat of his bill to eliminate the state convention. Before the special session was over, the committee's unusually broad mandate was augmented with specific authority to look into contributions and expenditures for statewide campaigns, including not only the governor's campaign for the direct primary bill but his own 1912 election campaign as well.[1]

After the decisive defeat of his direct primary proposal at the end of the regular session of 1913, the governor declared that the fight had only "just begun," generating a brief flurry of rumors to the effect that the governor was getting tired of the battle and was ready for reasonable compromise to save face. Speaker Al Smith and majority leader Robert Wagner were concerned about the impact of this public battle on Tammany's prospects for the city mayoral election in the fall and they saw the value of compromise. Mr. Murphy was not interested.

The entire state government was in turmoil. The comptroller's office, controlled by Tammany, held up approval of various expenditures on contracts and payroll emanating from those agencies of government that were controlled by the governor. Loyal Tammany stalwarts were losing their jobs and anti-Tammany politicos were filling the vacancies. The senate was refusing to confirm gubernatorial nominees and the new department of efficiency and economy was hampered by the lack of a legislative appropriation. Vendors, their workers, and state employees were suffering from loss of income. Large numbers of people became battle-scarred victims of the war. Collateral damage in today's terms.

Meanwhile, Frawley's lawyers, investigators, and a group of private detectives hired by the committee dug into every corner of the governor's life and a series of destructive allegations were brought to public attention beginning on the first of July with a story out of Philadelphia about the filing of a lawsuit against Governor Sulzer for breach of promise of marriage to Miss Mignon Hopkins, a salesgirl and cloak model at the John Wannamaker Department Store in Philadelphia. The suit itself was mysterious because the governor had already been married for the past five years to Clara Rodelheim, a nurse. Their courtship had been especially romantic because Sulzer, who was then an attractive congressman with an active social life and political prominence in Washington and New York, was an especially eligible bachelor. He was forty-five years old when he met and married Miss Rodelheim, who had nursed him back to health while he was a patient at a New York City hospital.

Miss Hopkins's complaint in her court case, filed and released by an attorney in Philadelphia, said that Sulzer had proposed marriage to her in 1903 but asked her to keep their engagement secret because it might interfere with his political career. She alleged that they had been seeing each other extensively during those years. Miss Hopkins never explained why she waited five years after the governor's marriage to initiate this legal action seeking financial reparations. Neither Miss Hopkins nor her attorney was willing to speak to the press or explain anything about the allegations in the written complaint her lawyer filed on her behalf. When confronted with the story, Governor Sulzer said, "Nothing to it. Merely another story started by my enemies."[2]

When the governor reached Gettysburg, Pennsylvania, on July 2nd, to celebrate New York's role in the Civil War, he answered questions from the *New York Times* reporter about Miss Hopkins's claims. Her lawyers intended to serve their complaint on the governor at Gettysburg but failed to do so. The governor told the *Times* reporter, who turned it into a front-page story on July 3rd:

> [T]he suit of this woman Hopkins is blackmail . . . instigated by my enemies and is part of the plot of Boss Murphy and his political conspirators to discredit me because they cannot use me for their nefarious schemes to loot the State of New York. If I were willing to be Murphy's kind of a governor, no one would have heard of this. . . . Mr. Murphy and his hirelings are doing everything in their power to destroy me politically. They have been threatening me ever since I became governor. . . . I shall go forward without fear, come what may. I never did a thing in my life of which I am ashamed. . . . Suffice it to say that I knew this Hopkins woman years ago . . . but I deny emphatically that I ever agreed to marry her, that I ever wronged her, that I ever lived with her, or that I ever held her out to be my wife. Miss Hopkins sued me in New York for breach of promise sometime after I married, about six years ago. She could not sustain her charges and admitted she brought the suit for ulterior purposes. That case was settled and my lawyer holds a general release from this woman to me. My reason for settling then was on account of the precarious condition of Mrs. Sulzer.

The governor was asked if he would become the Fusion candidate for mayor in New York City. He responded, "I would not take the nomination if it were tendered me by every party in the city. I am having too much fun in the job I have got."[3]

The Frawley Committee was going to have something detrimental to Sulzer to reveal nearly every day in July. On the first, the committee leaked information that it was expecting to begin work in Albany on Thursday afternoon, July 5th, letting it be known that they had already gathered a mass of material that would discredit the governor with the people. On the eve of the committee's first public meeting, key members of the committee staff leaked some examples of the subjects of the forthcoming inquiry.

> That the governor had received large contributions from individuals and corporations that he failed to report and that some of his campaign expenditures had not been reported as required by law.
>
> That William Randolph Hearst had helped to finance the Sulzer campaign in exchange for specific favors designed to leave Hearst and Sulzer as leaders of the Democratic Party in New York and make Mr. Hearst a U.S. senator.
>
> That the governor had vetoed a hydroelectric power bill earlier in the regular session as a favor to an upstate anti-Tammany political boss in exchange for substantial financial support.
>
> That the governor had made secret pledges to the railway labor unions in which he promised to sign a full crew bill.

When the governor was interviewed about these details of the proposed investigation, he called them "rot," and pointed out that under the Constitution, when the legislature was summoned by the governor to meet in extraordinary session, it could only consider those items put on the agenda by the governor. (This "defense" ignored the fact that the legislative inquiry had been authorized before the governor called the special session.)[4]

The leaked effort to embarrass the governor about his relationship with Miss Hopkins was followed by stories in the *New York Times* about the governor's involvement in mineral mining in Alaska. Those reports charged that an Alaskan missionary had sued Sulzer for $100,000 over a mining claim that the governor settled for $40,000.

A few days earlier, Patrick McCabe, the governor's nemesis from Albany County and the Tammany man who had been replaced as patronage dispenser by the governor's own man in Albany, gave out a story charging the governor with unprofessional conduct in relation to his work as a lawyer back in 1890. McCabe released a copy of what he claimed was a court document alleging that Sulzer had committed perjury in a Vermont case in which he was representing a client. That charge was authenticated by a former Brooklyn supreme court justice who had been associated with Sulzer at the time as a lawyer in the Vermont litigation. Fortunately, it was promptly denied by the Vermont trial judge who heard the case and whose statement vindicated Sulzer.

By the Fourth of July, it was apparent to anyone reading the newspapers that Sulzer's enemies were piling on in an effort to destroy his credibility, or what remained of it. A series of charges were leveled at Sulzer throughout July attacking his congressional career. Those included allegations charging him with use of his position as chairman of the House Committee on Foreign Affairs to help American business interests obtain some valuable mining concessions in Guatemala.

Sulzer promptly labeled these allegations as "a tissue of falsehoods and exaggerations." (However, late in August the *Times* published a series of letters and other documents that seemed to refute Sulzer's disavowal. Those documents revealed that, while he was a member of the Foreign Affairs Committee, Sulzer was serving as an advisor to a Cuban firm attempting to get the state department to intervene on its behalf in collecting a claim from the government of Cuba.)[5]

The Frawley Committee's first public hearing on July 3rd looked into the work of George W. Blake, the governor's special commissioner to investigate the prison department, which had already released rather dynamic charges about major corruption in the prison department. The committee took testimony to discredit Mr. Blake's initial reports about the performance of state prison superintendent Colonel Joseph Scott who had been removed by the governor. The committee attempted to subpoena Chester C. Platt, secretary to the governor (a statutory office similar to chief of staff), who refused to accept the subpoena and produce the papers it required, arguing that the traditional constitutional separation of powers should prevent a legislative committee from subpoenaing documents of the executive branch and that such a subpoena was unprecedented under New York law. As the investigation began, leaks from the legislature repeatedly made it clear that they had enough information to "show the governor in his true light to the voters" and that "big things on the governor" were forthcoming.[6]

When it came time for Mr. Blake to testify, his interrogators referred to the portion of his report where he asserted that $500,000 spent on the new Great Meadow Prison was pure graft. They pointed out that Blake had spent only three or four days investigating the construction work on this new prison. When asked how he had come to this conclusion, Blake told them that he had done so based on the statement of an "expert" who asserted that the job was worth $400,000 and the state had spent $955,000. It turned out that the expert, a Mr. T. E. Burney, had volunteered his services to Blake and was previously unknown to Mr. Blake. Burney had been recommended by a friend whose name Mr. Blake said he forgot. Blake admitted that he knew nothing about Burney's qualifications or if he had ever built a single building. The committee's counsel produced the original contract from the files of the office of the state comptroller and established that the contract Mr. Blake had looked at was a draft and not the original. Most importantly, Mr. Blake admitted that he was not aware of the clearly recorded fact that the contract had been awarded to the lowest bidder out of six. By the time he was finished testifying, Mr. Blake's hasty and careless investigation, which had yielded such startling headlines for the governor, was fairly well established by committee counsel as unfair and unreliable and had done a disservice to Colonel Scott.

Counsel to the governor, Valentine Taylor, appeared before the committee on the governor's instructions and asked that he be allowed to appear as counsel for any employee of the governor's staff who would be called as a witness, but that request was denied by the chairman who told Taylor, "this is an investigation to ascertain facts, nothing more. No one's life or liberty is in jeopardy. There is no need of counsel."[7]

To make matters worse, after two days' consideration of the legal impediments to Chester Platt's resistance to the legislative subpoena, the governor agreed to produce the papers from his office relating to the appointment of George Blake as his special commissioner. However, by the 15th of July, the governor qualified his promise to produce the subpoenaed documents. He told the committee that he would only produce those documents that he thought the committee was entitled to. Chairman Frawley promptly responded by instructing the committee's counsel to report the governor's refusal to comply with the subpoena to the legislature to determine what could be done to enforce the subpoena.

On July 17th, the *New York Times* reported that "Mr. Blake was compelled to admit that most of his allegations were based on belief, vague suspicion, and rumors circulating in the prison." That news story was headlined "GREAT MEADOW LOOT CHARGES SHATTERED," and the detailed story of Mr. Blake's investigation revealed, among other things, that Mr. Blake had engaged his own brother-in-law as an expert on building construction materials and saw his experts' qualifications "smashed into smithereens." The cross-examination of Blake was framed by testimony from a qualified deputy state architect who testified that Mr. Blake's reports were "falsehoods," "untrue," "without foundation," and "taken out of empty air."

The Frawley Committee certainly succeeded in undermining the governor's preliminary investigation of the state prisons by demonstrating the governor's reliance on Blake, whose report appeared in retrospect to have been what Colonel Scott's supporters said it was, a crude justification to fire Scott.

By virtue of Blake's own testimony about how he had gone about his work, Sulzer could no longer explain away some of his other investigations that had cast Tammany operations as corrupt, in light of the unreliability of the governor's own investigators.

The next day the Frawley Committee moved to a new area—examining a number of legislators, both senators and assemblymen, who described their conferences with the governor about bills they had introduced and were now awaiting his signature or veto. Several members told the same story; in short, when they came to see the governor to lobby for their own bills, the governor engaged them in a discussion of his direct primary bill and clearly expressed his belief in reciprocity and his repeated use of the phrase "you for me, me for you," but none of the members, several of whom had been genuinely aggrieved by the governor's attitude, could or would testify to any more specific threats or promises aimed at the particular bill they had come to discuss.[8]

The *New York Times* editorial writers were obviously troubled by the testimony. On Saturday, July 19th, they wrote a long editorial calling attention to the fact that "one legislator after another had testified that the governor was seeking to gain support for his direct primary bill by trick and deception." The *Times* editors wrote that the governor should put himself above suspicion in such matters by forgetting politics and attending strictly to the business before him. They acknowledged that the governor needed help and took him to task for "calling upon men who get him deeper into trouble. With his opportunities and with the intentions he has proclaimed he ought by this time to have the people of the state solidly behind him. He has failed chiefly because of his own mistakes," but they said it is not too late and encouraged the governor to retrieve the ground he lost, "and triumph over his enemies. He will have all the support he needs if he will deserve it."

That thoughtful editorial fairly well summarized the appropriate reaction of objective observers of the evidence that was revealed during the previous six weeks or so. The outcome of the Sulzer-Murphy war was still to be determined.

In what appeared to be as insightful a summary of the situation as anyone could have expected at that time, a detailed *New York Times* story on July 20th attributed to "a good authority," said the governor indicated to reliable intermediaries that "if the organization will yield an inch, Governor Sulzer will yield a foot," but the *Times'* source reported that Mr. Murphy was not in the mood for making either peace with or war on the governor. In Mr. Murphy's view, the legislature and the governor should fight it out among themselves. The knowledgeable sources promised that before the Frawley Committee investigation had gone much further, "the people of the state will understand why the organization is not willing to meet the governor half way."

They reported that, when the Frawley Committee was created, the legislative leaders intended to "show the governor in his true light before the people of the state," but that since the committee began its work, the situation had become much worse and bitterer. The *Times* reported that "the testimony taken in the latest session of the committee on Thursday afternoon, July 17th, in the estimation of some of the politicians here, could have been of only one purpose, that of laying the foundation for impeachment proceedings." They were referring to the examination of the individual legislators, which had failed to yield evidence that the governor had actually threatened to veto their bills if they did not vote for his bill. "Such evidence would constitute legally inappropriate conduct on behalf of the governor," but the committee had failed to get such testimony.

The same critical article revealed that the governor had admitted to a close friend that he did see Mr. Murphy at his home on April 13th, a meeting that had previously been denied by Sulzer and Murphy but authenticated by others. Mr. Murphy told the governor on that occasion that "I will have you out of office in six weeks. I spent $300,000 to ruin George P. McClellan who turned traitor. I will spend a million to put you out of business."[9] Sulzer had only revealed that Murphy had abused him at that meeting, but never reported on what Murphy actually said.

On July 23rd, the special session of the legislature was over for all practical purposes. It had refused to enact the governor's direct primary bill, which was its original purpose in convening, and any other items that the governor asked for had been promptly disposed of. Accordingly, they should have adjourned and gone home, but they did not do so. Instead, they decided to take a recess until Monday, August 11th. The recess had a specific purpose. By adjourning instead of ending the session, the governor would be unable to fill the vacancies in a series of key governmental jobs where men he had appointed were rejected by the senate. If the legislature were not in session, the governor could make interim appointments. If the legislature remained in session, the governor could only appoint people the senate would approve of. The governor announced that even though the legislature had not adjourned but was nominally in recess, he deemed that the legislature had really adjourned insofar as appointments are concerned if he could get the courts to so determine.

In the last week of July it had to become abundantly apparent to Governor Sulzer and his anti-Tammany stalwarts that the series of news stories leaked to the press in June and early July, topped by the initial hearings of the Frawley Committee, were having a dramatic impact on the governor's image. That the campaign to discredit the governor was taking its toll was best illustrated by the *New York Times* headline on July 26th: "PLOT TO MURDER ME, SAYS SULZER." On Friday, July 25th, the governor sat down with the *Times* reporter in Albany and poured his heart out in a most unusual interview, even for Sulzer, about his "war on the bosses" as the *Times* story called it and referred to it repeatedly as a war. At the very beginning of the story, the *Times* said, "the people of the state are mostly calm, but they are not unmoved. They are disgusted, and we wish Gov. Sulzer and Mr. Murphy would be made to realize the depth of their disgust. The decent people of New York have disapproved of many things done by Gov. Sulzer: it is their habit to disapprove of pretty nearly everything done or desired by Mr. Murphy. The spectacle now presented to the vision of decent and orderly persons is too unseemly to be passed by without protest."

The governor announced that, when the fall elections took place, he was going to stump every district in the state where an assemblyman who had opposed his program was running and campaign against him. In his long interview with the *Times* reporter, Sulzer referred to an alleged plot to put him out of the way. When the reporter pointed out that the governor ought to give his enemies credit for knowing that could be the worst thing that could happen to them, Sulzer told the reporter that "They know that. . . . But they won't let that stand in the way if they want their chance to achieve their murderous purpose. They won't think any more of that than Becker did when he went after Rosenthal. They are as desperate now as Becker was then."

It was only after he had been questioned at some length that the governor said that his information led him to believe that a plot to get him out of the way had been hatched by his political enemies in Tammany Hall and that he regarded it as serious enough to be made the subject of inquiry by the grand jury in New York County when District Attorney Whitman returned from his present trip to Nova Scotia.

Governor Sulzer said that threats or even plots against his life would not drive him from the firing line nor would they deter him from doing his full duty to the people as governor of the state.

This long and most unusual interview gave the governor the opportunity to expand on the details of his relationship with Mr. Murphy and reemphasized his argument that Murphy was trying to control his administration. He ended the interview with an explanation that he was not a wealthy man despite allegations that he had a considerable private fortune. "I wish that was true," he said reflectively, "but it isn't. I never could accumulate money. You can have all that I possess at this time for $5,000 and I will not be the loser on the bargain."

On the same day that the governor's long interview was reported, Lieutenant Governor Martin Glynn piled on. Sensing the political winds, Sulzer's heir apparent talked about the governor's "quenchless thirst for notoriety." Glynn said, "A little thing like the truth does not prevent Governor Sulzer from saying anything that will get him on the first page of the newspaper. He has a mania for seeing his name in print. He is suffering from first pageitis. His vanity is exceeded only by the peacock and he mistakes the sound of his own name for thunders of popular applause. Anyway he is guilty of the rankest kind of falsehoods in this matter."

When Sulzer's story of Tammany's threats and its plot against him were read to Charles F. Murphy at his country home, Good Ground, on Long Island, a reporter asked Mr. Murphy for a response. He said, "You can say for me that I refuse to take William Sulzer seriously." He was then asked about the governor's statement that he asked the district attorney of New York County to have Murphy indicted. Murphy laughed out loud at the governor and said, "You surely do not expect me to make a serious answer to things like that? . . . who does he think is plotting to kill him? Does he put me among the plotters?"[10]

The July 28th edition of the *New York Times* said one member of the Frawley Committee told the *Times* correspondent that the committee was investigating the governor's campaign fundraising and was looking into the contributions emanating from specific industries such as the racetrack operators and Wall Street, and especially into contributions that had not been reported to the secretary of state as required under New York's Corrupt Practices Act, which required reporting of campaign contributions. Certainly cognizant of the inherent impeachment threat that was being talked about in connection with the Frawley inquiry as the month of July drew to a close, Valentine Taylor, counsel to Governor Sulzer, expressed some legal arguments against the Frawley Committee's efforts to investigate Sulzer's campaign funding. The newspaper reported that Eugene Lamb Richards, counsel to the Frawley Committee, had sent a letter to many state officials and others soliciting detailed information about their campaign contributions to the Sulzer campaign. Taylor issued a statement from the Executive Chamber challenging the committee to call Charles F. Murphy and his close personal aide, Phil Donohue, to discuss campaign contributions that they had received and did not account for. The *Times* reported that the governor's attempt to question the Frawley Committee's outreach to his campaign contributions indicated to sophisticated people that the governor had concluded that his impeachment had been "decreed" by the powers at the wigwam.

As the month came to an end, the Frawley Committee began paying attention to winding up its review of the governor's reports from Mr. Blake about corruption in the prison department, as well as Commissioner Hennessy's review of corruption in the highway department. Commissioner Hennessy was busy sending evidence of highway corruption to a variety of district attorneys in different counties across the state where the reported abuse had taken place.[11]

More important politically, the Frawley Committee scheduled a meeting on Wednesday the 30th to begin its work on the investigation of Sulzer's campaign finances as well as the administration of the $60,000 fund that Sulzer's friends had raised to support the campaign for his direct nominations bill, for which no campaign fundraising statements had been filed.

The day before the hearing was scheduled, in a bold effort to protect himself, the governor asked Attorney General Carmody for an opinion on the legality of the legislature's inquiry into Executive Chamber affairs. The appeal to Carmody was based on the previous record established by Valentine Taylor's objections to Chairman Frawley. The legal point was based on the governor's interpretation of the authority granted to the Frawley Committee in the legislative resolution creating the committee. The governor's letter to the attorney general also sought support for Sulzer's theory that the legislature's recess was tantamount to an adjournment for the purpose that the session had been called.

The governor's request for the attorney general's opinion specified issues concerning the authority and power of the Frawley Committee. It questioned the range of the committee's jurisdiction because its authority had been supplemented on June 25th during the special session to authorize it to inquire into campaign funds and expenditures and was, therefore an inappropriate use of its authority because the state constitution said that, in the special session, the legislature could only deal with those matters specified by the governor.

At the committee hearing on Wednesday the 30th evidence was revealed about the mishandling of funds from the governor's 1912 campaign. The governor's concern, according to the *Times* story of July 30th, was due to information leaked from the committee that several witnesses had been subpoenaed to testify about contributions they had made to the governor's election campaign that had not been reported in his campaign receipts filed with the secretary of state, including Jacob H. Schiff, head of Kuhn, Loeb & Company, who gave a $2,500 check that was not included in the report. Taylor also objected to the scope of the Frawley Committee's authority having been augmented to include the governor's election campaign financing during the special session called by the governor, because the expansion of the committee's authority was not among the items included in the governor's call for the special session.

A few days later, on August 2nd, Attorney General Carmody responded from his honeymoon camp in the Adirondacks with an extensive opinion that rejected most of Sulzer's arguments and provided no comfort to the governor. The attorney general confirmed that the supplemental powers given to the Frawley Committee during the special session of the legislature were appropriate and the committee had the right to subpoena and examine witnesses pertinent to the subject that the committee was authorized to investigate, and that any witness who refused could be guilty of contempt.

The attorney general pointed out that the Frawley Committee's power to investigate the governor's campaign financing was justified because in the governor's call for the special session, he had asked specifically for legislation to strengthen the election laws.

The attorney general also pointed out that the legislature certainly had the power to adjourn a special session to a date certain without the consent of the governor. The governor's inquiry had also raised issues about whether or not both houses had a quorum present when the legislature determined to recess, and Carmody said that, because the official journals of each house showed that a quorum was present and voting and that no question had been raised in either house, the journals were, therefore, conclusive evidence. The attorney general took the opportunity of his own opinion to conclude it by saying that the Frawley Committee's investigation "should be welcomed by every right thinking citizen, anxious to preserve the purity of the ballot."[12]

On July 30th, the Frawley Committee held the first of its two most significant hearings. It started the day by introducing the governor's official campaign finance statement, filed on November 13, 1912, with the secretary of state and sworn to by Sulzer in accordance with the existing corrupt practices section of the election law. In the statement he filed, the governor acknowledged receiving $5,460 from sixty-eight named contributors to his gubernatorial campaign and that he expended $7,724.09 in that campaign. At that time, Article 16, Sections 750 and 776 of the Penal Law required every candidate for public office to file an itemized statement with the secretary of state detailing "all the moneys contributed or expended by him, directly or indirectly." The law said the statement must be accompanied by an affidavit subscribed and sworn by the candidate certifying its truthfulness.

The committee counsel then introduced two checks into evidence, one for $2,500 issued by Kuhn, Loeb & Company to the order to Louis A. Sarecky, who was then a confidential clerk to Congressman Sulzer and administrator of his campaign fund. The face of the check bore a notation by Jacob H. Schiff that it constituted Mr. Schiff's contribution to the Sulzer campaign fund. The back of the check revealed that the check had been deposited by Mr. Sarecky to his personal account with the Mutual Alliance Trust Company of New York. The second check was for $500, contributed by Abraham I. Elkus, a New York lawyer. This check bore the endorsement of William Sulzer who deposited it to his account with the Farmers Loan and Trust Company. Neither check had been listed in the governor's sworn campaign finance report.

Mr. Sarecky was the first person called to the witness chair before the committee that day. Described in the newspapers as "short and slim with a smooth face and rosy cheeks," he said he was twenty-seven years old. Sarecky testified in response to the questions from Eugene Richards, the committee's counsel, that he lived in Brooklyn and was employed as a deportation agent for the alien insane at the New York State Hospital Commission at a salary of $4,000 per year. Sarecky said he was a law school graduate and had been employed by Governor Sulzer as a confidential stenographer ever since December 1902 at a salary that went from $1,500 when he was hired and gradually raised to $2,500. After admitting in response to Mr. Richard's questioning that he had acted as secretary and treasurer of some of the companies that Governor Sulzer was interested in, Sarecky started refusing to answer Richards's questioning by saying, "I do not want to answer that question on the ground that it does not come within the jurisdiction of the committee." After admitting that he was in the position of secretary, stenographer, and clerk to the governor during the 1912 campaign and that he had an account with the Mutual Alliance Trust Company, he refused to answer questions about depositing checks received by the governor and endorsed by himself in his personal account. At that point, Sarecky said to Richards, "if you are delving into the governor's campaign expenses, I am willing to tell everything on condition that I be represented by counsel because, if the story is to be told, I want both sides told."

Throughout a long cross-examination by Richards, Sarecky continued to refuse to cooperate based on advice of counsel who he identified as Louis Marshall, and refused to answer questions about where he had met with Mr. Marshall. When Sarecky left the witness stand, committee chairman Frawley instructed Mr. Richards to take up the necessary papers to cite Sarecky for contempt to punish him for being an employee of the state and refusing to answer the questions of a legislative committee.

Before the day was over, Governor Sulzer issued a statement in reply to what he had heard about the preparation for the hearing. The governor's angry statement said that his attention had been called to the story about Mr. Schiff's contribution, and the fact that he had $25,000 in the bank before he was nominated for governor and $100,000 in the bank after he was elected. The governor said, "Most of this stuff is false and I demand that the Frawley Committee produce everything they have in connection with the matter. I have nothing to conceal." He went on to accuse Senator Frawley of meeting with Mr. Murphy and stated that, during the campaign, he was so busy making speeches around the state he knew little about campaign contributions. His official campaign financing statement was made up by men in his office and he signed it based on their assurances that it was as accurate as could be made. "I took the word of others in whom I had implicit confidence. I was too busy during the campaign to attend to these details. Others did it for me and I relied on them."[13]

It was only after he became governor, he said, that several people told him they had contributed to his campaign, but he knew nothing about it and most of the contributions from his friends in New York City were small contributions. The governor said he spent some of his own money on the campaign. "My friends, I was comparatively poor before I was nominated and I was poorer after I was elected." The governor said, "However, the large contributions from the contractors, the office holders, the special interests, and of prominent Democrats interested in the campaign were made through the bag man, directly to Mr. Murphy." He went on to say, "I want Mr. Murphy to explain the difference between what he accounted for through the state committee and what he received through the bag man. Mr. Murphy is trying to destroy me because I will not be a party to the looting of the state."

The next day, Mr. Murphy himself answered Sulzer's repeated attacks on him. He sent a letter to Chairman Frawley responding to Sulzer's statements that Murphy had a bag man collecting from big contributions. In his letter, Murphy stated, "These insinuations are untrue. If Governor Sulzer has any information as to misconduct on my part relating to campaign contributions, I request him to furnish it to the committee and I will appear for examination at any time."

On August 4th, the governor opened a campaign to secure the nomination and election of assemblymen who are pledged to support his proposal on direct primaries. He made this plea at a gathering of his friends from around the state who the governor called to a conference in the Executive Chamber. He told those in attendance, "my

friends, I am carrying a heavy burden. . . . I have been hounded, tra-
duced, vilified, and threatened as no other man has been who occupied
this office in all of the history of the state." The audience of Sulzer's
partisans expressed unwavering confidence in him. Those same friends
urged him to make a straightforward explanation or denial of the accusations that had been brought against him and vindicate his personal
honor. They advised him that, if he were guilty of carelessness or negli-
gence in handling his campaign, he should have frankly said so. They
made it clear that accusing Murphy of pocketing campaign funds was
not an answer to the allegation that he had falsified the statutory statement of campaign receipts and expenditures. People friendly to Sulzer
felt strongly that the only explanation Sulzer offered was that he had
been away from New York campaigning when the Schiff and Elkus contributions came in was not enough. However, at the next hearing, committee counsel Richards defeated Sulzer's story with evidence that
Sulzer's upstate speaking tour did not begin until several days after the
Schiff and Elkus checks were received and deposited.[14]

On August 6th, the Frawley Committee delivered its final shot at the
governor's head. This time, the scene was the council chamber in New
York City Hall. The committee had decided to move its hearings to New
York City to facilitate the participation of a number of bank officials who
were going to be called as witnesses. This hearing turned out to be monumental because the committee staff revealed additional contributions
that Sulzer had failed to report to the secretary of state and significant
evidence that the governor had diverted large sums contributed to his
campaign. More checks were produced showing contributions from
prominent New Yorkers that had been deposited in Sulzer's personal
account in the Farmers Loan and Trust Company. The evidence produced at that hearing also showed that Sulzer, who had always claimed
to be poor, had deposited some $24,000 of campaign contributions to
his own account between September 1, 1912, and January 1, 1913, and
many of these deposits were in substantial amounts of cash. The committee subpoenaed Sulzer's stockbrokers and showed how he used num-
bered accounts to hide his identity and specific investments. According
to the records produced before the New York City hearing, going back
to the beginning of the year when Sulzer was still a member of Congress,
one of his accounts had some $48,000 in shares. The brokers reported
that, when his account was finally closed out on July 13, 1913, just a few
weeks before the hearing, a little over $26,000 was due to the brokers

and that was paid off by Lt. Commander Louis M. Josephthal, a member of the governor's military staff. As Senator Frawley summed up the situation, "when our committee began work we had a hunch that the full account of the governor's campaign expenditures had not been published as the law requires, but it was a surprise to all of us to find that he had used some of the money contributed for his political expenditures to try a flyer on Wall Street."[15]

The impact of the Frawley Committee's work was dramatic. The governor, who had crisscrossed the state calling the people's attention to his battle against crooks and grafters, had personally raised much more money than he had sworn to having received and had used the campaign contributions to speculate in securities. While an ordinary man might have been forgiven, everyone could see that the man who so publicly espoused his own integrity had been caught red-handed violating the laws that he was sworn to enforce.

The exposure of the governor's malfeasance by the Frawley Committee was a stark lesson to political campaign advisors in 1913 because it became so obvious to sophisticated observers that some of the governor's political problems could have been so easily avoided, or at least diminished, had he disclosed the error of his campaign finance revelations when he first learned of them from friends telling him of contributions they made that he said he didn't know of until after the campaign. In today's times of instant cable television news, candidates of all types are constantly seen to be making public apologies about potentially embarrassing stories before they are exposed by their adversaries or the media. Self-exposure is an accepted political procedure—far preferable to denial of indefensible allegations.

20

The Impeachment Drama

The Frawley Committee's last public hearing on August 6th sealed the fate of Governor William Sulzer. Despite the motivations of those who instigated the investigation, the reputation of a political colleague so carefully constructed and successfully promoted over a quarter of a century was permanently damaged, if not completely destroyed. Only the details of its ending remained to be worked out. He could resign, he could continue to defend himself by attacking the motives of his persecutors, or perhaps he could actually refute the evidence and conceivably survive however unlikely it seemed at the moment.

Among the members of the Frawley Committee, the responsible legislative leaders, and the sachems of the Society of Tammany, there was a commitment that Sulzer's governorship should end before the end of his term. Now, they had to decide which road to take to reach their objective. Choices had to be made. As elected officials, they naturally gravitated to the decisions that would impress the constituents who elect them. Some believed that justice would prevail if they sought an indictment of the governor for violating state law because conviction would automatically disbar him from holding public office. Those who believed in taking this route were convinced that conviction of a crime would take the political heat off Tammany Hall and its elected legislators, and avoid the accusations that were sure to come if they relied on impeachment, which would likely arouse sympathetic public sentiment for a man who only so recently won an impressive elective victory.

Most of the legislators realized that constitutional impeachment by legislative action was the fastest and most certain means to their objective. Besides, there was a realistic concern that the defendant in a criminal case could create sufficient delay to defer a final decision until after the November election when those voters who still supported Sulzer could elect a new assembly that might exonerate him and keep him in office for another year. On the other hand, impeachment could be accomplished before the next election and leave no possibility of appeal. It was only a matter of counting votes—the assemblymen who would impeach and the senators sitting with the court of appeals as the court of impeachment, which would be the deciding tribunal.

Another serious political miscalculation by the governor led to the legislative decision that would be fatal to him. Although he had promptly responded with denials to each of the public revelations against his character—Miss Hopkins, the Vermont case, and his alleged congressional misdeeds—the governor remained silent about embarrassing charges of personal dishonesty involving his campaign funds and the evidence that he diverted campaign cash to himself.

Because the governor had remained silent while the hearings were exposing his mishandling of campaign contributions, reacting instead with repeated challenges to the legitimacy of the hearings and the influence of Mr. Murphy, Sulzer was losing supporters who had been loyal to him in his direct primary battle. His most reliable friends seemed ready to give him the benefit of the doubt if he would explain his side of the accusations that needed to be explained. But, no such explanation was yet forthcoming.

By Thursday, August 7th, the legislative leaders met and resolved their dilemma by deciding to impeach the elected governor of the state of New York. On Friday, August 8, 1913, the *New York Times* reported that, when the legislature reconvened in the following week, the governor would be impeached. The legislative leadership concluded that the Frawley Committee had already produced enough evidence to prove that Sulzer had violated the state's Corrupt Practices Act, and continuing evidence on this would only be cumulative. They believed that the governor's public efforts to block the committee's investigations, his colleagues' refusal to answer questions, and the nature of the evidence already introduced had convinced the public of his wrongful conduct and that he was unfit to hold office.

On the day that the press reported that the leadership made its decision, Governor Sulzer told the press that he had nothing to say.[1] The governor announced that he would refrain from responding to those charges until he had the opportunity to read the transcript of the

Frawley Committee testimony and he said nothing about the damaging evidence. He referred to a statement issued by his secretary, Chester C. Platt, as his only answer for the present. Platt's statement once again attacked the motivation of the legislative committee. He called the Frawley Committee's testimony "fragmentary and garbled." Platt promised, "A full and frank statement of all the facts will be made just as soon as the governor can learn exactly what the facts are. Money was received and paid out to promote the governor's election of which he had no knowledge. He necessarily must delay making any statement until investigations now under way are finished."[2]

On August 9th, despite differing political preferences, every major newspaper editorialized what we can presume, by virtue of the universality of their positions, provides an accurate picture of the public's view of the situation at that moment. The credibility of these views is enhanced by the fact that nearly every one of these newspapers was anti-Tammany. The widespread editorial reaction was effectively captured in Jacob Alexis Friedman's erudite 1938 Columbia University thesis, where he reported,

> "the people of New York do not want to believe these shocking things of the governor of the State," wrote the *Times*, "but if the charges are untrue, why does not Mr. Sulzer deny them at once? If he has any explanation, why does he not make it?" The *Times* said that making "countercharges against Mr. Murphy" were "no answer to the evidence affecting Mr. Sulzer's reputation and honor," and asked "can he be so blind as not to see that his silence will be construed as confession, that any attempt on his part to battle the committee in its work or to evade a full investigation will also be construed as confession?"

As Friedman summarized the editorials, the *Times* pointed out that Sulzer was being subjected to public disgrace only because he refused to remain subservient to the boss, but observed that "it was not Murphy who signed William Sulzer's name to a false statement of campaign contributions and expenditures" or diverted his campaign contributions to speculations on Wall Street. The *Times* considered Sulzer's public usefulness over, regardless of any defense he might offer, and called upon him to "save the State of New York further shame and humiliation" by resigning. The *Tribune* said there was no possibility for the governor to escape the issue and wrote that it was "sickening to see a Governor who went into office with bright prospects and who had the people's confidence and support while they believed he was honestly fighting corruption, remain silent under disgraceful charges affecting his personal integrity and his political honor." The *Evening Post*, unfriendly to Sulzer and Tammany, ridiculed the governor's hypocrisy and declared that it preferred "a plain unadulterated Tammany rascal, who stands for what he is, to a politician sinner turned saint for a moment." Even Hearst's *American* told the governor to stop quibbling about the legality of the investigation and stop attacking the motives of his accusers.

Sulzer got the message. At one o'clock in the morning of August 11, 1913, with the assembly due to convene that same evening, after a long midnight conference with his close political and legal advisors, the governor finally issued a statement denying that he used campaign contributions for his personal use or that he had used campaign contributions to speculate in Wall Street in his name or otherwise. He specifically denied that he had accounts with some of the firms whose officers had testified that he did, and he claimed that whatever contributions were deposited in his personal accounts were subsequently paid into his campaign account with his own checks. He said that, when he filed his campaign statement with the secretary of state, he relied on information provided by his staff and believed those statements to be accurate and true.

His denial did not dispose of many of the specific allegations in the testimony against him. As the denial was not backed by any evidence, it was unsatisfactory, even to those who supported him, according to the *Times* of August 11th.

The next day, after receiving the governor's general denial, with impeachment imminent, many of the state's newspaper editorials modified their commentary, universally moving toward questioning whether impeachment was appropriate under the circumstances. The *Times* editorial of August 12th picked apart the governor's "denial" point by point and called on the Frawley Committee to continue its investigation and give the governor "every chance to clear himself." The *Times* also summarized the editorials of many of the leading newspapers across the state. Although calling Sulzer "a political wreck beyond repair," the *Syracuse Post Standard* said, "but it by no means follows that he will be impeached," and concluded that, if he made a complete confession, "while he would stand convicted of gross hypocrisy—perhaps of personal dishonesty—we doubt whether he would be guilty of an offense properly punished by impeachment."

The *Rochester Democrat and Chronicle* urged conviction under the Corrupt Practices Act as the appropriate means to end his political career. The *Buffalo Express* called the governor's denial an "amazing" feature of the Frawley Committee's investigation, but advocated giving him an opportunity to provide evidence before the assembly impeached him. All of these upstate papers were generally considered to be Republican. The *Times*, which had been a strong Sulzer admirer in New York City, pointed out that the governor's "public shame and disgrace" was "only because he broke with the organization and refused to take further orders from Murphy," otherwise Tammany would have protected him as it did other miscreants. Hearst's *American*, owned by Sulzer's friend and frequent ally, said, "the denial issued by Governor Sulzer is too late and too sweeping to help him." The Republican *Tribune* warned the governor against trying to defend himself with technicalities which only confirmed the "despicable impression" that his delay in responding had already produced.[3]

The legislative drama approached its pinnacle on August 11th, the Monday to which the special session had been adjourned in July. The day of drama had begun at 1 a.m. with the release of "Governor Sulzer's Midnight Denial," as the press named it. After the sun rose, the Frawley Committee issued its detailed interim report summarizing the results of its hearings over the past few weeks, analyzing the significance of the evidence it had collected, and the testimony it had heard under oath. It contained very few surprises as the hearings were well covered. The report concluded with a call for "an answer from Governor Sulzer, because both his obstructive tactics and his silence warrant the conclusion that the charges can neither be answered nor explained."[4]

Then, as now, Monday sessions usually began each week of legislative activity in the evening to allow members time to travel to Albany during the day. On this historic day, Albany was full of tremendous anticipation. The galleries of the legislative chambers were crowded with spectators who had arrived early to secure seats in the limited space available in the chamber. Many others were allowed into standing room behind a rail at the back of the Assembly Chamber where the initial action was expected to occur (three or four men actually stood inside of the three great fireplaces that line the chamber's rear wall).

Alfred E. Smith, Speaker of Assembly. *The New York Red Book*, 1913.

Speaker Al Smith did not call the assembly to order until 10 p.m. The majority leader, Assemblyman Aaron J. Levy, a short, somewhat pudgy, and bespectacled practicing litigator from Senator Frawley's assembly district in lower Manhattan, who, with Tammany support, had consistently won his seat overwhelmingly in five elections, had been elected unanimously as majority leader in 1913. Levy introduced a resolution detailing Sulzer's offenses and calling for his impeachment "for willful and corrupt conduct in office and for high crimes and misdemeanors." The resolution summarized the important charges emanating from the Frawley Committee about the fake campaign finance report he had signed under oath, his conversion of campaign contributions to "purchase of securities or other private uses," his engagement in stock speculation while he was governor vigorously pressing for legislation that would affect the business and prices of the New York Stock Exchange, his use of his gubernatorial office to "suppress the truth" and "prevent the production of evidence in relation to the investigation" while directing witnesses, including state employees, to act in contempt of the investigating committee, and that he had "punished legislators who disagreed or differed with him."

With 150 members, the assembly needed only a majority—seventy-six votes—to adopt the impeachment resolution. The assembly leadership had been counting noses assiduously, seeking eighty as a wise cushion, but a sufficient number of Democrats had not yet arrived in the assembly chamber. Less than one hundred assemblymen were already in attendance. As a result, at about 1 a.m., both houses of the legislature adjourned until 11 a.m. the next day—Tuesday, August 12th.[5]

Some objections were promptly raised to the plans for impeachment. The Democrats were taken by surprise when the assembly minority leader, Harold J. Hinman of Albany, moved to delay the impeachment resolution, arguing that the Democratic leadership was moving too fast. The Democrats were taken by surprise because they had presumed that William J. Barnes, the powerful state Republican Party boss, would be sympathetic to his Democratic counterpart, Charles F. Murphy, but the Republicans had decided to leave the dirty work to Democrats in hope it might inure to their benefit in the next election. The motion to delay by Assemblyman Hinman was defeated on a straight party vote.

The Frawley Committee report was introduced for acceptance and, after a long debate, it was adopted by the assembly by a vote of 65 to 35. Most of the Democrats were in favor and four Republicans joined them. Nineteen Democrats and fifteen Republicans voted nay, along with one Progressive. Afterward, Hinman called it "precipitate action" and noted that the Republicans "have held aloof . . . and taken no part in this disgraceful proceeding." Hinman was obviously establishing a political posture for the Republican future when he said, "while Sulzer may not have been a good official, he is entitled to fair treatment. We are not concerned in Sulzer, the man, but Sulzer the governor."

Assemblyman Louis A. Cuvillier, a Spanish-American War veteran and a lawyer from Manhattan, challenged Hinman, saying that, if Sulzer had collected $65,000 instead of the reported $5,000, he was committing perjury when he signed the report and swore to its accuracy. Then he read from Sulzer's own gubernatorial campaign literature where he claimed credit for introducing legislation for the New York Corrupt Practices Act years ago when he was an assemblyman himself.[6]

The events of the next day, August 12th, would be more dramatic than anything ever before or since in the Assembly Chamber.

Majority leader Aaron Levy had adjourned the assembly until 11 a.m. the next day, August 12, 1913—a date that would soon leave an indelible stain in the history of the Empire State, a date when the excitement of the anticipated events would be exceeded by the impact of what was about to take place. No governor of New York had ever been impeached.

During the debate about the impeachment resolution, Sulzer was holed up with his political and legal advisors in the Executive Mansion on Eagle Street, just a few blocks from the Capitol. He and his loyal staff were doing everything they could conceive of to avoid the inevitable disgrace of impeachment. He contacted several members of the legislature to appeal for their consideration or reconsideration. The most poignant conversation that was eventually reported was his personal confrontation with Senator Frawley, a longtime Tammany man who had spoken up on Sulzer's behalf on several occasions before his investigation began. According to the *Times* of August 14th, as Frawley told the story, the governor said, "Jim—this has gone too far. I didn't expect anything like this and I know you didn't." When Frawley indicated that there was nothing he could do, Sulzer said, "let me tell you that if I am impeached there will be a revolution in New York State

THE LEGISLATURE IN SESSION

Between three and five o'clock Wednesday morning, August 13, 1913
Aaron J. Levy's Speech at sunrise.

From Jay W. Forrest and James Malcolm, *Tammany's Treason,
Impeachment of Governor Sulzer: The Complete Story Written from behind
the Scenes, Showing How Tammany Plays the Game, How Men Are
Bought, Sold and Delivered* (Albany: The Fort Orange Press, 1913).

within twenty-four hours. The people elected me and they won't stand for my being removed this way."

Before the impeachment resolution was adopted, Chester Platt, secretary to the governor, was busy sending telegrams to friendly party leaders around the state, imploring them to influence their own assemblymen to support the governor. Sulzer's people also appealed by telegraph to assistant secretary of the navy and former senator Franklin D. Roosevelt, and to John Purroy Mitchel, federal appointee as collector of the port of New York, to try and get them to involve themselves on behalf of Sulzer with President Wilson, but nothing came of this effort according to the *Tribune* of November 2nd. Throughout the day, Charles F. Murphy was receiving periodic progress reports by telephone at his New York City residence.

When the assembly convened at 11 a.m., Majority Leader Levy saw that there were not yet enough of his supporters present to count on the eighty votes they had determined to be a safe number to assure the necessary seventy-six-vote majority, so Levy moved to adjourn until 8:30 that evening. Telegraphed commands were sent to members all day long to compel their attendance. The absentees began arriving in the afternoon and evening, but late for the session that had originally been called for 11 a.m. Meanwhile, the deputy sergeants-at-arms had been dispatched by the Speaker to go throughout Albany to round up those who were already in town. Other groups were meeting trains at the station to escort assemblymen up the hill to their desks on the assembly floor. At the same time a crowd was gathering to witness the anticipated event.

As the *Times* described the situation, "a throng eclipsing any that had stormed the capitol in the memory of the oldest attendant poured through its stone doorways. Two hours before the time set for calling the assembly to order in night session the first-comers had taken their stand outside the railing in the assembly chamber. Hundreds were standing at 7:30 o'clock. At 8 o'clock the great doors to the assembly chamber closed in the face of a grumbling crowd in the corridor. The galleries were packed. Hundreds of women were among the crowd."

Rumors were flying about all day long. One that started early in the day said the governor might call out the militia, of which he was the commander-in-chief, and attempt to keep his office by force of arms.

Another rumor in circulation that had reached the assembly leadership said that an attempt might be made to break up the impeachment session by physical force, and that a large squad of "strong arm men" was living in a rooming house on State Street for the past few months and they had been visited by people identified with the governor.

The assembly leaders, deciding to take no chance, established a security system that required—for the first time in a generation—that admission to the assembly chamber required a card signed by the speaker and cosigned by a member.

As tension rose among the members, hundreds of curious onlookers had already crowded into the chamber, filling the spectators' gallery and the standing room that had been created for them behind the rail at the back of the chamber.

The assembled members waited casually in their chairs, talking among themselves and occasionally with friends and constituents they spotted in the chamber, smoking cigars and cigarettes, filling the assembly's ashtrays and brass spittoons, reading newspapers, and not yet giving any sign of the momentous decisions that they were about to make, as the situation was described in the *Times* edition the next day. Eleven minutes past 10 o'clock, Speaker Al Smith banged his huge gavel and called the house to order. In his distinctive, Lower East Side accent, he demanded that "the gentlemen in the gallery will kindly stop smoking."[7]

"The Clerk will call the roll," ordered the Speaker. One hundred and twenty-three members responded, eighty-six Democrats, thirty-five Republicans, and two Progressives. Mr. Levy and his managers were now confident about who they could rely on. Mr. Hinman, the Republican leader, rose to argue that all of the offenses that the Frawley Committee report referred to predated the governor's swearing in on January 1st, and that he could not be legally impeached for offenses that occurred before he took office. Hinman also made the other pointed legal argument—that the state constitution limited the subjects of a special session of the legislature to only those specific matters that were included in the governor's call for the extraordinary session. Impeachment of the governor was certainly not an item on Governor Sulzer's proposed agenda. Others, of course, argued that the impeachment power rested with the assembly at its discretion, regardless of whether or not it was in session. Hinman also made the point that the governor was entitled to be represented by counsel before the Frawley Committee or the assembly before they could indict him, pointing out that the Frawley Committee had denied counsel to the governor's colleagues who appeared before them.

The real surprise of the morning was the sensational interruption of the debate at 2 a.m. by Republican leader Hinman's information that new evidence just revealed that the governor's wife had told a certain legislator that she was the one who diverted campaign contributions to the stock market and the governor did not know about it. Mr. Hinman argued that this was in the nature of new evidence and should at least justify a delay in the proceedings. Mr. Hinman made a motion to delay the proceedings because of his understanding that Mrs. Sulzer had admitted to having forged the governor's name to some of the checks that were used by the Frawley Committee because she was trying to use some of the campaign funds to make some money in the stock market to provide for their old age. The delaying motion was defeated by a vote of 78 to 49 and produced an early sign of the success of the majority in the eventual impeachment vote.

Mrs. Sulzer's last-minute story was anticipated by the Democratic Party leaders and considered to be just another fraud by Sulzer and they gave it no consideration. Mrs. Sulzer's story shared the blaring headlines of the day for just a moment.

The actual debate was enlightening and extensive, and certainly afforded a clear opportunity for expression by each of the factions in the chamber. Every member who chose to express his own perspective had the opportunity to do so. Different members rose during the wee hours of that fateful morning to make their arguments.

Representing an uptown Manhattan district that remained independent of Tammany was Democrat assemblyman Louis D. Gibbs. He was thirty-two years old and a well-educated lawyer serving his first term. Gibbs expressed the view that in the history of the nation no public official was ever impeached for offenses committed before taking office. If an elected official commits a crime before taking office, the remedy is to try him in a court of law as any other citizen would be tried. The purpose of impeachment is to punish an elected official for offenses committed while in office. "Why impeach the governor if he has committed a crime," he asked the other members of the assembly. "If the governor had been guilty of murder prior to his taking office, he could not be impeached."

Gibbs expressed the view of many others that "the men who are trying to drive the governor out of office are promoters of a vicious political system," and said, "at the same time they impeach the Democratic

Party. Maybe they have done so already. . . . Everybody knows that the reason why Sulzer is being demanded as a victim is that he had the manhood to refuse to be tied to the wheels of a certain political chariot."

The *Times* of August 13th published a detailed account of the events in and surrounding the Assembly Chamber, beginning on August 12th, leading up to the eventual impeachment vote early the next morning. In order to meet publication deadlines, the early edition had to go to press before the story was over. When the *Times* went to bed, its last dispatch from Albany generated the headline that the assembly was: "READY WITH VOTES TO IMPEACH HIM, ASSEMBLY DEBATING SULZER AT 3:30 AM, GOVERNOR'S WIFE WOULD TAKE BLAME." The story was dated "Albany, Wednesday, August 13" and marked the time of its last dispatch as 3 a.m., when the assembly was still debating Majority Leader Levy's impeachment resolution. When Levy addressed the house at that late hour it had been in session since eleven minutes after 10 p.m. the night before: "Mr. Levy spoke to a sleeping house." As the *Times* described it, "in every conceivable attitude of fatigue his fellow assemblymen lay back in their chairs, most of them with their eyes closed, or their heads sunk forward on their bosoms. Those not assuredly asleep were not discernibly awake, save for the party leaders and their active lieutenants."

The usually elegant and formidable Assembly Chamber was a chaotic mess with newspapers read and reread, and pages of bills and memos littering the floor. "Back of the railing where a crowd of hundreds had braved the long vigil and were still wide awake and waiting, newsboys did a thriving business in the morning papers featuring the deliberations. . . . Some of the assemblymen bought papers and read at their desks accounts of what had been said and done by themselves a few hours before." By the *Times'* last report at 3 a.m., the spectator galleries that had been full when the session began, "with a standing throng of spectators, were deserted, except for the strong detail of uniformed police on guard at the door of the chamber."

By that time most of the substance of the debate had been heard when at 3 a.m., Mr. Levy began his own peroration, summarizing the case for the majority. Mr. Levy had delayed the debate until he and his cohorts were certain that they had gathered up a sufficient number of supportive assemblymen to be assured of enacting the impeachment resolution.

New York senate receiving impeachment resolution, August 13, 1913.
From Jay W. Forrest and James Malcolm, *Tammany's Treason, Impeach-
ment of Governor Sulzer: The Complete Story Written from behind the Scenes,
Showing How Tammany Plays the Game, How Men Are Bought, Sold and
Delivered* (Albany: The Fort Orange Press, 1913).

Mr. Levy spoke for two hours—summarizing his case and responding to every issue raised by those members who were firmly opposed to
impeachment—or merely sought to delay it. Just after 5 a.m. the roll
call began. When it was over, William Sulzer was assured of his place in
history as the only governor of New York ever impeached. He was
charged with "willful and corrupt conduct in office and high crimes
and misdemeanors." The vote was 79 in favor and 45 opposed. Seventy-
two Democrats joined by seven Republicans constituted the majority.
The opposition was comprised of twenty-six Democrats, sixteen Republicans and all three Progressives.

The well-planned procedures were then instituted. A committee of
three was dispatched to the waiting senate to ask that body to order the
appearance of William Sulzer to answer the charges. Another committee of five members was appointed by the Speaker to prepare the arti-

cles of impeachment that the assembly was obligated to provide. Majority leader Levy was designated as the head of that committee. Within the allotted time, the committee returned with specifications, similar to an indictment in a criminal case. It combined the results of the Frawley Committee's report with citations of the appropriate sections of the Penal Law. As summarized in the aforementioned work of Jacob Alexis Friedman:

> Article I accused Sulzer of "willfully, knowingly, and corruptly 'making and filing with the Secretary of State a false statement of campaign receipts and expenditures in connection with his campaign for Governor,' in express violation of the statutes of the state." (Eleven contributions, aggregating $8,500 were specified as having been omitted.)
>
> Article II accused him of "willful and corrupt perjury" in making oath that his statement of campaign receipts was correct, in violation of section 1620 of the Penal Code.
>
> Article III accused him of "bribing witnesses" and, in violation of section 2440 of the Penal Law, "fraudulently" inducing Louis A. Sarecky, Frederick L. Colwell, and Melville B. Fuller "to withhold true testimony" from the legislative investigating committee.
>
> Article IV accused him of suppressing evidence by "practicing deceit and fraud and using threats and menaces" to prevent the investigating committee to procure the attendance and testimony of those same witnesses, in violation of section 814 of the Penal Law.
>
> Article V accuses him of "preventing and dissuading" a witness, Frederick L. Colwell, from answering the subpoena of the same committee, in violation of the statutes of the state and of section 2441 of the Penal Law.
>
> Article VI accused him of larceny, in having converted and appropriated to his own use and to stock speculation eleven checks totaling $8,500 and 32,850 in cash contributed to his campaign fund, in violation of sections 1290 and 1294 of the Penal Law.
>
> Article VII accused him of improperly using his Executive authority and influence "for the purpose of affecting the vote

or political action" of certain members of the Legislature by promising to sign or threatening to veto bills in which they were interested, in violation of section 775 of the Penal Law. (Assemblymen Prime and Sweet were specified as persons to whom such promises of threats were made.)

Article VIII accused him of corruptly using the influence of his office to affect the prices of securities selling on the New York Stock Exchange, in some of which he was at the time speculating, in violation of the statutes of the state and section 775 of the Penal Law.

These were the specific charges the governor would have to answer at the forthcoming trial, set to take place before the court of impeachment to commence in the Capitol on September 18, 1913, at noon. The Constitution of the State of New York created the court of impeachment to consist of the entire senate and the judges of the court of appeals, the chief judge to be the presiding officer. Each member of the court would have one vote and the court's decision would require a majority of two-thirds.

The assembly's constitutional business was concluded with the adoption of the impeachment articles by a vote of 79 to 29 after only a brief debate, and the appointment by the Speaker of nine members as "managers" to prosecute the case on behalf of the assembly before the court of impeachment. The managers designated by Speaker Smith included seven Democrats and two Republicans, who were authorized to employ counsel and have all the powers of a legislative committee, which included the right to issue subpoenas and take testimony under oath. The managers were also required to convey the articles of impeachment to the senate.

As the final act of the assembly before adjourning in the early morning of August 13th, the special session passed the Blauvelt bill on reforming the election law by a vote of 108 to 5—the bill the governor had denounced as a "fraud and a show."

After setting the date for the impeachment court to meet, the senate concurred unanimously in passing the Blauvelt bill and adjourned until August 19th.[8]

21

Reactions

Sulzer was badly beaten by Murphy in the biggest battle of their war—but the war was not yet over. Both the pros and cons of the impeachment issue were galvanized by the fact that it had actually happened and how it came about. Despite the scandalous personal conduct of Sulzer that was revealed, or at least alleged by the Frawley Committee, great segments of the American public, even some beyond the state's borders, were aghast at the extent of Tammany's power and the length of its reach.

In 1913 there was no television or radio to spread the news. Newspapers and popular magazines, of which there were many, were the only way for Americans to know what was going on in the times or in their own state or locality.

For political information, attending a meeting, rally, or a speech provided the interested public with firsthand information and also explained why those events were attended by large audiences that far exceeded the numbers who attend such opportunities today.

Once again, we can turn to the op-ed pages to examine the range of thought and differing positions that constituted the people's reaction to the assembly's achievement and the governor's humiliation. Sulzer himself had forewarned Senator Frawley and others who spoke to him on the eve of impeachment that there would be a revolt against Tammany if they went through with their plan. Sulzer warned several legislators that the people would not support those who were responsible for his embarrassment. Sulzer would turn out to be right. Following the impeachment, editorials and letters to the editor almost universally expressed contempt for Tammany, but were divided on whether Sulzer deserved what he got and if he was a good guy or a bad guy. On August 14th the *Buffalo Courier*, a paper generally supportive of Democrats, summed it up well: "Whatever may be the failings of Gov. Sulzer, the gunman method of seizing the executive office and turning the whole administrative branch of the State Government into a Murphy annex deserves the severest popular condemnation."

Even the *New York Times*, which had long been known as the enemy of Tammany, pointed out in its own editorial reaction on August 14th that Sulzer had invited his own impeachment by his betrayal of the principles of honesty that he had so frequently professed, by playing "fast and loose with his own integrity" and "betraying the principles which he pretends to represent, he must take the consequences."

The *Elmira Advertiser* took a harder position on August 13th: "The people honored him thoroughly, and this very fact makes his usefulness as Governor at an end, come what will." On August 13th, the *Rochester Democrat and Chronicle* said the governor had forfeited his future but criticized the assembly's "uncalled for haste in voting for impeachment," and the *Syracuse Post-Standard*, an avowedly Republican newspaper, said that the governor "probably deserved impeachment, but he was not impeached because he deserves it," and blamed Tammany because "he had proven faithless to Tammany Hall." On the same day, however, the *Utica Press* added an interesting perspective: "The overwhelming majority of opinion among the better element would sooner see Sulzer succeed." Back in New York City, where the attention was intense, the *Times* editorial of August 19th asked the question "because Murphy is known to be a sinner, must the Sulzer transgressions be overlooked?"

The impeachment of Governor Sulzer by the New York State Assembly became national news. The dispatches and editorials of a century ago reveal the significance to the nation of what happened in Albany in 1913. Editors and columnists around the country were inclined toward the view that New York was going through a crisis between a flawed governor and the power of Tammany to control vital government agencies, patronage, and government contracts. *The Nation* magazine pointed out that "hatred" of Murphy "almost takes on the guise of love of Sulzer."

The fact that the story of Sulzer's impeachment has been so completely overlooked today is even more remarkable when we see how it grabbed national attention a century ago, when people elsewhere paid major attention to it in the form of the editorials and stories by American's most well-known newspapers and magazines at a time when they were the only sources of news. The *Philadelphia Record* found it was unable "to believe that a man who had the moral courage to defy the powerful boss, with foreknowledge of the consequences, could have been guilty of such mean and dishonorable conduct in the administration of his campaign funds." The *Independent* wrote on August 7th, "the nation has before it the edifying spectacle of the administration of a great state hamstrung because its chief executive, the representative of the sovereign people of the state, will not obey the dictates of a political boss." The magazine *Times Work* asserted that the real reason for the governor's humiliation was "his refusal to hand over the powers of his office to Tammany" and expressed its concern as to whether "corrupt bossism and special privilege shall by 'constitutional' methods strangle popular government in New York State." The range of views was exemplified by an article in the Louisville, Kentucky, *Courier Journal* on April 23rd saying that Sulzer's impeachment proved that the people of New York were "incapable of self-government." The Norfolk *Virginia Pilot* said that "The whole proceeding smacks of persecution of a retaliatory nature and is therefore to be viewed with extreme suspicion." The *Baltimore Sun* expressed its concern that people saw news of the impeachment as "the organized effort of an unscrupulous political machine, which has always stood, and still stands, for all that is worst in politics and business, to maintain its supremacy and to keep the people out of their rights," and the *Atlantic Journal* disclosed that "though Sulzer be guilty, the really dangerous criminal is not he, but his hypocritical accuser." *Harper's Weekly* attacked the leadership of Tammany Hall for turning on a governor of their own selection, but nevertheless concluded that "Governor Sulzer cannot excuse himself by showing how bad Tammany Hall is. He must stand or fall by his own performances."[1]

Theodore Roosevelt remained supportive and on the eve of the impeachment trial wrote to Governor Sulzer: "I have yet to meet a single person who believes, or even pretends to believe, that a single honest motive has animated the proceedings of your antagonists . . . we have never seen a more startling example of the power of the invisible government under the present system." But Roosevelt's letter also advised him that he owed it to himself and his supporters to give a "full and straightforward explanation."[2]

For the past few months the state had been in utter chaos because of the Sulzer-Murphy war with different state agencies responding to the governor and firing loyal Tammany Braves while hiring people loyal to him, or at least opposed to Tammany. Questions now arose as to which governor's signature would be required by the state comptroller on pay vouchers. Would anybody ask the attorney general for an opinion? Chaos reigned.

A great issue arose immediately following adoption of the impeachment resolution and its transmission to the senate to set up the court of impeachment. Lieutenant Governor Martin Glynn had automatically become acting governor of New York State by virtue of the impeachment. According to the state constitution in effect in August of 1913, it was very clear that at the moment when the assembly presented its impeachment resolution to the senate, the governor's responsibilities were to be performed by the lieutenant governor until the trial was over. The constitution anticipated that, if the governor were acquitted, he would resume his duties and, if he were removed from office, the lieutenant governor then became the governor for the balance of his term. The operative section of the constitution was one long sentence known as article 4, section 6, which read as follows: "In case of the impeachment of the governor or his removal from office, death, inability to discharge the powers and duties of the said office, resignation, or absence from the State, the powers and duties of the office shall devolve upon the Lieutenant Governor for the residue of the term, or until the disability shall cease."

To some it seemed quite clear that the word "impeachment" was intended to be treated as a separate item in addition to the word "removal" and the lieutenant governor was expected to take over. Governor Sulzer and his legal experts read it differently. They asserted that as the word "impeachment" was used in the state constitution it was implicit that the intent was to apply only to impeachment that resulted in removal. To do otherwise would violate the basic American principle of innocent until proven guilty. They pointed to the not too distant past. In 1868 when President Andrew Johnson was impeached in Washington, no one expected him to give up his office pending the outcome of the trial in which he was acquitted. The U.S. Constitution contains no provision for an impeached president to surrender his duties unless he is removed from office.

Nevertheless, the lieutenant governor announced that, by virtue of the language of the constitution, he regarded himself as acting governor of the state and that until the trial was over he was going to conduct the business of the governor's office. He most sensitively announced that he would not seek to occupy the Executive Chamber and would not resort to force to get into it, but that he would conduct the affairs of the state from the smaller office he occupied on the third floor of the Capitol as lieutenant governor.[3]

When the governor announced his position he was surrounded by the several prominent lawyers who had agreed to represent him. They made it clear that the dispute over who was the momentary governor would only be resolved by the courts and there were several ways to accomplish that, including a test of a pardon issued by Governor Sulzer before his impeachment, which had not yet been sent to the Bureau of Prisons, to see whether or not the pardoned prisoner would be released.

Because he was firmly committed to his own interpretation of the constitution, Sulzer was easily convinced that he was responsible for carrying out the duties of the office of governor until the impeachment court made a decision, and he steadfastly refused to leave the Executive Chamber. Lieutenant Governor Glynn, a former two-term congressman and state comptroller in the administration of Governor Charles Evans Hughes, relying on the clear language of the state constitution believed that it was now his responsibility to carry on as acting governor. Sulzer suggested that they avoid "any unseemly struggle" and submit the issue to the courts for a decision. Glynn rejected the suggestion, stating his view that the constitution devolved the duties on himself and Sulzer should know that it was "beyond his power to barter away any of the few items attached to the office of which I am placed by your impeachment," and that the matter could only be resolved by the court of impeachment and no lower court's decision would apply. Both of them publicly rejected suggestions that they should enforce their position by use of the military or police forces and each let it be known that they would not resort to force. Glynn also said he would stay in his lieutenant governor's office and work from there to avoid challenging Sulzer's use of the Executive Chamber until the matter was legally resolved. Sulzer kept the Executive Chamber locked and guarded by armed guards anyway and actually secured the executive privy seal with chains. As a result, state government was seriously imperiled, people did not get paid as the state comptroller refused to honor Sulzer's signature on pay vouchers, contractors stopped work on highway and construction projects, and governors of other states did not know to which office they should direct extradition warrants.[4]

Finally, on August 18th, Attorney General Carmody (a Tammany man) issued a formal opinion totally supporting Glynn's position with appropriate legal arguments interpreting the constitution. In his opinion, the attorney general also addressed the frequently repeated claim that the governor could not be impeached during a special session of the legislature. He explained that impeachment was a judicial function assigned to the assembly by the constitution, and could not be restricted because the assembly was obligated to exercise that function at any time it determined to do so.[5] This opinion was subsequently sustained by the impeachment court.

Glynn acted in a wise and responsible manner. He announced that he had no intention of making any new policies or radical changes in the civil personnel pending the decision of the court of impeachment. Glynn reassured the public that "there would be no political earthquakes and no factional reprisals." The legislature accepted Glynn as acting governor. Meanwhile, the New York City corporate counsel advised the city's correction department that they should not surrender prisoners on any warrants issued by Sulzer. By the end of the month, a state superior court justice presiding over a habeas corpus proceeding designed to free a prisoner who had been pardoned by Governor Sulzer ruled Sulzer's pardon void, pointing out that the assembly had acted under its constitutional powers and that the governor's impeachment eliminated the governor's powers, however, "unjustifiable and unreasonable" the constitution might be. The superior court justice pointed out that by making the governor's suspension mandatory the state constitution had indeed usurped the fundamental rule of justice in America that a man is innocent until proven guilty.[6] An appeal on behalf of Sulzer was also rejected on the grounds that the matter could only be determined by a court of impeachment.

Eventually, on the day after the impeachment trial began, Sulzer formally recognized Glynn as acting governor and had his secretary send some official documents to Glynn for his signature.

Interestingly enough the state constitution was changed in 1963 to clarify the point and now makes it clear that when a governor is impeached, absent from the state, or unable to discharge his duties, the lieutenant governor acts as governor "until the liability shall cease," thus creating a constitutional exception in New York to the basic American principle of innocence until proven guilty.

Two major legal issues had been raised by Sulzer, his supporters, and his attorneys prior to the actual impeachment. They had been mentioned in the impeachment debate. Eventually those issues would have to be resolved at the actual impeachment trial and the governor's defenders hoped they would prove to be determinative.

First, the point had been expressed that most of the more serious, easily evidenced, and proven allegations against the governor arose out of matters that occurred during his 1912 campaign and before his 1913 inauguration. Specifically, the charge of violating the state Corrupt Practices Act by filing a false report of his campaign funds with the secretary of state, a filing that was made under oath as required by a statute that Assemblyman Sulzer had himself sponsored (but did not pass) at least twenty years earlier, resulting in a charge of the crime of perjury. Sulzer and his supporters asserted that a governor could not be impeached for offenses committed before he became governor and that, in the whole history of impeachment across the United States of America, nobody had ever been successfully impeached for misconduct prior to their election.

The other major legal issue was the claim of Sulzer's friends and attorneys that, once the legislature adjourns and the governor calls a special or extraordinary session (which the governor is empowered to do under the state constitution), the subjects to be considered at that session are only those laid out in the governor's call and no other subjects can be addressed. Accordingly, said Sulzer's supporters, as the governor's agenda for the special session did not list his own impeachment as one of the items, there was no authority for the legislature to vote to impeach him while they were in attendance at that extraordinary session. Because they had adjourned *sine die* at the beginning of May they could not come into session again until the next legislature convened in January 1914, unless the governor called them for the special purposes specified in his call. Parenthetically, the foresight of the legislative leadership was such that the Frawley Committee was created on the very eve of the adjournment in May so that its ongoing functions could not be legally objectionable. (A few amendments to the committee's authority were made during the special session.) The legislature's army of lawyers paid little heed to the Sulzer side's arguments on this because they reasoned that the power of impeachment was an inherent power of the assembly and that it was inconceivable that the framers of the state constitution intended to limit that power to only the days when they were in regular session. They distinguished between the assembly's judicial power, which did not require them to be in session in order to act and allowed them to gather at their own call at any time for judicial purposes, or to allow legislative committees to function when the body was not in session, and its administrative power to legislate, which could only be done during a regular session or a special session. It is interesting to note that in today's times, the legislature usually does not adjourn *sine die* when it completes its first session at the beginning of the year, but merely adjourns so it can be called back into session by its leaders whenever appropriate or convenient for them to do so. The attorney general's recent opinion had argued against Sulzer's position. However, the final resolution of this issue would have to wait adjudication at the trial of the impeachment, the date of which had been set for September 18th. These legal issues, while of great interest to the lawyers and of some interest to the public, could await resolution without having any more detrimental impact than had the impeachment itself.

22

The Trial of Governor Sulzer

The court for the trial of impeachments convened as scheduled, in . the elegant Senate Chamber in the Capitol at noon on Thursday, September 18, 1913. Pursuant to the rules, the Honorable Edgar M. Cullen, chief judge of the court of appeals, would be the presiding judge of the impeachment court created by the state constitution. The court consisted of the judges of the court of appeals (seven had been elected and three selected by the governor from among the judges of the state supreme court), plus all fifty-one elected state senators. One of the ten court of appeals judges was missing on a long-scheduled European vacation. Three of the elected senators were missing, Senator Franklin D. Roosevelt, who had resigned earlier in the year, when he was appointed assistant secretary of the navy by President Wilson; Senator Stephen Stilwell was unable to get to Albany from Sing Sing prison, where he was serving a term for attempted extortion; and a third senator, John C. Fitzgerald, was absent due to illness.

During the weeks before the trial began, the Senate Chamber had been carefully prepared for the historic event. Changes were thoughtfully designed by the state architect in order to provide an awesome setting for the occasion. Henry Morganthau,[1] an important Sulzer friend and supporter who played a small part in the case, described the appearance of the chamber in his 1922 autobiography, *All in a Lifetime*. There were three tiers of seats with a high single seat for the presiding judge of the high court of impeachment; a tier below provided a long seat for the eight associate judges, which was followed by two ascending tiers of seats for the forty-eight state senators. Morganthau said that the setting "gave the event a fictitious dignity."

Honorable Edgar M. Cullen, chief judge of the court of appeals, 1913.
From Jay W. Forrest and James Malcolm, *Tammany's Treason, Impeachment of Governor Sulzer: The Complete Story Written from behind the Scenes, Showing How Tammany Plays the Game, How Men Are Bought, Sold and Delivered* (Albany: The Fort Orange Press, 1913).

The impeachment court opened with a degree of pomp and circumstance never before seen in Albany. At 12 noon, the designated hour, the Senate Chamber's doors opened to what the *Times* called "a solemn and exalted tribunal," which actually commenced with senate majority leader Robert Wagner banging his oversized gavel to demand the senators vote approval of a resolution appointing a committee of senators to notify the judges of the court of appeals, then also located in the Capitol, that the senate was ready to go ahead with the trial of William Sulzer, and to escort them to the senate chamber.

There was a clang of metal as brass bolts were drawn and brass bars shifted to swing open the big doors to the Senate Chamber. The committee of senators preceded the nine judges of the court of appeals, led by Chief Judge Cullen, as everyone in the courtroom stood and a hush of solemnity fell in the room. The judges of the court of appeals marched down the center isle wearing their judicial robes. Their solid black attire provided a somber contrast to the gay attire of the many women among the spectators in the gallery. The judges were followed by the long line of senators.[2] The scene was reminiscent of the opening of parliament.

Chief Judge Edgar M. Cullen of the court of appeals was formidable, wearing an oversized, well-groomed white walrus mustache under his dark brows and thinning white hair. His appearance and his courtly manner were always impeccable. He could well have been typecast for the part.

The stage was set and each member of the talented cast was fully prepared to play his role as the curtain rose on what was destined to be a unique legal contest. The quality of justice was about to be tested. The lawyers for each side had been carefully selected to provide their respective clients with the variety of skills that the parties anticipated they would need to persuade a unique court. Sulzer's team was headed by D. Cady Herrick, a sixty-seven-year-old retired justice of the New York State Supreme Court. Herrick himself had been the unsuccessful Democratic candidate for governor in 1904, a former district attorney, as well the political boss of Albany County who, to the chagrin of some, had kept that job even after he was elected to the supreme court. A tall man with an impressively large head, topped with a receding forehead and thinning gray hair, he was an eloquent and extremely courteous advocate. Known as a persuasive and knowledgeable lawyer, he was a man who exuded a combination of leadership, power, grace, and wisdom.

The managers' team, the prosecutors, was led by sixty-one-year-old Alton B. Parker as the chief counsel. Also an unsuccessful candidate in 1904, Parker had resigned as chief judge of the court of appeals, the

D. Cady Herrick, chief counsel for Governor Sulzer. From Jay W. Forrest and James Malcolm, *Tammany's Treason, Impeachment of Governor Sulzer: The Complete Story Written from behind the Scenes, Showing How Tammany Plays the Game, How Men Are Bought, Sold and Delivered* (Albany: The Fort Orange Press, 1913).

state's highest court, to run as the Democratic Party candidate for president of the United States against Theodore Roosevelt. Parker had been the state's chief judge for six years, preceded by twelve years as a justice of the state supreme court. He had been chairman of the 1912 state Democratic convention that nominated Governor Sulzer. Balding, and wearing a dark, full walrus mustache, he was especially impressive and well groomed in an elegant cutaway coat. He was highly respected for his extensive legal acumen acquired over eighteen years on the bench, after a successful career as a lawyer.

Parker was assisted by John B. Stanchfield, a prominent corporate lawyer and litigator who had been the Democratic candidate for governor in 1900. He was considered to be a political reactionary who had distinguished himself over the years as a favorite Tammany orator, and a highly experienced litigator capable of tough cross-examination of witnesses.

The managers' lawyers also included Edgar Truman Brackett, a former senate Republican leader; Eugene Lamb Richards, a Tammany state committeeman who had served as the aggressive counsel to the

Alton B. Parker, chief counsel for the impeachment managers. From Jay W. Forrest and James Malcolm, *Tammany's Treason, Impeachment of Governor Sulzer: The Complete Story Written from behind the Scenes, Showing How Tammany Plays the Game, How Men Are Bought, Sold and Delivered* (Albany: The Fort Orange Press, 1913).

Frawley Committee; and Isidor J. Kresel, a former assistant district attorney in Manhattan, and also a veteran lawyer for the Frawley Committee.

Assisting Judge Herrick on Governor Sulzer's defense team were Irving G. Vann, a former associate justice of the state court of appeals; Harvey D. Hinman, once an influential Republican state senator from Binghamton, New York, who had been associated with former governor Charles Evans Hughes and was highly respected for his advocacy; Austen G. Fox, a special assistant district attorney from Manhattan, a prosecutor who made his reputation in the successful Lexow investigation of corruption in New York City; and Louis Marshall, a very well-known constitutional law expert from Syracuse who was a longtime advisor to Governor Sulzer. Marshall was a founder of the American Jewish Committee, who had distinguished himself as an early civil rights lawyer as well. Other lawyers on the Sulzer team included Elihu Root, Jr., the son of Republican U.S. Senator Elihu Root; Robert P. Clark, a former Broome County Democratic sheriff; and Judge James Gay Gordon, a Sulzer friend from Philadelphia where he had also been a judge.

The first legal issue arose when counsel Herrick raised objections over the swearing in of three senators as each rose to take the oath. Herrick objected to the eligibility of Senators James Frawley, Samuel Ramsperger, and Felix Sanner because they were members of the Frawley Committee. He argued that it should be assumed that they had already made up their minds and could not be presumed to judge objectively. Herrick raised the same objection to Senator Robert F. Wagner; as the senate majority leader he would automatically become lieutenant governor if Sulzer were impeached. Herrick said that fundamental principles of justice afforded every accused the right to be tried by an impartial tribunal.

Parker responded that the court had no authority to exclude any of the constitutionally qualified members of the court. He was obviously well prepared with research supporting his position with the citation of a number of applicable precedents, including some emanating from the impeachment of President Andrew Johnson.

The presiding judge agreed with Parker, stating his own view that each member of the court had to decide for himself if it were proper for him to be a judge under the circumstances. As presiding officer, Judge Cullen ruled that such objections had to be laid aside until after the court had adopted its rules. The role was called and the court voted

LAWYERS FOR IMPEACHMENT MANAGERS

From left to right   Eugene Lamb Richards, Isodor J. Kresel,
Edgar Truman Brackett, John B. Stanchfield

Lawyers for the impeachment managers. From Jay W. Forrest and
James Malcolm, *Tammany's Treason, Impeachment of Governor Sulzer: The
Complete Story Written from behind the Scenes, Showing How Tammany Plays
the Game, How Men Are Bought, Sold and Delivered* (Albany: The Fort
Orange Press, 1913).

unanimously that they would not entertain the challenge. Appropriately, the four senators who had been objected to requested to be excused from voting.

The second day of the impeachment trial began at 10 a.m. on Friday, September 19th. Adopting the rules to govern the proceeding was the first order of business. The rules, based on customary state court procedure, had been proposed in advance by the senate Committee on Rules and were introduced by Senator Wagner. Copies were distributed to each member before they were adopted unanimously by a voice vote. At that point, Judge Cullen announced that the time had come to consider the objections made by Sulzer's counsel to the participation of certain of the senators. Chief defense counsel Herrick rose to present his argument. In the introduction to his presentation, Herrick said that this was not merely a perfunctory point, that this case was the greatest "in all respects of any that has been heard in this country since the trial of President Johnson," and "is arousing the attention of the whole country. What shall be done now and here is a precedent for future time."[3]

Herrick went on at considerable length and detail, citing precedent from specific New York and federal cases, as well as old English cases, to support his argument that justice and fairness required the abstention of the four senators, concluding with a quotation from Edmund Burke, that all we ask is "the cold neutrality of an impartial judge."[4]

Alton Parker rose to respond, refuting Herrick's arguments and his interpretation of the authorities he cited. He presented additional authorities of his own, relying principally on the fact that the state constitution had decreed who should act as judges of the court of impeachment, and that no disqualification was available on the grounds cited by his adversary.[5]

Each of the learned lawyers were afforded ample time to respond to the other's arguments, after which Judge Cullen announced that, although he had the power under the rules adopted by the court to make decisions, he would express his opinion on the issue and give the final decision to the entire court. Cullen pointed out that all the precedents were against the respondent's challenge, but he also believed that the challenge could not be "sustained by principle,"[6] as Herrick had argued. The roll was called again and the members of the court unanimously rejected the governor's challenge, with the four challenged senators again excused from voting at their own request.

The articles of impeachment were then introduced by having the clerk of the court read them into the record in their entirety.

After that, the court turned again to D. Cady Herrick and asked, "What answer does the respondent interpose to the articles presented by the assembly?"

Herrick advised the court that his side had filed a notice of special appearance for the purpose of reserving their right to make certain objections to the legality of the proceedings without condoning it by actually appearing. He introduced his colleague, Louis Marshall, to present their arguments. The Sulzer side had clearly signaled their strategy. Make use of every possible legal precedent, constitutional clause, and appeal to justice and fairness to preclude the proceedings at hand. Leave their adversaries to denigrate the defense for relying on "technicalities" to avoid the bigger issues concealed in the revelation of facts.

Marshall began by announcing that, on behalf of the respondent, William Sulzer, he asked the court to dismiss the proceedings on the ground that the assembly's impeachment was null and void and of no effect. He then began to argue that this impeachment was accomplished during an extraordinary session of the legislature called by the governor after the legislature had adjourned *sine die*, that the legislature had convened the extraordinary session as called by the governor on June 16th and remained in session until July 23rd when it undertook to adjourn until August 11th, but Marshall challenged the legality of the August session because he said that the adjournment motion was made in fact by a vote of less than the necessary majority. Marshall argued that the call for the extraordinary session by the governor had not included the subject of impeachment or any charge against the governor whatsoever. He added that no notice of the subject of impeachment had been issued prior to the August 11th reconvening of the assembly. He claimed that when the subject was first put under consideration on August 11th, twenty-six members of the assembly were absent, "none of whom were given any notice of the proposed action." The consequences therefore, said Marshall, was to deprive Governor Sulzer at that time of the "benefit and advantage" of attendance of those assemblymen who were absent. Therefore, he argued, Sulzer was deprived of due process of law in violation of the constitution of the state and the Fourteenth Amendment to the United States Constitution. Therefore, the court of impeachment was without jurisdiction to entertain a discussion of the issue.[7]

It was 12:25 p.m. when Louis Marshall finished his introductory argument and the court recessed until 2 p.m.

That afternoon, Mr. Marshall continued his argument, citing support of his position from impeachment cases around the nation, and a number of erudite articles on constitutional law and relevant New York cases on related principles of law until 3:35 in the afternoon, when Judge Cullen decided to adjourn until 2 p.m. on the following Monday, September 22nd. Mr. Marshall, the defense constitutional expert, resumed his presentation on Monday. He went further, introducing as an appendix to his brief a compilation of the law of every state in the union related to extraordinary sessions of the state legislature, most of which contained provisions similar to New York's about limiting the action to the specific issues for which the chief executive called the session. (This appendix is a gift to every lawyer in the future who may ever need to deal with the subject of impeachment.)

When Marshall finished, both Parker and Brackett gave equally extensive arguments to refute his case. The session culminated with a vote of 51 to 1 against the eloquent defense argument by Mr. Marshall seeking dismissal of the proceedings. Only Senator Gottfried H. Wende, a committed Sulzer loyalist from Erie County, voted to support the governor's position, arguing that once the legislature had adjourned *sine die*, the assembly could no longer exercise its impeachment powers.[8]

When the court convened at 10 a.m. on Tuesday, September 23rd, Herrick announced that, having lost its case for dismissal of the proceedings, counsel for the

Louis Marshall, of counsel for Governor Sulzer, from *Tammany's Treason, Impeachment of Governor Sulzer*, by Jay W. Forrest and James Malcolm.

respondent were now appearing generally to defend Sulzer against the charges, explaining that the governor now understood that their questioning of the legality of the proceeding had been dismissed. Herrick also announced that the governor was no longer contesting the necessity of giving up his functions until the trial was over. The governor's office began to transfer current matters to Lieutenant Governor Martin Glynn as acting governor.

It was now appropriate for defense counsel to argue another important basic legal issue in their case; that certain articles of impeachment, I, II, and VI, should be quashed because they were all entirely related to matters that, if they had actually occurred, occurred prior to Governor Sulzer's inauguration and, therefore, could not be considered to be "willful and corrupt misconduct in office."[9] Accordingly, Herrick also alleged that the court should set aside these specific articles and take no further cognizance of them. Herrick continued that, as to the first article, charging the governor with filing a false campaign finance statement, the law did not require a candidate to report contributions received by him while he was a candidate. Herrick said it only applied to contributions made by the candidate himself to his own campaign.

As to the second article, charging the governor with filing a false statement under oath, Herrick argued that the law did not actually require him to file a statement under oath and, therefore, not having been required to file an affidavit under oath, the statement he filed could not be proper grounds for an accusation of perjury.

Herrick repeated his argument that the impeachment charged that the governor's offenses constituted willful and corrupt misconduct "in office," and high crimes and misdemeanors, but none of the accusations contained in Articles I, II, or VI actually accused the governor of any misconduct while in office, and should, therefore, be dismissed. Defense counsel buttressed their case with numerous examples of impeachments in New York and elsewhere, in all of which the offenses occurred while the accused was actually in office. Counsel for Sulzer stated that "after reviewing every known case of impeachment in the United States; no case of impeachment has been found where a public official has been impeached for offenses prior to his assumption of office. All are cases of misconduct in office."[10]

The case was also made on Sulzer's behalf that, as the law did not require an affidavit under oath, such an affidavit filed erroneously could not be used to establish a charge of perjury. Additionally, they argued that the section of the Corrupt Practices Act, which Sulzer was charged with violating, was not applicable to contributions from others, but only applied to contributions and expenditures made by the candidate himself.

The arguments raised by Sulzer's lawyers consumed over two hundred pages of single-spaced exposition, which probably constitute the most exhaustive legal memoranda ever assembled on the issues raised in impeachment cases throughout the United State of America, and include over one hundred years of English precedent as well. Suffice it to say for the purposes of deciding the issues in the case, each side presented the most erudite legal analysis of history and applicable law that ever existed on the subject at hand, and each supplemented their presentation with valuable memoranda of law, all of which became part of the extensive 1,792-page record and a great source of information for future scholars on the law of impeachment.[11]

Toward the end of the morning session on Wednesday, September 24th, Judge Cullen spoke up. Cullen proposed that the respondent's motions to dismiss the three articles (I, II, and VI) should be decided at the end of the trial, a procedure that was common in ordinary jurisprudence because by doing so, it afforded the impeachment court far more flexibility as a two-thirds vote was required for impeachment and only a majority vote was required for a decision on the motion. Judge Cullen pointed out that, in ordinary legal cases, it is not an unusual practice to put off such a decision until the end of a trial when there are significant issues of fact as well as issues of law. In advocating this approach to his colleagues, the judges and all the senators who were also judges of the impeachment court, Judge Cullen reminded them that there was no subject "on which there has been more divergence of opinion than as to what constitute and what do not constitute impeachable offenses. On that question the greatest statesmen, the greatest publicists, the greatest advocates and text writers are not in accord but many times diametrically opposed one to the other."[12] Any one of the impeachment judges who had sat through the past two days of admirable advocacy attentively, and read the accompanying memoranda, would have to appreciate Judge Cullen's wisdom. When he called for a vote on his suggestion, it was 49 to 7 in favor of adopting Judge Cullen's decision, which meant that the court would now proceed to hear testimony.

The opening statement for the prosecution was delivered by Eugene Lamb Richards, who so recently had served as the strident chief counsel to the Frawley Committee. Richards described a summary of Sulzer's offenses. Clearly attempting to bridge the gap between Sulzer's alleged corruption in how he handled his campaign financing reports and the defense position that he was being impeached for offenses prior to assuming office, Richards argued creatively that the reporting requirements were "in the nature of a condition precedent to his taking office as governor." He pointed out that the purpose of the reports of campaign contributions and expenditures was to implement a progressive policy to let the people know "whether there are any strings on a candidate and who his backers are." In other words, is money paid to a candidate to influence his future action so that when a man takes office "his official acts can be scrutinized, weighed, and judged in the light of the interests, political or financial, that were behind him in his campaign."[13] He then summarized all of the Frawley Committee's long list of findings of the governor's diversion of campaign contributions to his own use, the things he had allegedly said to various people about his preference for cash, details of his different investment accounts, including the "facts" about the amounts of money he had spent on stocks. Richards charged that Sulzer was more interested in getting campaign contributions than he was in getting votes. Richards also addressed the instances where the governor had attempted to influence assemblymen when seeking support for his direct primary bill.[14]

The first witnesses called by the managers were the secretary of state, who testified about the receipt of Sulzer's campaign reports; then the assembly clerk who testified about the authenticity of the impeachment resolution, refuting defense arguments about the quality of the assembly quorums by authenticating the number of members present according to the official assembly journal.

They called Alfred J. Wolff, who was the commissioner of deeds who witnessed Sulzer's affidavit swearing to the accuracy of his campaign finance report. The defense lawyers cross-examined him extensively, trying unsuccessfully to raise questions about who else was present, whether or not Mr. Wolff's commission was current, whether or not he really saw Sulzer sign the finance report, what pen he used, what furniture was in his office, but they got nowhere. The young man could not be shaken from his testimony that his commission was in effect and that Sulzer had signed in his presence.[15]

The prosecutors introduced a copy of Governor Sulzer's "Statement of Receipts and Expenditures of a Candidate for Political Office." The official form begins with a recitation of sections 750 and 776 of the Penal Law, the applicable essence of which is the sentence in section 776 that says, "every candidate . . . shall . . . file . . . an itemized statement showing in detail, all the moneys contributed or expended by him, directly or indirectly, by himself or though any other person in and of his election." The same provision requires that the candidate's statement shall have attached to it "an affidavit, subscribed and sworn to by such candidate" describing the required details. This seemed to address the statutory argument that the defense had said it only referred to his own contributions and expenditures, and also argued that the sworn affidavit was not required.

Sulzer's statement listed seventy contributions totaling $5,460, all in amounts ranging from $5 to $250, except for one of $500.

The first important witness was Jacob Schiff, a partner at Kuhn, Loeb and Company, a major Wall Street brokerage firm. Schiff testified that Sulzer had come to his office to solicit a campaign contribution and he gave him a check for $2,500. On cross-examination, he told the court that it was intended for any purpose Sulzer wanted to use it. He could not be deterred from that point despite heavy pressure from the manager's counsel who now had good reason to regret bringing him as their witness.[16]

Schiff was immediately followed by Henry Morgenthau, then recently designated to be U.S. ambassador to Turkey. He testified that he gave Sulzer a $1,000 contribution to "help him." "Help him in what?" he was asked by the manager's counsel. Morgenthau replied, "In his election, in his canvass," and he was quickly dismissed as a witness, however, not before he was cross-examined by Louis Marshall for the Sulzer team, who asked him if he intended to limit Sulzer's use of the money. "I did not," Morgenthau responded.[17]

At the opening of the trial on Thursday, September 25, 1912, opposing counsel, Brackett for the managers, and Marshall for the defense, engaged in an argument about whether or not it was appropriate to allow the defense to elicit statements from the witnesses about their intent on cross-examination. Judge Cullen told the attorneys that his previous ruling to allow such testimony was proper because of the allegation of larceny in the impeachment charges, and he believed that his previous decision to allow the cross-examination on intent was therefore appropriate. This argument was refuted in different ways— after testimony of difficult witnesses—but eventually, Judge Cullen's decision was approved by the entire court by a 33 to 14 vote on Friday, September 26th.[18]

Over the next four days, one witness after another introduced by the managers were forced to admit on cross-examination by Mr. Marshall that he had made his contribution to Governor Sulzer for his personal disbursement as he saw fit. Several made the point that they were aware of the candidate's poor financial circumstances and understood that he needed money personally. In that sense, the prosecution's parade of people whose contributions were not reported by Sulzer on his financial report backfired. On the other hand, one after the other of the witnesses were shown to have his check deposited in one of Sulzer's three different personal investment accounts with one or the other brokers, and the managers easily demonstrated that all this money went, not to campaign expenditures, but to Sulzer's personal investments. However, one way or another, most of the long line of prosecution witnesses over a period of two days or more testified that they were aware of Sulzer's "impecunious condition," and were quite willing to have the candidate use the money they gave for any purpose he saw fit.

Despite all this rather exculpating testimony from prosecution witnesses, the managers did succeed in presenting the case they had originally established during the Frawley Committee hearings, that Sulzer, through three different accounts with brokerage houses, had used his personal campaign contributions to speculate on Wall Street, and he had not reported thousands of dollars he had received as personal gifts.

Even more damaging to the governor's image was the testimony subsequently introduced by Henry Morgenthau's second appearance. After he was called back to the stand, he was questioned by John Stanchfield for the managers, about a telephone conversation he had with Sulzer on September 2nd or 3rd, immediately after returning to New York from a trip abroad. Morganthau said he was staying at his daughter's house in Port Chester, Westchester County, when he received a call from the governor. After Morganthau told him that he could not come up to Albany to see him, Sulzer said, "If you are going to testify, I hope you will be easy with me." Morgenthau replied, "I told him I would testify to the facts." In response to a question from Stanchfield about whether or not he was going to discuss his contribution, Morgenthau said, "He said something about that I should treat the affair between us as personal." Stanchfield asked, "What did you say?" Morgenthau replied, "That I could not." Stanchfield then tried to get Morgenthau to repeat the comment. Morgenthau said, "I don't remember the exact words, but that states the substance." Louis Marshall rose to cross-examine. "You say you don't recollect the exact words of that conversation?" Answer, "I don't," and Morgenthau's testimony was over.[19]

Another prosecution witness, whose testimony was especially damaging to Sulzer, was called at the start of the afternoon session on the same day, Friday, September 26th. The witness was D. W. Peck, the state superintendent of public works, an appointee of Governor Dix who was held over by Governor Sulzer. Peck testified that he had given Sulzer a $500 bill at a political meeting in Troy, New York, after Sulzer was nominated in 1912. Peck said that on the day he gave the contribution to Sulzer he said to him, "there were no strings on it and he need not feel at all obligated to reappoint me."

Peck went on to testify that sometime after July 19, 1913, he saw Sulzer in the Executive Chamber in Albany, just after he had received a letter from the Frawley Committee asking for information about his contribution and whether it was by a check or otherwise. "I showed him the letter and I asked him what I should do about it?"

Stanchfield asked, "What did he say?" Peck replied, "He said, do as I shall; deny it. . . . That is nothing, forget it."

After a rather inept brief attempt at cross-examination by Mr. Hinman, which only confirmed the certainty of his recollection, Peck was dismissed.[20]

The managers' presentation of witnesses was clearly designed to establish that Sulzer had received far more money than he had reported. His report listed only $5,460 in contributions from seventy contributors. The evidence presented at the trial, supplementing and including the evidence included at the Frawley hearing, clearly established some $49,000 in contributions handed to or delivered to candidate Sulzer, although a very significant portion (over $30,000) of the unreported funds had been given by men who clearly intended, and so testified under oath, that Sulzer was free to use their money for his own personal preference. Other prosecution witnesses had provided detailed testimony about the three investment accounts he had funneled the money to and the stock purchases he made. Clearly, the accusation that he had converted the money to his own personal use was true, but not illegal, and not in violation of the contributors' intent, however unsavory or immoral it might have appeared to the public and however offensive when the facts of his intensive efforts to keep his activities secret were revealed.

This testimony was both related and unrelated to the three impeachment articles that the defense had tried hard to dismiss or at least nullify. Article I was the accusation that he filed a false campaign finance report by omitting $8,500 in specific contributions. The evidence introduced at trial was far more than that, but most of that came from people who said that their money was to be used at Sulzer's discretion.

Based on the same testimony, the prosecutors expected to establish the veracity of Article II—alleging that he had committed perjury with his false affidavit attesting to the accuracy of his incomplete report his affidavit supported.

Similarly, Article VI accused him of larceny in converting campaign contributions to his own use by investing those contributions in the stock market, a charge that Sulzer's counsel refuted by cross-examination showing that the contributors expected him to use their contributions for his own personal purposes.

When they finished their extensive presentation of testimony from all of the stockbrokers who had handled Sulzer's investments, the prosecutors turned their attention to Article VII, which charged the governor with improperly using his office to influence the political action of certain members of the legislature by implicitly threatening to veto bills they had introduced and passed in trade for their support for his direct primary bill. The managers' case on this article was a very weak one. The testimony at the trial was not very much more enlightening than the testimony already introduced at the Frawley Committee hearings. Two assemblymen, Thaddeus Sweet and Spencer Prime, repeated their previous accounts of their meetings with the governor when bills significant to their districts were before him. But, despite the skillful handling of their testimony by counsel for the managers, they were unable to produce hard substantiation of the charges, leaving the case reliant on implied threats, and the testimony that the governor had said, "You for me, I for you." Besides, Prince's bill was approved, even though he did not promise to support the direct primary bill.[21]

Finally, when the prosecutors attempted to introduce testimony from another assemblyman, J. L. Patrie from Greene County, Judge Cullen upheld a defense objection because his name had not been included in the impeachment articles, and he was unable to testify.

The managers' case in support of Article VIII, accusing the governor of using his office to affect prices on the New York Stock Exchange by advancing legislation to tighten regulation of the exchange while he speculated in stocks, was to introduce copies of the bills he proposed, and the supporting memoranda he delivered to the legislature, and copies of the bills that were enacted. The case they thus made was purely inferential and nothing was introduced to establish or even specify the alleged influence. In truth, the governor's bill would be more likely to reduce the value of his investments.

As to Article III, charging Sulzer with "bribing witnesses" by "fraudulently" inducing Louis Sarecky and stockbrokers Frederick Colwell and Melville Fuller "to withhold true testimony" from the Frawley Committee investigation, counsel for the managers introduced evidence to establish that Sarecky was appointed to his job as a deportation agent for the State Hospital Commission at $4,000 per annum, two weeks before his scheduled appearance at the Frawley Committee hearing, a $1,000 increase from his previous state job at $3,000 per annum as the governor's personal representative with the State Civil Service Commission.[22]

On October 1st, rather suddenly, the prosecution rested its case. It was reported that they had a number of additional witnesses available who the managers were holding in reserve for rebuttal in case the governor would actually testify. Furthermore, the lawyers who had not expected the sudden resting of the prosecution case needed more time to prepare their defense. They asked the court to adjourn until the following Monday, October 6th, because Mr. Marshall needed the time to complete his observation of the Jewish New Year, as did one of their intended witnesses. They also told the court that Mr. Hinman, who would present the opening argument, was exhausted to the point of incapacitation and needed rest.

Before the defense could open their case on October 6th, the prosecution obtained the court's permission to reopen their case for the introduction of a newly discovered witness, Allan A. Ryan, who was the son of Thomas F. Ryan, a financier whose testimony would be so sensational that even the governor's lawyers were taken by surprise.[23] Mr. Ryan told the court that, early in the gubernatorial campaign, he had taken a call from Sulzer trying to reach his father for a contribution to his "personal campaign," when the elder Ryan was abroad. Ryan said that the candidate had told him, "Tell your father I am the same old Bill." Ryan testified that he had sent him a contribution of $10,000 in $1,000 bills as a result of the call, another contribution that was never reported by Sulzer. Sulzer's lawyers tried to keep the testimony out, but they were unsuccessful. Subsequently, Ryan was recalled to the witness stand to describe another conversation he had with Sulzer only a week before the impeachment trial started. This testimony was ruled out by Judge Cullen, whose decision was sustained by the court, but only after the entire court heard Mr. Ryan say that he was told by Sulzer to ignore any subpoenas he might receive to testify before the impeachment court. He quoted Sulzer as saying to him, "They had no right to adopt a resolution to impeach me at an extraordinary session and the court has no right to try me." Ryan also testified that "he asked me to go to Washington to see Senator Root and request him to see Mr. William Barnes," the state Republican leader, to get him to have the Republican members of the court vote that the court had no right to try him and impeach him. Again, the Sulzer lawyers protested vigorously and Judge Cullen agreed that the testimony should be struck. However, for the first time, a member of the court, Senator Elan R. Brown, the Republican minority leader, objected to a ruling of Judge Cullen and asked for a roll call. Judge Cullen's ruling was adopted by a vote of 32 to 18.[24]

The next day, the court went into an executive session, and reversed its ruling, allowing the Ryan testimony to remain as part of the record.

Until the day the defense rested, no decision had yet been made about whether or not Governor Sulzer should testify, and this was a subject of great consequence. Reportedly, Sulzer himself intended to appear before the court and point an accusing finger at Charles F. Murphy and disclose what the governor perceived to be a plot by Tammany Hall and its legislative representatives to destroy his administration because of his consistent refusal to let the so-called invisible government control the state. Theodore Roosevelt, among many others, had publicly urged him to testify. Sulzer had been telling the press, almost daily, that his testimony would destroy the impeachment case, that "nothing short of death would keep him from testifying," and he promised "amazing revelations." On the other hand, the fact that the court had consistently ruled out testimony about matters not addressed in the articles of impeachment, his attorneys concluded that the court would not be likely to allow the governor to testify about his relations with Murphy. They were also generally concerned that one of the managers' lawyers had reportedly told a newspaperman that "Sulzer would get that sort of defense in only over our dead bodies. There is nothing in the rules governing this proceeding which would justify the admission of that sort of defense." The defense team had other concerns, specifically that if Sulzer testified, his credibility would be put in issue and he could be put under a withering cross-examination that could go into almost any phase of his career, and thereby raise a wide range of issues that had not yet been admitted to the proceeding. The *Times* reported that the internal dispute in the Sulzer camp had the governor's political advisors encouraging the governor's testimony and the legal team opposing it.[25]

Insofar as I am aware, the following correspondence is revealed here for the first time. Through the kindness of Albany County Judge Stephen Herrick, the grandson of D. Cady Herrick, I was given access to the following correspondence that settles the question of why Sulzer did not testify at his own impeachment trial. Prior to receiving this letter from Judge Herrick, a number of years earlier when I began my research into the story of Governor Sulzer at the library of Cornell University, the repository of Governor Sulzer's personal papers, I found a two-inch-thick onionskin transcript of a dry run of the testimony that the governor's lawyers took him through in preparation for his trial. Until I saw these letters, it seemed to me that his lawyers would decide that his testimony would be detrimental to his own cause because, when he was asked by his counsel if anyone else gave him money for himself (in addition to those who had testified to that effect), the governor answered substantially, "Yes, wherever I went during the campaign, people gave me money for myself." It seemed to me that such an answer, however honest, was certainly detrimental to his public image and to his legal position as well. However, the most factual explanation for his decision not to testify is set forth in those two letters. The first was the lawyerly letter to Governor Sulzer from his chief counsel, D. Cady Herrick, three days before the trial was to resume.

Dear Sir:
You have now reached a stage in your case when it becomes necessary to determine whether you will become a witness in

your own behalf. The decision of that question finally rests with you.

You must realize that should you become a witness, it will be necessary for you to run the gauntlet of your entire life, and to submit to an investigation into every phase of your record, in order to test the credibility of your evidence. The manner in which you undergo that test may prove to be the ultimate factor in determining the final results of the proceedings against you.

It has been our observation in criminal cases that the defendant who fails to become a witness in his own behalf, is usually convicted; whereas, one who does, and tells a truthful story in a convincing manner, is as a rule acquitted.

Whether you can tell such a story, unshaken by cross-examination, must be decided by you.

While we do not wish to shirk any responsibility, we feel that the importance of this case to you, and to the State, requires you to determine for yourself whether or not you are willing to undergo the ordeal of the searching examination to which you undoubtedly will be subjected, together with the attending risks.

We will loyally abide by any decision that you may reach, and exercise our best endeavors to protect and guard your interest. We must, however, request you to instruct us definitely as to your conclusion, so that we may guide our course accordingly.

October 3, 1913   D. Cady Herrick

The second was the governor's handwritten letter in response to Herrick's lawyerlike letter giving the governor his best advice:

October 8, 1913
Gentlemen:
Yours received in relation to my becoming a witness and my determination concerning same.

A very few words in answer will suffice. If I go on the stand I shall tell the truth regarding all persons and all matters, and that will mean the revealing of confidences, and the breaking of lifelong friendships.

Furthermore there are some things sacred and I believe which no mannerly man can shield himself; some sacrifices that no honorable man ought to accept to even save himself.

In view of these considerations I have concluded not to be a witness, otherwise I should insist upon being sworn in my own behalf irrespective of the personal consequences.
Very Truly Yours
Wm. Sulzer
To the –
Hon. D. Cady Herrick
Hon. Austen G. Fox
Hon. Louis Marshall
Hon. Harvey D. Hinman

Harvey Hinman was assigned to make the opening address to the court for the defense on the adjourned date of October 6th. The few days' rest during the adjournment gave Mr. Hinman sufficient time to get ready for the task. As soon as the reopened testimony of the prosecution witnesses was completed, Hinman rose to open the defense case. He began by reminding the court that the purpose of an impeachment proceeding is to "enable the people to rid themselves of public officials corrupt in office." His point was that if a man met the legal qualifications, and acted "honestly and faithfully in the discharge of his official duties" these were the only qualifications. "The morals or private life of the officeholder, provided they do not affect the performance of his official duties, do not disqualify him from holding office and cannot be made the ground for his removal—were the rule otherwise the people would have been deprived of some of the greatest men and statesmen."[26]

After the general introduction to the defense's position, Hinman then went on to discuss the charges contained in each of the articles of impeachment, claiming that the evidence was inadequate to establish the validity of Articles III, IV, V, VII, and VIII. Then he repeated the defense case against Articles I, II, and VI, as relevant to matters prior to Sulzer's inauguration on January 1, 1913, and, therefore, not fit subjects for impeachment. This concluded Hinman's opening presentation.

However, before Hinman could begin to introduce the defense witnesses, the court interrupted his plan and allowed the prosecution to go back again to hear additional testimony from Mr. Ryan.

Harvey Hinman, of counsel for Governor Sulzer. From Jay W. Forrest and James Malcolm, *Tammany's Treason, Impeachment of Governor Sulzer: The Complete Story Written from behind the Scenes, Showing How Tammany Plays the Game, How Men Are Bought, Sold and Delivered* (Albany: The Fort Orange Press, 1913).

Allan Ryan was then recalled to the witness stand, once again to add information to the story he had begun. He testified that he had refused to go to see Senator Root. Ryan said that he had told Sulzer that because certain charges had been made against him, he did not see how Sulzer could be satisfied to have the trial concluded without taking the opportunity to respond because he would put himself in a bad position if he did not answer the charges. Sulzer's response was notable. "He said that his reason was that he did not want to drag his wife into the situation and put her on the stand," Ryan said. Sulzer pursued the matter, however, and asked Ryan to go to his father's attorney, DeLancey Nicoll, and ask him to intercede with Charles Murphy, suggesting that he should ask Murphy to "get his following to vote that the court had no right, the assembly had no right to vote his impeachment." On further prodding by Stanchfield, who was conducting the examination of Ryan for the prosecution, Ryan testified that Sulzer wanted him to have Mr. Nicoll, the proposed go-between, go tell Murphy that if he did so, Sulzer "was willing to do whatever was right." Shortly thereafter, Stanchfield completed his examination of the witness, and offered D. Cady Herrick the opportunity to cross-examine him. Herrick declined to do so. Nevertheless, the hypocrisy inherent in Sulzer's reported effort to rely on the party boss to save himself had a powerful impact on friend and foe alike.

At the conclusion of Mr. Ryan's testimony, Judge Cullen turned to Mr. Herrick to begin with the defense witnesses. The first was Sam Beardsley, a lawyer from Ithaca, New York, with an office in New York City. The Sulzer defense team proposed to introduce him to testify about a major campaign contribution that Sulzer refused to accept. Their obvious purpose was to offset the embarrassing things about Sulzer that had already been testified to with a significant situation to demonstrate the governor's integrity. Herrick told the court that this witness was going to testify in refutation of the prosecutors' claim that Sulzer was going around seeking contributions for himself, and "we propose to show this man rejected contributions in large amounts, refused to accept them. . . ." Stanchfield vigorously objected to the relevancy of such testimony, and Judge Cullen seemed sympathetic. He said that they proposed to show that Mr. Beardsley offered Sulzer a $25,000 contribution and Sulzer refused to take it. After a brief, but sharp, adversarial debate among the opposing lawyers, Judge Cullen proposed to rule out Beardsley's testimony, and asked the court for a roll call vote to sustain his ruling, which they did by a small majority of 28 to 25.

Mr. Herrick called Herbert H. Lehman, then a young banker at Lehman Brothers in New York City.[27] Lehman testified that he met Sulzer for the first time in July of 1912, after he wrote to him in Congress. He produced a copy of the letter offering to help him get nominated and elected because he had admired his record and his personality, and thought that Sulzer would be the logical Democratic candidate. Lehman made a specific suggestion—that Sulzer should publicly and widely distribute a book of his speeches and offered to help defray this expense. Lehman testified that he paid Sulzer $5,000 in September of 1912 "for his personal use without any conditions."

The $5,000 contribution was paid in $1,000 bills. He also told how he had absorbed the expenses of publishing the books for Sulzer. He specified on cross-examination by Mr. Stanchfield that he personally paid for the publication of the book of the short speeches of Congressman Sulzer at 7.5 cents per copy for 50,000 copies. He also paid for the cost of mailing 7,500 of those copies across the state prior to the Democratic convention in October, a total expenditure of $6,000. After repeatedly trying to clarify the details of all of his expenditures for the Sulzer campaign, Mr. Lehman eventually agreed with Judge Cullen that he had spent a total of $12,000, including $5,000 for Sulzer personally, $1,000 for distribution of the book of speeches before the nomination, and $6,000 for publishing and distributing 50,000 copies after the nomination.[28]

After listening to Herbert Lehman's story, the court heard from the defense's next witness, Louis M. Josephthal, a banker and broker who had not been a contributor to the Sulzer campaign. Josephthal was appointed as a naval aide on the governor's military staff four days after Sulzer was declared governor. He was the one who had taken over Sulzer's $26,000 brokerage account with Harrison Fuller, and he testified that the governor had told him that the stock in that account belonged to Mrs. Sulzer, but, when he took it over, he found none of it in her name. Although he had not contributed to Sulzer's campaign fund, after Sulzer appointed him as his naval aide his firm retained Sulzer's former law partner as its counsel.[29]

The *New York Times* of October 8th called Louis Sarecky a "star witness." They said that "the galleries, crowded almost entirely with eager-eyed women folk," were especially impressed with the calm demeanor of twenty-seven-year-old Louis Sarecky as he testified articulately under rather constant and oppressive cross-examination by prosecutor John Stanchfield.

At the commencement of his testimony, Sarecky, responding to Harvey Hinman's careful examination, revealed that he was born in Odessa, Russia, and came to America with his parents when he was only two or three years old. Soon after graduation from DeWitt Clinton High School where he learned stenography, he took a job with Congressman Sulzer's New York City law office where he had been for ten and a half years prior to the 1912 election campaign. He was a cultured young man who spoke English well and had also mastered French, German, and Yiddish. He was able to read in each of those languages and used each on an almost daily basis in dealing with the congressman's visitors, clients, and constituents, and he could also understand, but not speak Spanish. By the time Sulzer was nominated for governor, Sarecky was running his law office, in which between one and two hundred visitors a day would crowd in, and he was supervising three permanent assistants, and as many as eight part-time volunteers. Sarecky opened the mail and responded to correspondence, signing the candidate's name to form letters he himself devised based on language he knew the congressman had used. The candidate, he said, had entirely left it up to him to deposit all the contributions, and keep whatever records were necessary, but Sulzer himself paid no attention to the management of the money because he entirely left it up to Sarecky, who was fully empowered to make the deposits, send out the thank you letters, and sign Sulzer's name to them so the candidate could be free to spend his own time writing speeches and campaigning. Sarecky admitted that the campaign committee of prominent friends of the governor was organized by himself, and that they had neglected to file their initial registration form when they organized, until the necessity of filing the campaign finance report was called to their attention just before it was time to file it. According to his testimony, Sarecky had to create the report from his deposit slips and he did it himself rather loosely and neglected significant contributions, but the governor signed it when he presented it. Sarecky testified that "Sulzer asked, 'is this alright?' and I said 'this is as accurate as I could get it and he signed it."

While Sarecky was only twenty-seven years old, he had genuinely been a close confidant of Sulzer for a long time and his loyalty was unquestionable. Sarecky was the same young man who refused to testify before the Frawley Committee without benefit of counsel and who took full responsibility for all of the violations of campaign finance laws that Sulzer had been charged with. Harvey Hinman, the defense counsel, gently guided his testimony as Sarecky explained the free and easy manner in which he accepted and disbursed thousands of dollars of campaign funds. Sarecky told the court how he had created the infamous and ambiguous letter that Sulzer wrote to so many of his contributors, saying, "I thank you for all you have said and done." Sarecky insisted that Sulzer did not know anything about the letters. He also denied that the commissioner of deeds who witnessed Sulzer's execution of the document had ever read it to Sulzer before affixing his signature. Sarecky described his free use of the power of attorney that Sulzer gave him some time ago and how he used it to sign letters purportedly coming from Sulzer personally, endorsed Sulzer's deposits, and how for many years, he had been signing Sulzer's name to checks and correspondence. In conclusion to that phase of his testimony, he gave the court a demonstration of his expertise in imitating the governor's signature as "Wm. Sulzer," and testified he never signed as "William Sulzer," and that he had a power of attorney to do so.

Sarecky candidly acknowledged that the campaign finance statement did not include everything they had received and that he knew that to be the case when the statement was prepared. He explained how he had pulled the contents of the campaign finance statement from his own daily memorandum sheets and deposit slips. During cross-examination Sarecky was confronted by the prosecution attorneys with questions that made it appear that he had deliberately omitted the contributions from liquor interests, Tammany district leaders, and Wall Street financiers. Despite the implications, Sarecky's rather serene response was that some of the records might have been missing. He made it clear, however, that he had never spoken to the governor about leaving out the names of certain large contributors on the official statement. He admitted that he had on his own initiative used some of the money that they received for other than campaign purposes and that he had not been in the habit of submitting all of the campaign checks to Sulzer.

According to accounts of his testimony, he was described as calm, self-possessed, and resourceful in dealing with the tough cross-examination by Stanchfield and he never lost his poise. When Stanchfield prodded him about his failure to appear before the Frawley Committee, he denied that Sulzer had advised him on how to handle it. He responded to cross-examination on the subject as to whether he had conferred with Louis Marshall prior to his appearance before the Frawley Committee, insisting that he had not done so, even though he had told the committee that Marshall was the attorney who advised him not to testify before that committee. When he was asked to produce documentation about the campaign contributions, he claimed that he had lost, mislaid, or destroyed all such materials except for the bound volumes that he had sent to the Executive Mansion when the Frawley Committee began its hearings. Finally, his cross-examination led to a review of the sources of his salary before he went on the state payroll and he was unable to testify clearly in response to those questions. Stanchfield led him through a review of his career as a state employee and repeated promotions he had received from his first state job as a clerk in the adjutant general's office, his promotion only weeks later as confidential stenographer to the governor at $2,500 per year, and then soon thereafter, his promotion to his current job as a $4,000-per-year deportation agent at the state health commission, a job which he had to concede he had no special training for and which sometimes required him to supervise physicians.

Near the end of his examination and cross-examination by the respective attorneys, and the presiding judge, Sarecky was made available to the senators, several of whom went over some of the testimony he had given during his two-day-long appearance. When it came the turn of senate majority leader Robert Wagner, he asked just two short questions, perhaps the most salient ones. First, "At the time you made up your statement you knew that you had received $12,000 in campaign contributions didn't you?" Sarecky calmly said, "I did." Wagner's second question was, "And in making out your statement you put in that you had received but $5,000 in campaign contributions?" and the young man answered, "Yes sir."[30] Very shortly thereafter, Sarecky's examination was concluded.

Through the prosecutor's counsel and then the senators' cross-examinations of Sarecky *ad nauseam*, they were never able to shake his confidence or self-assurance, even when scoring points.

The defense then called Hugh Reilly, a seventy-year-old friend of Sulzer who testified that he had long-standing interests in a Cuban cartel for the Cienfuegos Waterworks, that he had loaned Sulzer some $26,000 over a period of months, beginning in August 9th of 1912 through November 8th, that he had taken no written note or other writing from Sulzer, that all of the loans were in the form of cash, and none had yet been repaid. The prosecutor tried to tie the loan to some favors that Sulzer may have done during his congressional years, but after hearing just a little of the testimony, Judge Cullen sustained the defense objection that it was irrelevant and, after a few more questions about the loan, Reilly was dismissed.

The final witness called by the defense was John A. Hennessy, who was one of Sulzer's confidants and recently a close advisor to him on his strategy in responding to the impeachment.

Harvey Hinman asked Hennessy if he was the man the governor had appointed in March of 1913 to investigate the state highway department, and gave him the opportunity to tell the court what he had done, when Ed Brackett, part of the managers' legal team, interrupted with an objection claiming that the question was irrelevant and immaterial—causing Judge Cullen to ask Mr. Hinman why the witness's answer was material.

Hinman went into a long explanation, describing the highway investigation that Hennessy had conducted, and the fraud he had uncovered in the highway department and the public water department headed by Duncan Peck who had been implicated in fraudulent practices and that, when Peck testified at the impeachment trial a few days ago that Sulzer had advised him that when he went before the Frawley Committee he should deny making a contribution, Peck had an ulterior motive for that testimony. Hinman also took the opportunity to tell the judge that he intended to have Hennessy testify about the extent of his highway investigation and what he had discovered in his service to the governor.

Cullen ruled that the defense could not use Hennessy's testimony to discredit Peck, or to show that he had committed fraud. Hinman argued that he wanted to show that Peck had a motive to testify "in such a way as would eliminate the respondent from office" and stop Hennessy's investigation.

Judge Cullen ruled that Hinman could not discredit another witness generally unless he did it through that witnesses' own testimony. Hinman tried again, telling Cullen that through Hennessy's testimony he wanted to show that Sulzer was a good governor who "has been discharging the duties of his office faithfully and well." Cullen responded, "I don't think you can go into that."

Hinman was left with no alternative unless he wanted to challenge the presiding judge. He excused Mr. Hennessy. Judge Cullen then turned to the members of the court and asked if anyone wanted to question his ruling, otherwise it would stand. Nobody spoke up.[31]

On October 8th, D. Cady Herrick rose and said, "The respondent rests."

After introducing three rather meaningless witnesses for rebuttal, none of whom added anything significant, the prosecution announced that they had nothing further. Testimony in the impeachment trial was over, and each side was scheduled to sum up their case when the court convened at 10 a.m. the next day, October 9th.

The headline in the *Times* of October 9th was "SULZER EVIDENCE ENDS; GOVERNOR NOT TESTIFYING." The lead story was about the abrupt ending of the defense testimony without hearing from the governor. D. Cady Herrick, as chief counsel, was also the principal spinner on the point. He was asked why the governor had not been called to clear up what remained to be explained. Herrick said, "There is nothing to explain. The prosecution has utterly failed to make out a case against our client. For the rest, I refer you to the testimony given here yesterday by Mr. Allan A. Ryan." The reporters persisted, asking Herrick, "Do you refer to the part where Mr. Ryan told the court that Mr. Sulzer said he could not afford to go to trial because it would make it necessary to drag Mrs. Sulzer into the situation and drive her into taking the witness stand?" Herrick replied, "That is correct," and went on to explain that there would have been a unanimous demand for his removal if he had resorted to such a cowardly act as hiding behind a woman's skirts.

The court had adjourned until the next day, Thursday, October 9th, when by agreement each party, beginning with the defense, would have five hours to summarize their case. Louis Marshall was to open for the defense, followed by Alton B. Parker for the managers. On Friday, D. Cady Herrick would respond for the defense and Edgar Truman Brackett for the managers.

Louis Marshall's advocacy for Sulzer was passionate, eloquent, and elegant. His presentation took a total of three and a half hours, beginning promptly after the court convened at 10 a.m., and concluding halfway through the afternoon session. His opening paragraph was actually Lincolnesque, saying that he approached his "present duty, not with false modesty, but with extreme diffidence, and with a full realization of the disparity of my powers and the greatness of the task which has devolved upon me," telling the court that they were engaged in an event that would make "a permanent impression on the history of our beloved state," with "consequences far beyond our ken, which will determine whether or not the reign of law has ceased, and that of passion and prejudice has begun." With considerable subtlety, he went on to let the court know clearly that their own decisions would testify to the independence of public officials. He reminded the court that the man on trial had been elected only a few months ago as governor of the nation's greatest state by an unprecedented majority and now he was the man being subjected to "an everlasting stigma upon his name."[32] He proceeded with a detailed review of Sulzer's many accomplishments over his career in the assembly and the Congress, and outlined his substantial achievements as governor and his effective efforts to expose massive corruption in state government, and his improvements to the finances and organization of state government. Then, turning to each of the charges against Sulzer, he reviewed the testimony and articulated the defense position, pointing out that the court's power was limited to determining the evidence in each of the articles of impeachment. Included, of course, was the significant argument that

Sulzer could not be removed for offenses committed before he became governor, pointing out that "for more than three centuries, there has not been a case of impeachment which was not grounded on official misconduct." Marshall was armed with a slew of judicial documents to buttress his arguments, including several decisions of Judge Cullen himself and of Judge William Werner as well, interpreting New York law on points of precedent that were favorable to the defense positions. Marshall summed up his argument with "shall ours be a government of laws, or one of passion and caprice?"[33]

By mid-afternoon on October 9th, Alton Parker rose to begin his summary for the prosecution. Parker's case was presented on a much different level, claiming at its inception, that now that all the evidence is in, "there is no answer to any of the material facts which have been presented on the part of the managers. Not a word."[34] He began with an exposition of the campaign finance laws that had been enacted in the state, going back to 1892 when their original purpose was to alleviate the public's concern about a series of rich men who had financed their own campaigns, and leading up to 1906 when the current laws were enacted as a result of investigation of the corrupt influence of corporate contributions that were ended by Charles Evans Hughes, and the new laws of New York became a model for the rest of the nation. Parker went on to detail the facts of Sulzer's false statements and how he knew or must have known of the implications of concealing the contributions from Wall Street and other corporate entities, and how the managers had shown some $37,400 of such contributions that were not included in Sulzer's statement of $5,460 as his total contributions. He attacked Louis Sarecky as a "worthless character" and pointed out that Sulzer was far too experienced a candidate as to fail to understand the significance of the omissions of the contributions from so many men whose contributions and importance were well known to Sulzer. As Parker put it, "How Mr. Sulzer must have chuckled when he saw the ready shrewdness with which this apt pupil of his had suppressed the contributions received from the brewers and from other special interests in the final draft of the campaign statement."[35]

When Parker finished the presentation of the managers' case, the next day he summarized the situation with what the *Times* of October 11th aptly termed "an unusual feast of oratory." In the course of his concluding remarks, Parker said that there was "something of the pathetic in the defendant's frantic efforts to cover the nakedness of his wrongdoing. Defiance, defense, justification, prevarication, denunciation of his accusers, attempts to suppress and falsify testimony and efforts to cast blame elsewhere—each of them has been stripped from his quaking flesh until he stands now naked before the court, without a rag of his attempted vindication clinging to his deformed and mutilated manhood."

Parker did not avoid Sulzer's verbal attacks on Tammany, calling it "the armor of defiance in which he threatened to attack and expose a political leadership to which we had found him securing later for a merciful obliteration of his misdeeds, and offering the bribe of submission," explaining further that he was referring to "his effort to coerce members of this court through channels his warped intellect mistakenly instructed him held the power of coercion." Parker ended with a plea to the court, that it must "find in all the evidence that this defendant has been guilty of misconduct so gross as to necessitate his removal."

D. Cady Herrick's rebuttal took a new approach. Starting with a discussion of the Andrew Johnson impeachment process, he emphasized the point that a man's character or popularity was irrelevant to an impeachment proceeding that needed to confine itself to the man's conduct in office and stay with the specifics of the articles of impeachment. He said, "A man may be unfit in some respects. He may have committed ethical violations or worse in his private life, and yet we are to judge him as a public official, by what he does in public office and in no other way." Recognizing that Sulzer had antagonized a lot of the senators, by being abusive to them, even threatening to drive them from public life, or that some were sympathetic to the organization he fought with, and some considered him to be ungrateful for the years of support he had from that organization, he reminded them of their duty to judge him impartially, and he called on them for "fair play." He emphasized again the defense argument that there was no history of impeachment for acts committed when a defendant was not in a public office—and he even admitted for the first time that there were two or three cases in history where a man was convicted for "past official misconduct, but still acts committed in office." Then he proceeded to review the evidence against Sulzer in each of the articles. Herrick distributed a chart summarizing the testimony of thirty-nine different witnesses, citing the page in the trial transcript and the date they testified, stating the amount each had contributed and the extent to which each had left it up to Sulzer as to how he would use their money.[36] Their contributions ranged from $50 to $10,000 and added up to $31,500, to which Herrick added some others that were not included on the list, which brought the total to $41,000 Herrick said, plus the $26,500 and the Lehman $5,000.

Summarizing Sulzer's nearly twenty-five-year-long career in public service, as he neared the conclusion of his rebuttal speech, Herrick pointed out that, when Sulzer was in the state legislature twenty years before, it was a time when members were known to take graft in exchange for their political action—but there was never any taint or accusation against him. He said, "Now, after over a quarter century of public service, he is for the first time, charged with being a dissolute man, charged with stealing money, charged with plundering his friends, charged with seeking contributions for one purpose, using them for another, and committing perjury to conceal the fact."

According to the *Times* of October 11th, Herrick said, "The fact that a great party had nominated and the people had elected to be governor a man of the low ethical standards of this respondent must be conceded to be a shame and a disgrace to the State of New York, but it is not for these things that you are to remove him from office."

It is interesting that the *Proceedings* at page 1491 contain the same sentence, but without the word "low" preceding the word ethical. The *Times* inclusion of the word "low" is reflected in the next day's edition of the newspaper in which they covered a one-paragraph story about some of Sulzer's friends feeling resentment at Judge Herrick's reference to Sulzer's "low ethical standards," stating that Sulzer's kitchen cabinet had "looked askance at the eminent counsel of record" from the beginning.[37]

When Edgar Brackett, the final advocate for the managers, rose to make his rebuttal speech, the court had decided to listen to him even though they did not anticipate that he could not finish before the usual adjournment time. By a vote of 49 to 4, they agreed to stay as long as necessary to complete the lawyers' presentations that day. Brackett, also a former senator, had his own brand of eloquence, flowing and old-fashioned, but he pulled no punches and consistently kept the court's attention with extensive references to biblical analogy. This, combined with his tough description of Sulzer, made him especially effective.

Brackett finished far earlier than promised and, except for his enter-
taining biblical references and hard accusations assailing Sulzer's lack
of character, he added very little to the debate.[38]

The testimony was over. Each side had summed up. It was only 4:45
p.m. when the court adjourned until Monday, October 13th, but not
before Judge Cullen had admonished every member of the court to
refuse to engage in any conversations with anyone else over the weekend.

Governor Sulzer's people believed they had proven that no man
had ever been impeached for something done before taking office.
They had good reason to believe that precedent would make it difficult
to convict on the basis of Articles I, II, or VI. Although they realized
that the prosecution had made the governor look bad with his incomplete financial report, Louis Sarecky had done a good job of taking full
responsibility. They also felt pretty good about their legal argument
that a man could not be convicted of perjury for voluntarily filing a
sworn statement when he was not required to by law. They realized too
that, except for the evidence of the governor's attempt to suppress testimony, the prosecutors had not provided much evidentiary support for
any of the other articles.

The managers' attorneys had good reason to be optimistic about
the portrait they painted of Sulzer's character and integrity emanating
from the testimony of their witnesses. The evidence of Sulzer's success
at raising money for himself and his aggressive approach to collecting
cash and then covering it up was truly damaging. Clearly the court
could create new precedent and find him unfit for office based on his
conduct in preparing for office. While a significant number of senators
may have prejudged the case, nobody had revealed that during the testimony. Surely the fact that Sulzer had not testified would influence
some judges against him. Whether or not there would be a two-thirds
majority for removal was not crystal clear in light of the number of the
members of the court who came from the judiciary or the independent
democracy, or the Republican side of the senate aisle.

When the court reconvened on Monday, court of appeals judge
Nathan Miller raised a legal issue for consideration. Because witnesses
Peck, Morganthau, and Ryan had each testified that Sulzer had
attempted to influence their testimony, there was a legal question as to
whether that testimony could be considered under Article IV as it was
drafted, or whether the court had the right to amend the article to
include testimony that had not been anticipated when the impeach-

ment was drafted. The court went into executive session and there is no transcript of their deliberations.

On the day after the respective attorneys argued the point, Judge Cullen announced that the court would not attempt to amend the articles of impeachment, but it had decided that Article IV as written was sufficiently broad to encompass consideration of Peck's testimony about the Frawley Committee as evidence, but not the testimony of Morganthau or Ryan about the impeachment trial, which was considered to be merely corroborative. Afterward, the court adjourned again and went into executive session for another day.

Finally, at 3:00 p.m. on the afternoon of October 16th, after completing its private conversations, the court proceeded to take a public vote on each of the eight impeachment articles, one after the other. Once again the galleries filled with spectators seeking to become witnesses to history. The clerk of the court was asked to read the first article, which is the one that charged governor-elect Sulzer with filing a false statement of campaign receipts pursuant to the state's six-year-old Corrupt Practices Act.

Judge Cullen asked each member of the court, in alphabetical order, to stand and give his response when the clerk called his name. As each member rose, the presiding judge stated solemnly, "How say you, is the respondent guilty or not guilty." While a few merely said "guilty" or "not guilty," all of them were public men of one sort or another and quite used to expressing themselves. Some easily explained their vote with a few sentences giving their reasons. Several even filed written briefs to record the justification for their action. Some of the senators incorporated arguments that the judges of the court of appeals had made in their own statements. Most of those who voted for acquittal reasoned one way or the other that the acts that were charged, even though actually committed, did not constitute grounds for impeachment under the constitution or the laws of the state. While practically nobody denied the facts alleged, many differed on the question of whether Sulzer's action was an impeachable offense.

Judge Cullen said it best. He expressed the view that he believed the accusations of filing a false report were true because the amount actually received by Sulzer was "so grossly in excess" of what he actually reported that such a difference could not have occurred through inadvertence or error. Despite that conviction, Judge Cullen said he was nevertheless constrained to vote for acquittal because Sulzer had not committed an impeachable offense. Cullen said, "The objective of impeachment is to remove a corrupt and unworthy officer, but a corrupt and unworthy officer is an entirely different thing from an officer who has, before his office, been unworthy and corrupt." The presiding justice analogized such an impeachment to an *ex post facto* disqualification from office for an offense that had no such penalty when committed because, even if filing a false certificate was technically a crime, forfeiture of office was not the prescribed penalty. Driving his point home, Judge Cullen said, "Men have committed serious crimes, even felonies, and subsequently attained high public position."[39] Three court of appeals judges agreed with Judge Cullen's view.

On the other side, those who supported conviction on account of the first article believed that the state constitution gave the assembly the power of impeachment without any limitations and, therefore, violating the state's Corrupt Practices Act prior to election might constitute an impeachable offense. Most of those who thought that way relied on the fact that the specific acts charged against Sulzer, even though committed before his inauguration, were so connected with his official position as to be sufficiently related to the discharge of his duties as governor. Court of appeals judge Miller summed it up perfectly when he said of the impeachment power, "a more unlimited grant of power could not be expressed." Miller reasoned that "a grave offense committed before induction to office may constitute cause for impeachment . . . provided it so touches the office and bears such a relation to the discharge of its duties as to unfit the offender to discharge those duties."[40] He called the governor-elect "a quasi-public official." Four of the court of appeals judges shared Judge Miller's views.

After each member had expressed himself, it turned out that thirty-nine had voted "guilty" and only eighteen had voted "not guilty." Sulzer was convicted by one more vote than the necessary two-thirds. Of the thirty-four senators who voted for conviction, twenty-three were Democrats and eleven were Republicans. Of the senators voting for acquittal, eight were Democrats and six were Republicans.

Following the same procedure the members of the court then voted on the second article charging Sulzer with perjury in swearing to the accuracy of his campaign finance statement. The same procedure was followed and each man stood to give his vote and sometimes his reasons. The result was exactly the same, 39 to 18 and Sulzer also stood convicted under Article II. This time few of the members bothered to explain their vote at length because the reasons were mainly the same. On this point, Judge Cullen explained his vote against conviction because he believed that the perjury charge could not be based on falsely swearing to a matter that was not material. He agreed with the defense counsel that the election law did not require a candidate's statement to be verified by oath. Senator Blauvelt spoke up against the judge's argument explaining that he was guilty by moral standards and that was just as serious because the intent was there.[41]

By the time they got to the third article, which accused Sulzer of bribery in trying to influence witnesses before the Frawley Committee, the chief judge dispensed with the practice of asking the question of each one individually and, while each had to respond to his name being called, there was no discussion as the vote was unanimous for acquittal.[42]

The clerk read the fourth article, charging the governor with attempting to suppress evidence before the Frawley Committee. On this charge, he was found guilty by an even greater vote of 43 to 14. Obviously several members of the court had changed their position.[43]

The explanatory remarks made by the various members showed that Sulzer was convicted on this article largely on the basis of Peck's testimony. Once again, it was Judge Cullen who argued against conviction, asserting the position that the court of impeachment had no right to broaden the scope of the fourth article to include the testimony of Peck, which had not been included in the original indictment. He felt that Sulzer was being charged with one crime and being convicted of another. This time it was Judge Werner who disagreed with the chief and the majority agreed with him. Werner said, "It seems to me to require the narrowest kind of technical reasoning to hold that, because Peck was not mentioned by name in the fourth charge, it must be regarded as insufficient to charge the offense established by his testimony." On this count, Sulzer would have no argument that it did not apply to conduct while in office.[44]

By this time, the court had continued until 7:10 p.m., and they decided to adjourn until the next day, Friday, October 17th at 10:30 a.m.

When the court reconvened that morning, the members acted quickly to dispose of the remaining impeachment articles, V through VIII. On each of these articles, there was a unanimous vote for acquittal. Article V accused Sulzer of preventing Colwell from testifying before the Frawley Committee, generated very little substantive comment before the members voted "not guilty." There had been no evidence to support the accusation.

Article VI charging the governor with "larceny" for converting his campaign contributions to his personal purposes, generated comments about the fact that he had used his nomination as a means of generating cash for his own purposes, and those judges and senators who took the opportunity to explain their vote, all considered his behavior as "moral turpitude." In this case, it was Judge Cullen who said that his personal conduct was so bad that if he had done those things while he was an incumbent, "I think they would require his removal."

Article VII was the charge that the governor had misused the authority of his office to coerce members of the legislature with promises and threats to affect their vote on legislation. The court said that there was insufficient evidence to sustain the charge, although some senators expressed the view that if there had been senators called to testify, there would have been such evidence.

The last article, VIII, the accusation that he used his office as governor to manipulate the stock market when he was an investor, also generated a unanimous acquittal, but Senator James A. Foley of Manhattan, who was always considered to be the one closest to Mr. Murphy, could not resist the opportunity to say that the accusation demonstrated Sulzer's "hypocrisy, and all that may be condemned in the actions of a demagogue."

Finally, the court had arrived at the moment when it had to decide if Sulzer should be removed from office or not and whether or not he should be barred from ever holding office. On removal—the roll call went quickly, 43 to 12 in favor of removal. Judge Cullen did not vote because he said he was in the minority and had not voted for conviction.

The final action of the court was to vote on whether or not Sulzer should be barred from public office. Fifty-six voted no.[45] Those voting who made any comment seemed to agree that the decision about Sulzer's future should properly be left to the people. Whereupon, the presiding judge declared that William Sulzer "be, and he is hereby, removed from his said office as governor" and the clerk declared the court "adjourned *sine die.*"[46]

The last day's proceeding took one hour according to the *Times* of October 18th.

23

What Does an Impeached Governor Do?

Sulzer was surrounded by friends at the "People's House" when he was notified of his removal by a telephone call from someone at the Capitol at 11:57 am. When he heard the news, he "pressed his lips tightly together, smiled, and, turning to those around him as he hung up the receiver, said, nodding his head reflectively, 'well, they're through over there; they've done it.'" One of his intimates who had spent the morning with him said that "he was no more excited than if he had heard that someone had shot a rabbit."[1]

By the end of the day Sulzer released a long-awaited statement that purported to be the embodiment of the defense he did not make at the trial. It reiterated the defensive midnight statement of denial he had put out on the eve of his impeachment by the assembly. To nobody's surprise, it also contained a bitter attack on Boss Murphy.

As to some of the specific charges, he merely repeated his position that the campaign finance report had been prepared by people he trusted and still trusted. He denounced the participation of each of the senators who served on the Frawley Committee as men who had prejudged his guilt, without whose votes he would not have been convicted. He derided the impeachment proceeding as a "farce" and "political lynching, the consummation of a deep-laid political conspiracy to oust me from office," claiming that "Mr. Murphy controlled the assembly and ordered the impeachment," and that Murphy also "controlled most of the members of the court." Sulzer's said history will call the court "Murphy's High Court of Infamy." He was confident that future historians "will do me justice and posterity will reverse the findings of the court," expressing his confidence that "there is a higher court than Murphy's, the court of public opinion."

Sulzer explained that he had wanted to take the witness stand on his own behalf but was persuaded by his advisors that because the court had ruled out Hennessy's testimony, they would not hear the information he could give. He made the point that Peck and Ryan had lied about him, charging that Ryan had been put up to it by the managers of the prosecution. He also claimed that every dollar he put into his personal account was eventually "turned over by me to the committee in my office or to an agent of Mr. Murphy or the state committee."

Responding to a query from the *Times*, D. Cady Herrick said that he had expected "to put Mr. Sulzer on the stand up to the Monday before the closing of the trial, and that it was decided not to do so at the suggestion of Mr. Sulzer himself."[2]

Though many of Sulzer' supporters and friends were disappointed that his statement failed to specifically refute much of the evidence against him, they still considered Sulzer a victim and rallied to demonstrate their ongoing enthusiasm for him as the leader of the fight against the invisible government of Tammany Hall.

The day after his removal, Sulzer was treated to a parade of his ardent admirers who marched in a cold drizzling rain, led by a small brass band, gathering more and more people, through the streets of Albany to the Executive Mansion where they presented him with a silver loving cup bearing the inscription: "Presented to Hon. William Sulzer by the Citizens of Albany in loving remembrance of duties well performed—A martyr to the cause of honest government. October 18, 1913."[3]

The rain-soaked parade was warmly welcomed into the "People's House" by the tall and neatly refreshed ex-governor, wearing a pressed three-piece light gray suit, and the almost equally tall Mrs. Sulzer. As Sulzer addressed the standing room–only crowd, Platt, his former secretary, distributed copies of a supportive letter from Theodore Roosevelt, and several gracious telegrams from around the country, with offers of money for speeches, including an offer from a speaker's bureau in New York City, for $50,000 for fifty lectures. When the party was over, the famous slouch hat Sulzer traditionally wore at campaign events, at his own inauguration, and at the inaugural parade for President Wilson, was missing. The next day papers reported that a Brooklyn fan had it and was not going to give it back.[4]

Meanwhile, leading newspapers from all over the state were editorializing on the results of the impeachment. While most of the upstate papers were ardently Republican, their opinions were not unified. All were disappointed at least, but several were critical of Sulzer despite their recognition that Tammany Hall and/or Murphy were really responsible. All of the newspapers condemned Tammany's role, and generally found good and bad in Sulzer.[5]

It also appeared that the national press was not as interested in the removal of Governor Sulzer as they were of the initial impeachment. The fact that the court of appeals judges had distinguished between the governor's morality and the issue of legality made a big difference. Where the court of appeals judges disagreed on questions of legal liability, all of them agreed on moral guilt.[6]

On October 20th, Sulzer finally revealed his side of the story. He issued a detailed statement and gave an interview to James Creelman, a reporter for the *New York Evening Mail* that was deemed to be important enough by the *Times* that it repeated the entire interview itself in its October 21st edition. It contained Sulzer's revelation of his real relationship with Murphy. Sulzer claimed that he was telling it now for the first time because he was released from his "pledge of silence" to his impeachment attorneys.

According to Sulzer's account from the partial autobiography in the governor's personal files at Cornell University:

> Just prior to taking office as Governor, I spent an afternoon with Mr. Murphy, at his request, at his private room in Delmonico's. . . . He said he was my friend . . . and that he wished to help me out.
>
> To my astonishment he informed me that he knew I was heavily in debt. Then he offered me money to pay my debts, and have enough left to take things easy while governor. . . .
>
> He said that nobody would know anything about it; that I could pay what I owed, and go to Albany feeling easy financially. . . .
>
> I declined Mr. Murphy's offer, saying that I was paying off my debts gradually; that my creditors were friends and would not press me; that I was economical; and that I would try to get along on my salary as governor.

He went on to detail his version of each subsequent encounter with Murphy, and his resistance to appointing Murphy's friend and business partner, James Gaffney, as highway commissioner where he would be responsible for disbursing the sixty-five-million-dollar highway construction fund, that Sulzer already knew, as a result of Hennessy's investigation, was the source of great patronage money to Tammany-favored contractors. Sulzer gave details of Murphy's demands to appoint Gaffney:

> Mr. Murphy finally said, "I am for Gaffney. The organization demands his appointment and I want you to do it." I replied: "I will make no promise about it." He said: "It will be Gaffney or war. . . ."
>
> This is the Gaffney who, only a few months afterward on September 4, 1913, in undisputed testimony before the Supreme Court at Nyack, was shown to have demanded and received $30,000 in money (refusing to take a check) from one of the aqueduct contractors, nominally for "advice." This is the man who Mr. Murphy demanded should be put in a position where he would superintend and control the spending of sixty-five millions of the money of the state in road contracts. How could I, how could any honest governor consider such a man for such a place? How could I face the people after such surrender?

On October 27th, Murphy issued his own statement referring to Sulzer's conviction for perjury by the impeachment court and Sulzer's failure to testify after promising to tell his story there. Murphy argued that fair-minded men should question the truth of Sulzer's charges. Murphy then specifically refuted almost everything Sulzer had said about him, claiming that he had never offered him money, and denying that he had ever sent emissaries to Sulzer to ask him to do things, as Sulzer had said. He admitted meeting with Sulzer, at Sulzer's request, and specifically denied that he had ever uttered the statement "Gaffney or war," and Murphy actually said that he had never endorsed any candidate nor attempted to influence in any way the governor's appointments to judiciary positions, or that he ever threatened to wreck the governor's administration, or as Sulzer had charged, that he ever threatened him with impeachment unless Hennessy's investigation were called off.[7]

All of Sulzer's charges and even more of Hennessy's specific allegations against Judge McCall, the Tammany candidate for mayor, infused the ongoing mayoral campaign and became major issues attacking the credibility and integrity of McCall, so much so that McCall began to answer back to his own detriment.

On the front page of the *Times* of October 18th, the edition that carried the banner headlines announcing Governor Sulzer's removal and the elevation of Lieutenant Governor Glynn, there was a central box above the fold carrying the story that Sulzer might run for the assembly from his old 6th assembly district in the Lower East Side. Over the next few days, the governor's friends and his wife were urging him to make the run. They saw it as an opportunity for Sulzer to vindicate himself and humiliate Murphy, and perhaps provide an opportunity for a new political career. Sulzer was easily persuaded and the Progressives gave him the nomination. When the Sulzers left Albany on October 21st, on the New York Central's Empire State Express, arriving at Grand Central Station at 10:25 p.m., they were overwhelmed by a crowd of over five thousand people, blowing horns, shaking cowbells, and shrieking approval of Governor Sulzer. They wanted to shake his hand, or touch him, and the crowd followed the slow-moving procession of automobiles downtown to the Broadway Central Hotel where the Sulzers had decided to make their headquarters until they found a new home. The hotel had reluctantly agreed to allow "Patsy," the governor's Irish terrier, to stay with them rather than lose their business. Sulzer campaigned extensively, drawing huge and enthusiastic crowds everywhere he spoke. Usually his speeches were sharp denunciations of Murphy and the Tammany organization, drawing hard on his experience while governor. His campaign was an outstanding success and a disaster for Tammany.[8]

Hennessy, his chief investigator and strong ally, spoke all over the city on behalf of the Fusion ticket, reviewing the results of his investigation of corruption in the highway construction and maintenance contracts to the benefit of Tammany-favored contractors. Hennessy got great credit for helping to defeat Judge McCall, who was Murphy's candidate for mayor of New York City. Sulzer got considerable credit as well. The result was the election of John Purroy Mitchel, the Fusion candidate for mayor by a 120,000-vote majority, and the defeat of almost all of the Tammany candidates for office in New York City. Mitchell carried every one of New York City's five boroughs and his Fusion running mates swept the Board of Aldermen and all but one vote on the Board of Estimate. Tammany was, therefore, out of business in the city for four years.

Sulzer won his old assembly seat by defeating his Republican opponent by a three to one vote, and the Tammany Democratic candidate who opposed them came in last.

Throughout upstate New York, all of the Murphy Democrats lost their elections, and the Tammany machine was destroyed in Buffalo, and most of the other upstate cities they had controlled.

Most gratifying for Sulzer and his people, the Democrats lost control of the assembly. Of the seventy-nine Democratic assemblymen who voted for his impeachment, only forty-six were re-nominated, and of those only seventeen were reelected, all of whom were from New York City Tammany districts.[9] Sulzer was widely credited by most objective observers with Tammany's defeat, and he took great consolation claiming that "I was able to accomplish more out of office then all the governors in the last decade could accomplish in office. . . . In the theft of the governorship, Murphy decreed his own destruction."[10]

Although the Democrats also lost the next gubernatorial election, Murphy's hold on the Tammany leadership survived substantial, but short-lived, criticism and he maintained his position as "chief" until his death in 1924.

After an undistinguished term, in 1914, Assemblyman Sulzer sought the Progressive Party nomination for governor, to run against Governor Martin Glynn who was nominated by the Democratic Party to run against Charles Whitman, the highly respected Republican district attorney of New York County. The Progressives turned Sulzer down in favor of one of their own, Frederick Davenport, who beat him out by a small margin after being endorsed by Theodore Roosevelt. Sulzer did not give up his quest and he convinced the Prohibition Party to nominate him after he made a speech about his opposition to rum. Sulzer also got a second line on the ballot by having his friends create the American Party, whose emblem was the Liberty Bell and its motto was dedication "to God, the people, and the overthrow of the political bosses."[11]

During the campaign, Theodore Roosevelt denounced Sulzer because "he does not tell the truth."[12] Roosevelt added, "It is useless to expect a public servant to wage war on corruption if his own record is

Charles F. Murphy at his desk, 1924. Collection of the author.

vulnerable." Of course, Sulzer responded by questioning Roosevelt's honesty, and most preposterously accusing him of an alliance with Tammany Hall. When the votes were tallied, Sulzer did beat out Davenport, but Governor Glynn beat him five to one, while losing to Republican Whitman by 150,000 votes.

Attempts to overturn the impeachment trial through litigation were repelled by the state court of appeals and the U.S. Supreme Court in 1914.

Fortunately, the governor's tragic ending did not totally destroy his sense of humor. When the state comptroller in 1914 tried to collect 35¢ for dog biscuits charged by Sulzer as a resident of the Executive Mansion, Sulzer rebuffed him with a letter saying that Patsy, his Irish terrier, was a legitimate resident of the mansion and if the state wanted to collect they would have to impeach Patsy.

Sulzer's political career ended in 1916 when he sought unsuccessfully to obtain the Prohibition Party nomination for president of the United States, and was turned down at their national convention.[13]

Ex-governor Sulzer, 1914. Collection of the author.

In Sulzer's draft autobiography that I found in the Cornell University Library, Sulzer says that after his 1914 defeat in the gubernatorial election, he made a lecture trip throughout the United States to pay off his debts, earning over $138,000, which, added to money from his law practice, paid off all his debts in less than three years.

After 1916, Sulzer took no active participation in New York politics. His admirers continued to espouse his achievements and some even produced a play on Broadway called *The Boss and the Governor,* which folded after only six weeks. The governor practiced law and was an active investor in mining interests in Alaska. He had made his first trip to Alaska in 1893 and many times thereafter. His younger brother, Charles, lived there. Charles was Alaska's first congressman and served only one term. New York congressman William Sulzer was very well known and much beloved by Alaskans as he looked after their interest in Congress. He was familiar to many as "Sour Dough Bill." They even named a mining town and a mountain after him.

Paramount Pictures released *The Great McGinty* in 1940, starring Brian Donlevy, which some believed was loosely based on elements of Sulzer's colorful career.

In 1917, the *Times'* December 18th edition reported that during the mayoralty campaign of 1913, the Fusion Party paid Sulzer $5,000 in cash for making campaign speeches in support of John Purroy Mitchel's mayoralty campaign, but the campaign did not report this expenditure as required under the state's Corrupt Practices Act, the same law that was used to impeach Sulzer. When a *Times* reporter called Sulzer's attention to the story the night before it was published, Sulzer told him that Fusion still owed him $3,500, but the money was not personal to him, it represented campaign expenses.

The governor passed away at the age of seventy-eight on November 6, 1941, and he was buried at the family plot in the Evergreen Cemetery at Hillside, New Jersey.

Epilogue

Winners and Losers

That history repeats itself always amazes me. Mr. Murphy certainly got his way with Governor Sulzer, but Tammany paid a heavy penalty because the public reaction cost Mr. Murphy control of the state assembly and New York City. Murphy had overplayed his hand. However, he could take pride in his lifetime political achievements as well as his personal fortune. Mr. Murphy's endorsement had elected three governors of the state, although two were mistakes. The other one, Alfred E. Smith, was elected four times and achieved the presidential nomination of his party, although Mr. Murphy did not live to see that nomination, which had been his lifelong objective. Mr. Murphy could also claim credit for electing six mayors of New York City.

Carmine DeSapio, the last chief of Tammany Hall, could also take pride in electing a mayor and a governor, but DeSapio also paid a big price for publicly humiliating Governor Averell Harriman at the 1958 convention, an act that contributed to Harriman's loss and the party's defeat. Within three years, his defiance of the governor he had elected contributed to DeSapio's loss of his leadership of Tammany Hall and the end of Tammany's influence for all time.

Reacting to his impeachment, Governor Sulzer said that "posterity will do me justice." Actually, it did. Despite his personal flaws, Sulzer led an interesting and useful life, leaving a productive and progressive legislative record as an assemblyman, congressman, and governor whose achievements enriched the lives of the people who elected him and those who came after.

I hope that this light cast on his entire career and his gubernatorial administration might result in his portrait being hung in the Hall of Governors on the second floor of the Capitol.

Acknowledgments

Writing my first book, *Final Treatment: The File on Dr. X* (New York: W. W. Norton & Company, 1979), turned out to be an exciting and life-changing experience that I wanted to repeat. However, I encountered great difficulty in finding another subject that would motivate me to repeat the experience. Fortunately, I had the opportunity to meet the great author David McCullough at a PEN International fundraiser, and told him of my dilemma as a new author. His words of wisdom were: "Do what I do—find a subject that interests you personally and learn everything there is to know about it and you will have a book." I did that. This is the first chance I have had to thank him.

When world-class agent Amanda Urban took the time to read the beginning of my manuscript many years ago, her encouragement and suggestions meant more to me than she could possibly know. Many years later, Judy P. Hohmann, editor of the *New York Archives Magazine*, accepted my Spring 2010 article on the Sulzer impeachment, which brought the pending book to the attention of James Peltz, publisher of State University of New York Press. I am very grateful for the confidence that each of them expressed, which led to this publication.

After I completed the first draft of the entire manuscript, my son, Justin Lifflander, business editor of *The Moscow Times*, applied his editorial skill and gave me the exhaustive and tough review, as well as candid advice that I sorely needed. I am most appreciative of his contribution and very proud of his assertive wisdom in polishing and improving my effort.

A number of good friends were interested enough to take the time to read my manuscript, give me their honest impressions, provide real insights and useful tips on how to improve the work. I am thankful for their time, candor, and wisdom; specifically, my long-ago colleague in the Executive Chamber, distinguished author and superb writer Joseph Persico, and fellow student of the state capital and accomplished attorney, former state senator John Dunne, and those avid readers of good literature, Paul Luftig and Jay Wilker and several members of our history book club, who made valuable constructive suggestions, most of which were incorporated into the final effort, that made it a lot better book than it was when they read it.

Helen Guelpa, my assistant and longtime secretary, typed the entire manuscript, gave her valuable editorial suggestions, did key research, organized all the endnotes, and helped find the right photographs to enhance the story.

I hope the two anonymous readers for State University of New York Press will someday introduce themselves so I can thank them for their useful suggestions.

I am especially grateful to Kelli Williams-LeRoux, my careful managing editor at SUNY Press whose amazing breadth of knowledge and detailed review of my manuscript made a tremendous difference in the final product.

Obviously, I did not take all the advice I got, so any errors or omissions are mine alone.

Notes

PROLOGUE

1. Hogan lost the senate seat to Republican attorney general Jacob Javits. Fifteen years later as finance chairman of the State Democratic Committee, I raised the money to pay off the last $30,000 of the party's debt from Hogan's campaign.
2. Samuel Bell Thomas, *The Boss, or the Governor* (New York: The Truth Publishing Co., 1914).
3. Chester A. Platt, "Introduction," in *The Boss, or the Governor.*

CHAPTER 1. INAUGURATION DAY

1. *Public Papers of William Sulzer, Governor* January 1 to October 17, 1913 (Albany: J. B. Lyon Company, 1914), xii–xii.
2. *New York Times,* January 2, 1913.
3. *Public Papers of William Sulzer,* pp. 5–8.
4. *New York Times,* January 2, 1913.
5. *New York Times,* January 2, 1913.

CHAPTER 2. A RURAL CHILDHOOD

1. All of the material in this chapter is based on the actual description of the governor's own recollections I found in the extensive files at

the Cornell University Library in Ithaca, New York. The files were sent to Cornell by the governor after his impeachment. The information on his childhood is buttressed by his official biography written by Edgar L. Murlin, contained in the *Public Papers of William Sulzer, Governor,* at pages iii–xxix. The governor's recollections are part of an extensive draft of what appears to be intended as an autobiography that was in preparation in 1939 with the help of a collaborator named Charles D. Isaacson. He wrote a letter to Governor Sulzer dated January 4, 1939, which was also found in the Cornell file saying that "with the world in such a state of chaos, I don't suppose publishers would be interested in our manuscript at this time." Isaacson was then a student in his junior year at Columbia.

The draft autobiography provided a great deal of the information about Sulzer's life that has never before been published.

2. Sulzer's autobiographical notes never mention the Centennial Exposition.

CHAPTER 3. STUDYING LAW

1. The quotations in this and following paragraphs in this chapter come from Sulzer's draft of his incomplete autobiography in the file of the Cornell University Library.

Chapters 3–7 are based entirely on the draft autobiography found in the Cornell files. The description of Richard Croker and the history of Tammany Hall in chapter 7 and the description of the hall facilities relied on Alfred Henry Lewis's *Richard Croker* (New York: Life Publishing Company, 1901).

Unless otherwise noted, the quotations in chapters 3, 4, 5, 8, and 9 come from Sulzer's unpublished draft autobiography found in his files at the Cornell University Library. The draft autobiography provided a great deal of the information about Sulzer's life which has never before been published.

CHAPTER 5. BUILDING A LAW PRACTICE

1. I became a member of this club in 1960.

CHAPTER 6. POLITICS REARS ITS HEAD

1. While this chapter is also primarily based on the autobiography, it is supplemented and supported by extensive correspondence from Sulzer's constituents and clients of his law practice, and some from his family, that are contained in the Cornell file.

   Sulzer's own recollections are supported by the description of his early career described in *The Impeachment of Governor William Sulzer*, a graduate thesis by Jacob Alexis Friedman, published by Columbia University in 1939. Friedman's thesis is the single-most comprehensive history of the man and his career and was a great source of information on the Sulzer's assembly career, on pages 16–18. Sulzer's legislative record in the New York State Assembly is laid out in George W. Blake's *Sulzer's Short Speeches* (New York: J. S. Ogilvie Publishing Company, 1912), pp. 19–21.

2. Devery was for many years in charge of much police graft for Tammany Hall.

3. M. R. Werner *Tammany Hall* (New York: Doubleday & Company, 1928), 489.

4. William Riordan, *Plunkitt of Tammany Hall* (New York: E. P. Dutton & Co., 1963).

CHAPTER 7. A CONNECTED ASSEMBLYMAN

1. Gustavus Myers, *The History of Tammany Hall* (New York: Boni & Liveright, 1917)

2. Myers, *History of Tammany Hall.*

3. Myers, *History of Tammany Hall.*

4. Riordan, *Plunkitt of Tammany Hall*, pp. 3–6.

5. Werner, *Tammany Hall*, p. 336.

6. Werner, *Tammany Hall*, p. 341.

7. Werner, *Tammany Hall.*

8. Lincoln Steffens, *The Autobiography of Lincoln Steffens* (New York: Grosset and Dunlap, 1931), pp. 236–238.

9. Alfred Henry Lewis, *Richard Croker* (New York: Life Publishing Company, 1901), p. 98.

10. Lewis, *Richard Croker*, p. 72.

11. Lewis, *Richard Croker*, p. 73.
12. Werner, *Tammany Hall*, pp. 424–426.

CHAPTER 8. ASSEMBLYMAN RISING

1. The autobiography is once again the principal source of information in this chapter, along with the copies of correspondence mentioned. The politics of Sulzer's congressional years, and his participation in presidential campaigning, is extensively covered by Friedman in *The Impeachment of Governor William Sulzer*, pp. 19–24, who provides other sources for his information. Sulzer's congressional record was laid out in George W. Blake's *Sulzer's Short Speeches*.
2. *New York Times*, January 3, 1893.
3. *New York Times*, January 17, 1883.
4. *Cosmopolitan* 53 (July 1912): 248–249.
5. *New York Evening Post*, October 16, 1912.
6. *New York World*, Editorial, April 21, 1893.
7. *New York Tribune*, April 25, 1893.

CHAPTER 9. THE CONGRESSIONAL YEARS

1. The story of Tammany's place in the body politic after the turn of the century has been told and retold many times. For the purposes presented here, I relied on Lewis's *Richard Croker*; Myer's *The History of Tammany Hall*; Werner's *Tammany Hall*; Oliver E. Allen's *The Tiger: The Rise and Fall of Tammany Hall* (Reading, MA: Addison-Wesley Publishing Company, 1993); and Alfred Connable and Edward Silverfarb's *Tigers of Tammany: Nine Men Who Ran New York* (New York: Holt, Rinehart and Winston, 1967).
2. Blake, *Sulzer's Short Speeches*.
3. Paul F. Boller, *Congressional Anecdotes* (New York: Oxford University Press, 1992).
4. In a story describing the new Speaker of the assembly on January 2, 1893, the *New York Tribune*'s Albany correspondent said that "Sulzer bore a striking physical resemblance to Henry Clay and was commonly known about the Assembly chamber as 'Henry Clay Sulzer.'"

Another magazine of the same period, *Outlook*, January 11, 1893, described him as having "Clay's steep forehead, high cheekbones, large mouth, and deep-set eyes; also the same tall, loose-jointed figure."

5. Friedman, *Impeachment of Governor William Sulzer*, p. 20.
6. Morganthau, *All in a Lifetime*, p. 156.
7. Blake, *Sulzer's Short Speeches*, pp. 38–39.
8. Blake, *Sulzer's Short Speeches*, p. 94.
9. "Palladium of Our Liberties," *Current Leader* 53 (November 1912): 513.
10. *Philadelphia Public Ledger*, November 30, 1912.
11. *New York Times*, August 31, 1913.
12. Norman Hapgood, *Harper's Weekly*, August 23, 1913.

CHAPTER 10. THE TRAGEDY THAT CHANGED NEW YORK

1. Leon Stein, ed., *Out of the Sweatshop: The Struggle for Industrial Democracy* (New York: Quadrangle / New Times Book Company, 1977), pp. 188–193.

CHAPTER 11. SELECTING CONGRESSMAN SULZER

1. Jay W. Forrest and James Malcolm, *Tammany's Treason, Impeachment of Governor Sulzer: The Complete Story Written from behind the Scenes, Showing How Tammany Plays the Game, How Men Are Bought, Sold and Delivered* (Albany, NY: The Fort Orange Press, 1913).
2. Oscar S. Strauss, *Under Four Administrations* (Boston and New York: Houghton Mifflin Company; Cambridge: The Riverside Press, 1922), p. 320.
3. Friedman, *The Impeachment of Governor William Sulzer*, pp. 25–26.
4. Kenneth S. Davis, *FDR: The Beckoning of Destiny* (New York: G. Putnam's Sons, 1972).
5. Henry Morganthau, *All in a Lifetime* (New York: Doubleday Page & Company, 1922).
6. *New York Times*, October 2, 1912.
7. Friedman, *Impeachment of Governor William Sulzer*, p. 29.
8. Forrest and Malcolm, *Tammany's Treason*.

9. Friedman, *Impeachment of Governor William Sulzer*, p. 27.
10. *New York Evening Post*, October 3, 1912.

CHAPTER 12. SULZER'S SECOND DAY AS GOVERNOR

1. *New York Times*, January 3, 1913.

CHAPTER 13. MR. MURPHY

1. While much has been written about Charles Francis Murphy, who presided over Tammany Hall and the Democratic organization that ran New York City and state politics from 1902 until his death in 1924, the most comprehensive source of information about his entire life was completed in a graduate thesis by Nancy Joan Weiss, at Smith College, and was published in 1968; *Charles Francis Murphy, 1858–1924: Respectability and Responsibility in Tammany Politics* (Northampton, MA: Smith College, 1968). Ms. Weiss's work is an outstanding legacy to the history of politics in New York. The accuracy of her work is verified by the description of Murphy in almost every other published history of the events he was involved in.
2. *New York Tribune*, January 1, 1898.
3. Myers, *History of Tammany Hall*, p. 301.
4. Welch, *King of the Bowery*, p. 19.
5. *New York Times*, September 20, 1902, cited in Weiss, *Charles Francis Murphy*, p. 27, n. 10.
6. New York Evening Post, April 25, 1924, cited in Weiss, *Charles Francis Murphy*, p. 30, n. 22.

CHAPTER 14. THE SECRET OF TAMMANY'S POWER (AND WHAT WAS DONE WITH IT)

1. Myers, *History of Tammany Hall*, pp. 307–308.
2. Myers, *History of Tammany Hall*, pp. 317–318.
3. Myers, *History of Tammany Hall*, p. 318.

CHAPTER 15. WAR CLOUDS ON THE HORIZON

1. *Public Papers of William Sulzer*, p. 21.
2. *New York Times*, January 4, 1913.
3. *New York Times*, January 4, 1913.
4. *New York Times*, January 5, 1913.
5. *New York Times*, January 4, 1913.
6. *Public Papers of William Sulzer*, p. 40.
7. *New York Times*, January 14, 1913.
8. *Public Papers of William Sulzer*, p. 653.
9. *New York Times*, January 22, 1913.
10. There were still two Public Service Commissions, one from New York City and one from upstate.
11. *New York Times*, January 30, 1913.
12. *New York Times*, February 4, 1913.
13. *Public Papers of William Sulzer*, p. 1252.

CHAPTER 16. THE PATRONAGE BATTLE

1. *New York Times*, February 4, 1913.
2. *New York Times*, March 18, 1913.
3. *Public Papers of William Sulzer*, p. 1285.
4. Morgenthau, *All in a Lifetime*, p. 169.
5. *New York Times*, March 26, 1913.

CHAPTER 17. GOVERNMENT BY INVESTIGATION

1. Hughes's lieutenant governor became governor in the last month of Hughes's term when Hughes was appointed by the president to be an associate justice of the United States Supreme Court.
2. *New York Times*, January 8, 1913.
3. *New York Times*, February 4, 1913.
4. *Public Papers of William Sulzer*, p. 653.
5. See Wikipedia, Henry K. Thaw.
6. *Public Papers of William Sulzer*, p. 944, and Forrest and Malcolm, *Tammany's Treason*, p. 295.

7. The term "square-chalked" refers to a practice of locking prisoners in their cells with no opportunity to get out.
8. *Public Papers of William Sulzer*, p. 867.
9. *Public Papers of William Sulzer*, pp. 856, 885, and 985.
10. *Public Papers of William Sulzer*, p. 898.
11. *New York Times*, February 26, 1913.
12. *Public Papers of William Sulzer*, p. 944.
13. Governor Sulzer told the entire Stillwell story in *The Boss, or the Governor*, by Samuel Bell Thomas.

CHAPTER 18. THE DIRECT PRIMARY BATTLE

1. The author was then counsel to the New York State Association of Railroads, which drafted and lobbied for the repeal of the full crew law in 1959.
2. *Public Papers of William Sulzer*, p. 101.
3. *Public Papers of William Sulzer*, pp. 1312–1315.
4. Before his resignation in 2008, Governor Eliot Spitzer made some poorly executed efforts to denounce specific legislators in their own districts—efforts that rebounded against him.
5. *New York Times*, April 30, 1913.
6. *New York Times*, April 30, 1913.
7. *New York Times*, May 2, 1913.
8. *New York Times*, May 9, 1913.
9. *New York Times*, May 17, 1913.
10. *New York Times*, May 20, 1913.
11. *New York Times*, May 21, 1913.
12. *New York Times*, May 19, 1913.
13. *New York Times*, May 31, 1913.
14. *New York Times*, June 4, 1913.
15. *New York Times*, June 5, 1913.
16. *New York Times*, June 7, 1913.
17. *New York Times*, June 11, 1913.
18. *New York Times*, June 14, 1913.
19. *New York Times*, June 15, 1913.
20. *New York Times*, June 18, 1913.
21. *New York Times*, June 25, 1913.
22. *New York Times*, June 26, 1913.
23. Editorial, *Times Work* 26 (1913): 382.

CHAPTER 19. MURPHY'S REVENGE

1. *New York Times*, June 12, 1913.
2. *New York Times*, July 2, 1913.
3. *New York Times*, July 3, 1913.
4. *New York Times*, July 2, 1913.
5. *New York Times*, August 23, 1913.
6. *New York Times*, July 4, 1913.
7. *New York Times*, July 6, 1913.
8. *New York Times*, July 18, 1913.
9. McClellan was the son of the famous Civil War general who had been elected mayor of New York City with Mr. Murphy's support but then turned against Murphy by ignoring his patronage demands.
10. *New York Times*, July 27, 1913.
11. *New York Times*, July 29, 1913.
12. *New York Times*, August 3, 1913.
13. *New York Times*, July 31, 1913.
14. *New York Times*, August 4, 1913.
15. *New York Times*, August 7, 1913.

CHAPTER 20. THE IMPEACHMENT DRAMA

1. *New York Times*, August 9, 1913.
2. *New York Times*, August 8, 1913.
3. Friedman, *Impeachment of Governor William Sulzer*, pp. 149–151.
4. *New York Times*, August 12, 1913.
5. *New York Times*, August 12, 1913.
6. *New York Times*, August 12, 1913.
7. *New York Times*, August 13, 1913.
8. *New York Times*, August 14, 1913.

CHAPTER 21. REACTIONS

1. See Friedman, *Impeachment of Governor William Sulzer*, pp. 165–170, for a survey of the national press.
2. Forrest and Malcolm, *Tammany's Treason*, p. 396.
3. *New York Times*, August 14, 1913.

4. *New York Times*, August 14, 1913.
5. *New York Times*, August 7, 1913.
6. 82 NYMISC. 164–74; (Appealed, 163 App. Div. 725–30; 212 N.Y. 603).

CHAPTER 22. THE TRIAL OF GOVERNOR SULZER

1. Morgenthau was the finance chairman of Woodrow Wilson's presidential campaign in 1912 and later became the U.S. ambassador to Turkey. (His son, Henry, became President Franklin D. Roosevelt's secretary of the treasury, and his grandson, Robert, was the long-serving district attorney of Manhattan.)
2. *New York Times*, September 19, 1913.
3. *Proceedings of the Court for the Trial of Impeachments, in the Matter of the Impeachment of William Sulzer, Governor of the State, September 18, 1913–October 17, 1913* (Albany, NY: J. B. Lyon Company, 1913), p. 18. (Hereafter *Proceedings.*)
4. *Proceedings*, p 28.
5. *Proceedings*, pp. 28–39.
6. *Proceedings*, p. 44.
7. *Proceedings*, pp. 56–59.
8. *Proceedings*, pp. 132–226.
9. *Proceedings*, p. 228.
10. *Proceedings*, p. 235.
11. *Proceedings*, pp. 228–427.
12. *Proceedings*, p. 430.
13. Not very different from the avowed purpose of campaign finance disclosure laws today—and not any more or less effective either.
14. *Proceedings*, pp. 435–444.
15. *Proceedings*, pp. 469–484.
16. *Proceedings*, pp. 485–491.
17. *Proceedings*, pp. 493–494.
18. *Proceedings*, p. 737.
19. *Proceedings*, p. 702–704.
20. *Proceedings*, p. 720.
21. *Proceedings*, pp. 808–809, 818–819.
22. Considering the relevance of the amounts of money people contributed to candidates in 1913, in order to put 1913 dollars in con-

text with today's dollars, there are a variety of acceptable formulas for making the calculation. The most conservative conversion tables would use the consumer price index, and the experts tell us that $25,000 in 1913 would be converted to $559,000 today. From my perspective as an experienced political fundraiser who has run campaign finance committees and fundraising dinners in New York for several decades, a typical political dinner today for a statewide or a presidential candidate in New York City charges at least $1,000 per person, with more intimate events ranging from a minimum of $5,000 to $25,000 per couple. The maximum permitted personal contribution to a gubernatorial candidate in New York under the law today is in the range of $90,000. These numbers can be verified by the published state and federal reports of the official agencies, all of which are available on the internet. Fundraising dinners for gubernatorial candidates today typically have a menu of tickets from $500 to $1,000, with sponsorship listings in the program ranging up to $25,000 and sometimes more for successful bundlers.

23. Friedman, *Impeachment of Governor William Sulzer*, p. 206.
24. *New York Times*, October 7, 1913.
25. *New York Times*, October 2, 1913.
26. *Proceedings*, pp. 1065–1066.
27. Lehman later became lieutenant governor of New York under Governor Franklin D. Roosevelt, and was governor 1932–1942, and U.S. senator 1950–1957.
28. *Proceedings*, pp. 1114–1135.
29. *Proceedings*, pp. 1135–1148.
30. *Proceedings*, pp. 1148–1288.
31. *Proceedings*, p. 1302.
32. *Proceedings*, pp. 1314 et seq.
33. *Proceedings*, p. 1404.
34. *Proceedings*, p. 1405.
35. *Proceedings*, pp. 1407–1417.
36. Reprinted at pages 1470–1473 of the transcript.
37. *New York Times*, October 12, 1913.
38. *Proceedings*, p. 1437.
39. *Proceedings*, p. 1625.
40. *Proceedings*, pp. 1649–1658.
41. *Proceedings*, p. 1689.
42. *Proceedings*, p. 1700.

43. *Proceedings*, p. 1723.

44. *Proceedings*, p. 1722.

45. *Proceedings*, p. 1763.

46. *Proceedings*, p. 1765.

CHAPTER 23. WHAT DOES AN IMPEACHED GOVERNOR DO?

1. *New York Times*, October 18, 1913.

2. *New York Times*, October 18, 1913.

3. Myers, *History of Tammany Hall*, p. 185.

4. *New York Times*, October 19, 1913.

5. *New York Times*, October 19, 1913.

6. See *The Nation*, October 23, 1913; *The Outlook*, October 25, 1913; and *Current Opinion* 55, no. 5 (November 1913).

7. *New York Times*, October 28, 1913.

8. Myers, *History of Tammany Hall*, p. 201.

9. Friedman, *Impeachment of Governor William Sulzer*, p. 260.

10. *New York Times*, November 5, 1913.

11. Friedman, *Impeachment of Governor William Sulzer*, p. 266.

12. Friedman, *Impeachment of Governor William Sulzer*, p. 266.

13. Friedman, *Impeachment of Governor William Sulzer*, pp. 267–268.

Bibliography

Allen, Oliver E. *The Tiger: The Rise and Fall of Tammany Hall.* Reading, MA: Addison-Wesley Publishing Co., 1993.

Barcus, James S. *The Governor's Boss: A Drama in Four Acts.* New York: The Boss Publishing Co., 1914..

Blake, George W. *Sulzer's Short Speeches.* New York: J. S. Ogilvie Publishing Co., 1912.

Boller, Paul F. *Congressional Anecdotes.* New York: Oxford University Press, 1992.

Brownlow, Kevin. *Behind the Mask of Innocence.* Berkeley and Los Angeles: University of California Press, 1992.

Bryan, William J. *The First Battle.* Chicago: W. B. Conkey Co., 1896.

Connable, Alfred, and Edward Silberfarb. *Tigers of Tammany: Nine Men Who Ran New York.* New York: Holt, Rinehart and Winston, 1967.

Davis, Kenneth S. *FDR: The Beckoning of Destiny.* New York: G. Putnam's Sons, 1972.

Fleming, Thomas. *Around the Capital with Uncle Hank.* New York: The Nutshell Publishing Co., 1902.

Forrest, Jay W., and James Malcolm. *Tammany's Treason, Impeachment of Governor William Sulzer: The Complete Story Written from Behind the Scenes, Showing How Tammany Plays the Game, How Men Are Bought, Sold and Delivered.* Albany: The Fort Orange Press, 1913.

Franklin, Allan. *The Trail of the Tiger.* New York: Allan Franklin, 1928.

Friedman, Jacob Alexis. *The Impeachment of Governor William Sulzer.* New York: Columbia University Press; London: P. S. King & Son, 1939; Reprint, New York: AMS Press, 1968.

335

Gould, Lewis L., ed. *The Progressive Era.* Syracuse: Syracuse University Press, 1974.

Huthmacher, J. Joseph. "Charles Evans Hughes and Charles Francis Murphy: The Metamorphosis of Progressivism." *New York State Historical Association Quarterly* 47, no. 1 (January 1965): 25.

LaCerra, Charles. *Franklin Delano Roosevelt and Tammany Hall of New York.* Lanham, MD: University Press of America, 1997.

Lewis, Alfred Henry. *Richard Croker.* New York: Life Publishing Co., 1901.

Morganthau, Henry. *All in a Lifetime.* New York: Doubleday Page & Co., 1922.

Myers, Gustavus. *The History of Tammany Hall.* New York: Boni & Liveright, 1917.

The New York Red Book: An Illustrated Legislative Manual. Albany, NY: J. B. Lyon Co., 1913.

Perkins, Frances. *The Roosevelt I Knew.* New York: Viking Press, 1942 (Second Edition).

Proceedings of the Court for the Trial of Impeachments, in the Matter of the Impeachment of William Sulzer, Governor of the State, September 18, 1913–October 17, 1913. Albany, NY: J. B. Lyon Co., 1913.

Public Papers of William Sulzer, Governor, January 1 to October 17, 1913. Albany, NY: J. B. Lyon Co., 1914.

Riordan, William L. *Plunkitt of Tammany Hall.* New York: E. P. Dutton & Co., 1963.

Slayton, Robert A. *Empire Statesman: The Rise and Redemption of Al Smith.* New York: Free Press, 2001.

Sloan, Kay. *The Loud Silents.* Urbana and Chicago: University of Illinois Press, 1988.

Smith, Alfred E. *Up to Now: An Autobiography.* New York: Viking Press, 1929.

Steffens, Lincoln. *The Autobiography of Lincoln Steffens.* New York: Grosset and Dunlap, 1931.

Stein, Leon, ed. *Out of the Sweatshop: The Struggle for Industrial Democracy.* New York: Quadrangle / New Times Book Co., 1977.

Strauss, Oscar S. *Under Four Administrations.* Boston and New York: Houghton Mifflin Co., The Riverside Press Cambridge, 1922.

Thomas, Samuel Bell. *The Boss, or the Governor.* New York: The Truth Publishing Co., 1914.

Von Drehle, David. *Triangle: The Fire That Changed America.* New York: Atlantic Monthly Press, 2003.

Wald, Lillian D. *The House on Henry Street.* New York: Henry Holt and Co., 1915.

Weiss, Nancy Joan. *Charles Francis Murphy, 1858–1924: Respectability and Responsibility in Tammany Politics.* Northampton, MA: Smith College, 1968.

Welch, Richard F. *King of the Bowery: Big Tim Sullivan, Tammany Hall, and New York City from the Gilded Age to the Progressive Era.* Albany, NY: State University of New York Press, 2009.

Werner, M. R. *Tammany Hall.* New York: Doubleday & Co., 1928.

Wesser, Robert F. "The Impeachment of a Governor: William Sulzer and the Politics of Excess." *New York State Historical Association Quarterly* 60, no. 4 (October 1979): 407.

Index